Praise for *Journey t*

"For all who love to bask in the light riences in beautifully crafted language, I warmly recommend this book. Characteristic of John Pontius, the pages are filled with breathtaking spiritual stories and doctrine described in actionable ways, infused with the Spirit that tells us we can also partake.

John Pontius is a masterful teacher and painter of words. For those who have read previous books from John Pontius, followed his blog, or are fellow seekers of Christ, this book gives a great last testament to John's life work."

—**Kevin Ball, IT manager, Global Energy Company**

"Magnificent. Powerful. Beautiful. Poignant. Sublime. I've loved all of John Pontius's earlier works and consider his UnBlogs to be his finest writings, the majestic pinnacle of a lifetime of faithful service to the Lord. The story line added by Terri is beautiful and compelling, offering tender insights into the personal life of a truly amazing modern-day giant. A highly recommended read for anyone who loves the gospel and desires to be buoyed by the Spirit. My only regret was that as with our fellowship with Brother John, it ended all too soon. I could have read and read and read, only wishing for more."

—**Robert L. Bolick, attorney**

"This magnificent collection of stories and writings from John Pontius, compiled after his death by his wife, Terri, teaches important and profound lessons from a well-lived life that might have been lost if he did not complete this final work. With *Visions of Glory* and now *Journey to the Veil*, John Pontius enjoys the honor of being one of the most widely read LDS doctrinal authors in the world."

—**Lee Nelson, bestselling author**

"*Journey to the Veil* is, without a doubt, one of the five best books I have ever read in my life. If you are ready to receive magnificent insights, learn on a deep level, witness testimony, and be profoundly inspired, read this book. If you are ready to discover how to be a humble follower of Christ and dedicate your life, your hands, and your heart to Him, read this book. If you are ready to be taught how to use your divine gifts and receive heavenly manifestations, read John Pontius's book. When you do, you will never, ever be the same."

—Dr. Paula Fellingham, founder of The Women's Information Network, author, and international speaker and trainer

"*Journey to the Veil,* authored by John Pontius, is a beautiful labor of love compiled by his devoted wife. Her personal input has provided an even closer look into the spiritual and every day life of John Pontius.

Not only did John's faith-promoting true stories remind me of the endless love for and strong testimony he had of the Savior, but it also left me with a burning desire to lay hold of the great blessings and miracles the gospel offers to us all. It has inspired me to reach for the true potential, as a disciple of Jesus Christ, in my own journey to the veil. . . .

Even after death, John found a way to, once again, offer the comfort and enlightenment I needed to lift my very soul a little closer to heaven. I wholeheartedly recommend this wonderful book."

—Amber Joy Giles, mother, lecturer, and cofounder and writer of the blog "Eponym"

"*Journey to the Veil* is a compilation of profound truths about the greatest blessings promised to the extraordinarily faithful who seek to enjoy the literal presence of God in this life. . . . Its insights will give us the context and perspectives we need to understand and enjoy our journey to our ultimate destination: God's presence."

—Eric Cawley, marketing and website development professional

"*Journey to the Veil* is a precious gift to its readers. It is an expression of John's love for Christ from beginning to end. Not many books I read add to my perspective on life and the eternities the way this book has. It is original and provocative and motivates me to be better. It is filled with great stories and personal accounts of the author's experiences through his sojourn on earth. His insights on so many gospel topics have broadened my thinking and expanded my mind. This book has brought me closer to Christ as it is a beautiful tribute to Him and His gospel. This book will change lives!"

—Sandi Suarez, stay-at-home mom

"A gospel of Christ 'How To' book. Blessed by John Pontius's counsel in Alaska, I am blessed again by *Journey to the Veil*. He tells of changed lives filling me with the Spirit and compelling me to tears of joy. Brother John teaches us how to achieve the glorious gifts of heaven while in mortality. He testifies the Church is true, operating as Jesus directs, and that it will build the latter-day Zion we seek. Thank you, Brother John, for a life full of love for the Savior and righteous living—we will meet again in Zion."

—Neil "Kiwi" Holland, USAF Lt. Col., author of *The USA and the Millennial Kingdom of God*, publisher

"John's desire was 'I wanted them to know that God does answer when asked, that He is found when sought, and that He does open when we knock.' *Journey to the Veil* [teaches] just that in a 'come follow me,' gentle, inviting way."

—Evan Swensen, author and publisher

Also by John Pontius

Visions of Glory
Following the Light of Christ into His Presence

Millennial Quest Series:
Spirit of Fire (Formerly *Angels in Coveralls*)
Angels among Us
Angels Forged in Fire
Angels and a Flaming Sword, Part 1
Angels and a Flaming Sword Part 2

We Three Kings
The Triumph of Zion

Additional books, essays, and
fireside sound tracks are available at:
www.followingthelight.org
and on the UnBlog
http://UnBlogmysoul.wordpress.com

Journey
to the VEIL

Journey
to the VEIL

by JOHN PONTIUS

Compiled by Terri Pontius

CFI
An Imprint of Cedar Fort, Inc.
Springville, Utah

ISBN 13: 978-1-4621-1389-7

Published by CFI, an imprint of Cedar Fort, Inc.
2373 W. 700 S., Springville, UT 84663
Distributed by Cedar Fort, Inc., www.cedarfort.com

LIBRARY OF CONGRESS CATALOGING-IN-PUBLICATION DATA

Pontius, John M., author.
Journey to the veil : selections from UnBlog my soul / written by John Pontius ; compiled by Terri J. Pontius.
   pages cm
Compilation of John M. Pontius's blogs.
Includes bibliographical references and index.
ISBN 978-1-4621-1389-7 (alk. paper)
1. Christian life--Mormon authors. 2. Church of Jesus Christ of Latter-day Saints--Doctrines.
3. Mormon Church--Doctrines. 4. Blogs. I. Pontius, Terri J., 1953- editor. II. Title. III. Title: Journey to the veil : selections from UnBlogmysoul.

BX8656.P66 2013
230'.9332--dc23

2013032907

Cover design by Shawnda T. Craig
Cover design © 2013 Lyle Mortimer
Edited and typeset by Emily S. Chambers

Printed in the United States of America

10 9 8 7 6 5 4 3

Printed on acid-free paper

To the UnBlog Family, whose incredible love, support, and rich commentary made John's last few years so sweet. If it were possible, I would have included all of your beautiful postings in this book as well.

Heartfelt thanks to Sanford Okura for answering John's call to help me and volunteering countless hours of careful editing and invaluable spiritual perspective. I could not have completed this project without you, my friend.

Contents

Foreword

John Pontius came into my life very unexpectedly and exited it a year ago (December 2012) in the same fashion. He was taken in the impeccable timing and love and mercy of the Lord. We were not ready to have him leave us, but he lived out all the days that were allotted to him from the beginning by the Father.

He loved the Lord and endeavored with all the energy of his soul to follow Christ's precepts and indefatigably served him and proclaimed his principles and teachings to all he met.

Not many of God's children have the ability and opportunity to influence the world for good after they have laid their bodies down in the grave; however, John continues to inspire, influence, and bless the lives of tens of thousands of Saints and true believers from his present station on the other side of the veil. His words are still resonating with those who seek after the truth and desire to follow the light into the presence of the Lord.

John knew sorrow and was acquainted with grief. He was stretched by that which he suffered. He learned to reach to the highest heights and understood the lowest depths. He was conversant with pain and suffering and could hold his own in a conversation with Job and Abraham. He knew how to succor the weak and lift up the hands that hang down.

With this newly published compilation of his many wonderful and spirit-raising stories, experiences, and writings, we are again lifted and refreshed by his faith-filled words and spirit. We again have the blessing of becoming reacquainted with John, or for some, knowing and learning from him for the first time.

John, thank you for your life and faithful devotion to Christ and His gospel. We long to be with you again and learn from you all that you now know, as you have had the opportunity to search the depths of eternity and to learn firsthand from the Lord Jesus Christ and His Father and our Father.

We will continue to learn from you and will wait for the Time of Refreshing to again learn from and with you at the glorious throne of God.

Your eternal friend,

"Spencer"

Introduction

Five months ago, my Johnnie left me.

He didn't mean to. He didn't want to. It was just his time. We both freely acknowledged, and discussed endlessly, the exciting and glorious mission awaiting John on the other side. I called him my Captain Moroni . . . he would prepare both sides of the veil for the latter-day Zion! Oh, but he was sick, so very sick. And because he was my best friend, and we always did everything together, I unwittingly made his sickness my sickness too. In the everyday busyness of serving this extraordinary dying man, I couldn't quite make myself believe that our earth life together was really coming to an end. I have no excuse for such indulgence; six years to prepare should have been long enough.

But I was brave. I told him, "Don't you worry about me! I am going to be just fine. I have my priorities straight: I know in Whom I trust. Go on, get out of here, and have all that spiritual fun on the other side of the veil, while I suffer and grovel down here!" I loved to tease him, because his tired, brown eyes lit up when I teased. Then I would kiss the top of his bald head a dozen times while my eyes filled with tears. I always tried to hide the tears, but he knew.

We spoke endlessly about—everything. When your husband has cancer, you have many bittersweet hours to talk about life and what lies beyond. These conversations, much to John's chagrin, were almost always late at night. I'm a night owl; he isn't. Right after I would give him his final morphine shot and fix his pillows and blankets just right, the "talkies" would kick in for me, just as his sleeping pill was kicking in for him.

"You have to come back and see me!" I'd tell him.

"I don't know if I will be permitted."

"Well then—gosh, John—beg! Come on, you've been so good . . . surely Father will let you!"

His eyes were gleaming now, but his voice was too hoarse to reply. I persisted, of course.

"At least—you gotta come back and give me a sign!"

He smiled as best he could, and brushed my cheek with his warm, now-trembling hand. "I will ask."

Then we would call our two daughters at home to come for family prayers. As we three girls knelt by his bedside, John would pray. During the last weeks of his life, he always wanted to be the one to pray. His faint voice would suddenly grow stronger as he boldly called down the angels, cast out our fears, and consecrated his all to God. The power in the priesthood that flowed mightily from John's pain-racked body and cracked lips was miraculous. Our weeping hearts were healed for yet another day.

Weeks passed, and the end was growing nearer. One night, I had an inspiration.

"Do you know what I'm going to do after you're gone? I'm going to compile the UnBlogs into a book. They are just too wonderful not to publish!" ("UnBlog My Soul" is a blog that John had begun in 2010 when he was told he had only six months to live. In this forum, John recorded his powerful witness of Christ and of the gospel he loved, initially intended only for his family and closest friends. But the blog became growingly popular, because its humble writer had such a unique gift for gospel clarity and expression. The UnBlog family was born, and soon thousands of UnBloggers enjoyed the posts that John wrote almost daily, despite his ongoing chemo treatments and failing body.)

But John resisted the idea of publishing the posts. "That's too big of a job. There are over five hundred of them! You'll kill yourself doing that."

"No I won't. I have edited all your other books; how hard could it be? Everything's already been written. Come on, Honey, those are amazing posts! You never know how it could touch a life." I knew that would get to him; he had only one burning desire—to touch lives for his Savior, Jesus Christ.

Finally John gave his permission rather reluctantly, with the caveat that I give whatever praise or good that came of it to the Lord. That was John; his focus was always on giving all thanks and any credit to God.

Then, just before Christmas 2012, my Johnnie was gone. I mourned wretchedly for months, wondering how I could have been so naive as to ever think I could live without him. Finally, a few months afterward, I found new energy and joy in compiling this book. I also know without *a doubt that John has personally and intimately assisted in this work. It's been a delight to sit here at John's desk using his well-loved computer, with him unmistakably by my side, and those thundering horses (my favorite painting of his) charging overhead to urge me onward.*

I have arranged the blogs according to subject rather than chronologically and have omitted the posting dates. There were so many excellent blogs to choose from that it was a daunting task to decide between them. If you'd like to read additional blogs, you are welcome to go online to "UnBlog My Soul," where you will find any that are not included in this book. Also, please note that most of the names of persons referenced have been changed.

I will dance between the chapters with the personal story of John's final mortal journey home. As you read these words penned by a man who was nearing his journey's end, it is my prayer that you may find truth and clarity for your own journey.

—Terri J. Pontius

Chapter One

UnBlogging Defined

All the Precious Fruit

*M*ost of my life, I have viewed mortality and the gospel somewhat differently than most people. By that I mean that I have an unusual relationship with truth; I am attracted to it, and it seems to come find me. I discovered this in my teens when I had long gospel talks with my dad. Dad was a righteous man who studied every morning and most evenings, who faithfully called family prayers and home evening, and who loved the Lord. I was a young teen chafing at having to do chores, milk cows, and work on a farm all day every day of summer vacation.

One day, a seminary teacher said something that didn't sound right to me. The next evening as I was going out to milk the (much hated) cows, I saw Dad sitting in his study reading. He was a doctor, and he had a large study filled with beautiful books. I walked up to the door, and he looked up. I asked him if he could answer a question for me, and then something unexpected happened. He closed his book and invited me to sit down. He listened intently to every word I said without comment. It was honestly the first time I can remember that my dad had really listened to anything I said!

In that moment, I realized that this was my father's garage door–size opening into his heart. He was rejoicing that I had come to him with a gospel question! Dad smiled and said, "Let's see what the scriptures say about that," and invited me to turn to a passage in the Book of Mormon. We talked for quite a while until I was satisfied. He listened to my ideas and seemed to genuinely value them. I was happily overwhelmed with this experience, both spiritually and as a rite of passage with my father.

As the years passed, we had these discussions often and continually. Without exaggerating at all, I estimate that during our lifetime of working side-by-side and living near one another, we spoke twenty thousand hours about gospel topics. What was intriguing to us both was that he would teach me something that he had acquired through scholarship, and I would feel the Spirit lighting my mind and then affirm with something like, "Well, then this also has to be true, and that means this other principle has to be right also." He would listen, look up a few things, consult the scriptures and his books, and without exception, he came to agree. Often he would add additional understanding, and we leap-frogged through the gospel, exchanging the teacher and student roles often.

As the years have passed, I realized that my understanding of the gospel is perfectly aligned with what all faithful people view; but for some reason only the Lord knows, He has occasionally gifted me with a peek into the sublime mysteries of eternity. I'm not saying this to boast. Anyone who knows me knows that I do not desire attention, and I work hard to stay far away from fringy people and the opportunity to acquire worldly status. Every insight I have been given has been but a tender mercy and a confirmation that the Lord answers the prayers of even a humble farm boy.

But all my adult life, the Lord has kept me silent about these little bits of additional light. For over thirty years, I have sat and listened and said very little. The first time I was given leave to voice any of it was in my first book, *Following the Light of Christ into His Presence*. After that, nearly twenty years passed before I obtained the information in *The Triumph of Zion* and was allowed to write and publish it. Now, probably because I was recently given six months to live, or because the potential inductees of Zion are hungering, or because the time for Zion is approaching fast, I no longer feel the same degree of sanction regarding what the Lord has taught me over the years. As a matter of fact, I feel a little urgency to spread these things as quickly and as far as I am given opportunity and utterance.

In pondering how I would best like to spend the twilight months of my life, I found that I wanted to take these precious memories, these hard-won truths and glorious gifts, and paint them in the sky. I didn't want them to be lost, buried within my head. I wanted them before the eyes, hearts, and minds of anyone who could reverence them, and I wanted them to be readily available when my precious children and grandchildren sought for their own light. I wanted them to know that God *does* answer when asked, that He *is* found when sought, and that He *does* open when we knock.

As I considered this growing desire, the unlikely thought of writing a blog came to me in a flash. Since I am not generally attracted to the whole concept of blogging, which appeared to me as a way of promoting one's self, the term "un-blogging" seemed to fit me better—thus the genesis of "UnBlog My Soul."

I realized last night that the name "UnBlog My Soul" also means to unburden my soul, to take all this precious fruit and lay it out as plainly and as sweetly as the Lord will give me words to do so. It means to unplug the storm drains of my fear, to unleash the lightning of the Holy Spirit in whatever way comes to my mind and my hands. It also means to me to complete my mortal assignment, and to not die with light under my bushel that should have been held aloft to cast away whatever shadows it may reach, that I might go to my next assignment without checked boxes on the "should-have-been-more-valiant page" the angels are keeping against my final report.

So, if you will forgive my late understanding, and accept that this is in no possible way an act of conceit or self-promotion, that my whole life and whole desire is only to do the Lord's will, and in so doing to help bring about the closing scenes of this telestial world we call home, I hope that you will accompany me through the process of UnBlogging My Soul.

Brother John

The Journey Home
Part I: The Beginning

It was late September 2006, and the glorious Alaskan summer was surrendering its blaze of fireweed and wildflowers to the inevitability of the long winter ahead. I always loved the fall, which spoke of misty mornings and colder nights, campfires that warmed, and the promise of darker evenings and northern stars. That summer had been very busy for John and me, with our children coming home from college, frequent visitors from the Lower 48, and the expansion of our self-storage business. But now life had slowed down. Our ten-year-old daughter had happily begun fifth grade, and John and I were gearing up for community Messiah rehearsals in October.

At first it seemed like such a little thing—perhaps a cold coming on. Although he was ill, John kept on working as a contracted consultant for Alyeska and writing his book. Finally at my insistence, he took a day off and swallowed some antibiotics we had lying around the house. The next day, I heard him feebly crying out for me from the bathroom. I walked in to find him in a hot bath, shaking violently and unable to get warm. That was enough for me. "I know you hate going to the doctor," I said, "but I'm sorry, I'm calling her right now!"

The doctor was as alarmed as I was and insisted that John come to her office immediately for tests. One hour later, he was admitted into the hospital. He had a massive liver abscess, which had apparently resulted from dental work done six weeks previously. After stabilization, he was ambulanced to a larger hospital in Anchorage to save his life.

Two weeks later, we knew two things: The first was that not only was John fighting this abscess, but he also had stage three colon cancer; the second was that our lives would never be the same again.

—Terri

Chapter Two

The First and Greatest Step

The First and Greatest Step

I have discovered that there is a specific pathway that will take any person upon it into the grand and glorious blessings of the gospel. These blessings are so fantastic that the mortal mind can't understand or even perceive of them without the benefit of direct revelation. They are so much broader than any mortal imagination or invention as to make them quite truthfully beyond man to comprehend, even when explained in great detail with charts and graphs and every art of language.

Yet, in the soul is a tiny engine of truth. It is not a part of man but resides within each of us. Its source is divine, engineered and paid for in advance by the Atonement of Christ, and when obeyed, it can open the very curtains that the genius of humankind alone cannot even budge.

I am speaking of the Light of Christ—that tiny voice of truth that we all possess, which first manifests itself as the conscience of man. It begins as tiny, but it is the first and greatest step to spiritual greatness, even godhood. Those who cast it aside and reject its counsels will forever disqualify themselves from those things that we most ardently desire—eternal life, eternal family, and eternal joy.

Those who embrace it, who recognize it as revelation, who discipline themselves to obedience to it—though it may take years of failure and repentance—and who ultimately make their eye single to the glory of God, will find this tiny spark of truth growing into a mighty blaze of truth and glory. They will walk in joy, work miracles, and receive profound blessings beyond the veil.

But it all starts with this first and greatest step: obedience to the Spirit.

A few of us may be called to spill our blood as martyrs. But it is not the single great sacrifice that exalts; it is a lifetime of small obediences—saying family prayers when it is inconvenient, reading the scriptures when prompted, apologizing when innocent, being kind to the unkind and merciful to the abuser, all when the voice of Christ whispers that it is the right thing to do.

Those who at last do these things will find themselves watching the veil part and angels descend, and it could be long before they are laid to rest at this mortal journey's end.

Brother John

Getting the Hang of Revelation

I woke up this morning thinking of an event that occurred in South Africa in 1971 and what it taught me. A great deal of my present thinking, my belief in revelation and my determination to be diligently obedient to the voice of the Spirit, originated with the happening I am about to recite. I promise this is a true story. I'm not making any part of this up, even though it sounds somewhat fantastic.

I was serving as a missionary in Bulawayo, Rhodesia, and had been on my mission for just short of a year. I had just been made a senior companion and transferred to Johannesburg. It was a two-day trip from Rhodesia on a train pulled by an old coal-fired puffer billy steam engine.

When I arrived, I was assigned to work with a missionary who had a reputation for two things: working very hard, and being very hard to like. Every companion he had had essentially despised him. The mission president actually apologized to me when he gave me this assignment as this guy's companion, and he promised me that in a few months I would get my own area and a junior companion.

On the car trip from Johannesburg to our area, Elder Snyder (not his real name) lectured me on how *he* was the senior companion and that my only job was to do everything he told me. He said the only reason he needed me there was because the mission rules required it, and that I was to shut up, say nothing, not think, and just be present so that we would meet the requirement of a companionship of two elders. He would make all of the decisions and teach all of the lessons.

Well, I had been warned about Elder Snyder and had thought long and hard about what I assumed was coming. When he "put me in my place," I actually felt the Spirit and replied, "You're right, Elder; I am here to do anything you need. Just tell me what you expect, and I will do everything you ask."

He looked at me to see if I was being sarcastic. I wasn't, so he replied, "I think we're going to get along just fine."

We tracted hard. We fasted many days. We worked and walked and walked and worked until we were physically and emotionally depleted. We were rewarded with zero success. Elder Snyder decided that we just had to work harder, so we slept less, studied more, drove to our area on our own time, and did everything he could think of to work harder.

One morning, after I polished his shoes and made his bed (I'm not even kidding), I asked him, "Why can't the Spirit just lead us to someone who is ready for the gospel?" He laughed and replied that I was so young and inexperienced that I couldn't possibly know that the gospel doesn't work that way. He told me flatly that we have to *work* and *do* everything; that the Lord only intervenes when something very important is happening and not in small things like missionary work. I didn't believe a word of it and shook my head, but I kept quiet as usual.

We had a handful of media referrals, which are slips from Temple Square that people filled out while visiting. They were usually fun and rewarding. We had several left for which we could not find addresses. We were driving our new missionary VW beetle and had driven around fruitlessly for a long time when Elder Snyder gave up, shoved the names into his pocket, and said he was going to throw them away. I felt a sense of deep loss and said so. I reminded him that the Holy Ghost could lead us to their homes if we would pray about it.

Elder Snyder scoffed. "I told you, it doesn't work that way."

I replied, "I think it would if we prayed about it."

He became angry and began mocking me. "Tell you what. We'll start right now, and you listen to the Spirit, and each time we come to an intersection, you tell me which way the Spirit wants us to go, and we'll just settle this once and for all."

It was a challenge spoken in resentment; nevertheless, I felt the Spirit distinctly say to me, "Just choose the opposite of whatever Elder Snyder says."

I replied, "I will accept your challenge, but at every intersection, you have to say which way you think we should go; then I'll choose and we'll go the way I say. Okay?"

"Fine!" he retorted and took off in a huff down the street. As he did so, my first impression was that he had chosen this direction, so I said, "We're going the wrong direction."

He made a fast U-turn, and we headed down a busy street. As we progressed, we came to a dirt road that crossed a railroad track. He said, "Well, there aren't even any houses down there."

I said, "That's the right road; turn in," again only speaking the opposite of what he had said.

"It can't be," he argued.

"It is," I replied, only relying upon that one whispering to do the opposite of him.

We came to an intersection, and he stopped. It was just about dark. He said, "We're lost."

"No, this is the right place," I assured him.

"Well, there's nothing to the left, but a few houses are on the right. Let's go right."

I reminded him of our agreement, and I insisted that we turn left.

"But there aren't any houses on this road, Elder!" he cried.

"The house we are looking for is on this road," I replied, just speaking the opposite of him.

Finally, the road swept to the right, and there was a row of new houses on the left. A few of them had lights on. "Oh, I guess there are houses," he conceded. "But they're all under construction. Nobody lives here."

I said, "One of these is the right house."

"There aren't even numbers on the houses; we could never find the right house, even if it accidentally was the right street!" He was angry now.

"Their house has a number on it," I said.

"I doubt it. Look, there's one with a light on; let's try that side of the street," he said.

"No, it's on the opposite side, without a light on."

"You couldn't possibly know that," he insisted angrily.

I pointed to the only house on that side of the street. It was under construction, and there were no lights visible.

"That house is deserted. Nobody's home," he said. "Let's go home."

"No, that house is not deserted, and there is someone home. Let's go knock." Again, I was just saying the opposite.

He slammed his door and stomped up to the front door. "This isn't their home!" he cried out as he knocked.

"This is the right house," I answered softly, actually unsure myself, because it had been a very unusual process, but I had faith in what I had been clearly told to do.

After a moment, a light snapped on, and a lady opened the door. Elder Snyder smiled snidely and introduced us. He asked if they were the Jones family who had recently visited Temple Square.

She brightened and laughed. "We were there a few months ago, and we were beginning to fear nobody was going to come. We loved it, and we've been reading the Book of Mormon. Do you have time to tell us more about your church? We're really interested."

As I said, I'm not making this up. It was so startling that both of us were immobilized for a moment. Elder Snyder looked at me with raised eyebrows and then stepped inside. We spoke to them about the restoration of the Church and Joseph Smith. They said they were pretty sure Smith was a prophet, having accomplished all that he had. We made an appointment to return.

Back in the car, we drove away in silence. Finally, Elder Snyder looked at me and said, "I know what you're thinking, that the Holy Spirit led you to their home. But, I've been thinking about it, and it wasn't the Spirit at all. All you did was say the opposite of what I thought—so it was actually me who got us there."

I looked at him and felt like crying. "Elder, what you saw tonight was a miracle, and you're like the children of Israel who refused to believe in God even when Moses showed them miracles!"

"That's not true!" he said.

I said, "From now on, I'm going to continue to do what you, my senior companion, tell me to do. But when the Spirit whispers something to me, I'm going to go that direction. I don't care what you say. I'm done following you through purgatory because you refuse to be directed by the Lord. My suggestion is, unless you want us walking in different directions, you just believe the Spirit when it says we need to go or do something else. Because that is the direction I will be headed!"

It was the first time since we had met that I had even proposed I had a brain, or that I would be so insane as to use it. He sputtered, coughed, and started to lecture me, but the Spirit was in the room. He finally laughed. "You have a deal, Elder," he said.

From that moment on, we began having success, meeting people, and teaching lessons. Elder Snyder got the hang of revelation, and I rarely felt like we needed to change course. I was transferred a short time later and became a district leader. I didn't know what happened to Elder Snyder after that; he went home a few months later. However, many years after my mission, I heard his name read in general conference as a new member of one of the Quorums of the Seventy. I'll bet with his work ethic, and with his ability to perceive and obey the Holy Spirit, that things really began to happen.

Brother John

Learning to Fly

*E*very journey begins with a single step. No matter how distant or near the destination, that first step is not optional. To fail to make it is to fail the entire journey. Failure of this one thing is failure of all things.

When it comes to the process of obtaining great priesthood blessings and an elevated stature of righteousness, the first step is learning to hear and then obey the voice of revelation in one's soul. There is no other first step. There is no other process. There is no other path. I think the reason the Holy Spirit has moved me toward this topic so many times on the UnBlog is because this concept is key to everything else we can discuss, or everything else we can ever hope to achieve.

Any precept of the gospel that I have mercifully learned—from the very existence of God to the meaning of temple truths—has come to me because long ago our gracious Savior led me down a long pathway to teach me to listen to His voice. Over the last few months, I have related quite a few of these experiences, and each one taught me in one way or another to listen carefully and obey with all of the courage I can. I'm certainly not as good at it as I wish to be, but over the years, the sum of obedience has literally opened the heavens and poured out joyous blessings.

Now we live in a dispensation of the gospel whose primary God-given objective is to build a society worthy to dwell in the presence of our returning Christ. When we actually understand what we are being asked—or rather commanded—to do, it is a calling and obligation that is so far beyond our present understanding as to make it seemingly incomprehensible. It is somewhat like trying to make a goldfish comprehend feathers and flight.

But like Nephi, the Lord has provided a way for us to do that which He has commanded us to do. He has specifically given each of us the Holy Spirit to lift us from the fishbowl of our inadequacies and to not only give us wings, but to make us worthy to possess them.

The process is very simple. When we allow Christ to become our shepherd by taking His voice as our guide, then He begins to change us. This is the empowering aspect of the Atonement. He not only causes us to see our potential, He vastly upgrades it. He doesn't just forgive us of our sins, He armors us against them. He not only shows us that goldfish really can fly, He causes us to grow wings, to become something that belongs in the air and can't wait to get there! Every time we yield our will to Christ's, something divine happens: we become more and more like Him.

Not only do we grow wings through this process, but we grow eyes that can see the things of eternity and ears that can hear the things of God.

When you read the scriptures and survey the lives of the noble and great ones of previous gospel dispensations, you are not reading the lives of the extraordinarily talented. You are reading the lives of the extraordinarily obedient. They each started with no greater advantage, genius, or strength than most of us.

Their great first step was when they learned to hear, and then to obey, and then to fly.

Brother John

Time to Swerve

Ever since I was a child, the Holy Spirit has been working on me—mostly to get me to learn to hear the voice of revelation and to respond with faith. I would like to tell you three stories lifted from the pages of my past that illustrate a few of the many times our merciful Savior attempted to teach me.

The first event occurred when I was in my teens on a Boy Scout camp. We were in the Uinta Mountains and had hiked a long ways up a crumbling shale mountainside. It was hard climbing because for every three steps forward, you slid backward two. When we finally reached the top, we found that it was as flat as a tabletop. I suppose the area was several acres in size, and it was interspersed with rows of willow bushes. It looked like a randomly planted maze, with big grassy areas cut into sections by these rows of willows. We began running and playing tag. You couldn't see through the willow rows, but you could run around the end of a row and disappear from sight. We also found that you could jump through the rows and land in the next meadow. The effect was almost magical. One instant you were there; the next, you were gone.

At some point, I became the person being chased. I ran around a corner and found myself at a dead end. I decided to jump through the willow row, and I ran hard toward it with another scout closing on me. As I approached, I had a bad feeling. Somehow I "knew" I shouldn't do it. I slowed down and then looked back and saw the scout behind me just about to catch me. I ran full speed at the hedge and jumped.

I felt something very solid hit my chest, and I fell backward back into the meadow. My pursuer was now just a few feet away, so I jumped up and ran at the hedge again. This time, I distinctly felt a hand on my chest, which caught me halfway through the row and pushed me back into the meadow. I fell hard enough to knock the wind out of me.

My friend waited for me to catch my breath. I opened my shirt to see if there was a welt on my chest the shape of a hand. There was nothing. Together, we slowly parted the willows, and to our utter amazement, we found a two hundred-foot vertical drop on the other side of the hedge.

Things like this happened many times, I'm sorry to say. I should have been a quicker learner.

Some years later, I was tasked by my dad to disk up a corn field. The field had been harvested, and running the disk through it in the fall made it a lot easier to plant the next spring. I started the big Farmall Model M tractor and filled it with gas, hooked on the disk, and climbed into the seat. The Farmall M was a tricycle design, with two wheels close together in the nose and two big exposed traction wheels.

I started across the field in fourth gear, which is the fastest "slow" gear on the machine. I grew impatient and pushed in the clutch to shift to fifth gear, which is a road gear and is way too fast for a field. As I did so, I had the distinct impression that I should not use that gear.

Of course, I did it anyway. It seemed safe enough; the field was only a hundred yards away, and I was on a dirt road worn hard by harvesting. The tractor took off. In front of me was an irrigation ditch, which we had plowed closed for harvesting. This let us drive trucks and tractors easily across it without spilling the load. As I approached, bouncing up and down on this barely controlled tractor, to my horror, I saw that my dad had plowed the ditch back open!

I slammed on the brakes as the front pair of tricycle wheels hit the ditch. The rear end bounded into the air and nearly flipped over forward. My foot came off of the clutch. The engine was roaring full speed, and the wheels dug in, flipping the nose of the tractor up into the air. The steering wheel spun to the left, almost breaking my wrists. The rear wheels dropped into the ditch with the nose in the air. The only reason I did not flip over backward was because the disk was still attached to the back end. When those big wheels dropped into the ditch, I came off the seat and flew onto the traction wheels. The wheels bit into my arm and side, rolled me around in the air, and plopped me back into the driver's seat. If I had fallen forward, I would have been fatally thrown under the big wheels and then the disk. If I had fallen backward, I would have been cut to ribbons by the disk.

The big wheels clawed up the opposite side of the bank, and I fell off again, this time to the right, and the big wheels again slapped me back into the seat. I grabbed the steering wheel, slammed my foot on the clutch, and hit the brakes. The tractor turned hard, skidded to a stop, and all the wheels finally dropped. Shaking and sweating profusely, I shut off the tractor and climbed down. My knees buckled, and I fell to the ground. As I knelt there, I remembered the strong impression that I should not use fifth gear in the field.

Fast forward to the year 2000, nearly thirty-five years later. It was after midnight in late October, and I was almost late to catch an airplane in Anchorage, Alaska, a full hour's drive away. The roads were snow packed, with a heavy fall of snow coursing out of the sky. I could just see about two car lengths ahead of me and should have slowed down, but I didn't want to miss my plane. There didn't appear to be any other cars on the road, and it was not particularly slick, just very cold and difficult to see through the dense snow.

As I was driving, the Spirit distinctly said, "Change lanes." It was only an impression, no louder than the previous "Don't use fifth gear" from many years ago. This time, however, I instantly changed lanes, which caused the car to fishtail and slide sideways. As I fought to get the car back under control, a large moose flashed by on my right. He had been standing in my lane and most likely would have killed me.

I have since pondered the spiritual training of my youth and have remembered some of the thousands of times the Lord tried to speak to me. Each of them was a chance to avoid pain, to not leave something behind, or even to save my life. Most of the time, the Lord spared me in spite of my disobedience, which warms my soul with gratitude and makes me feel loved and protected. It also seems very parental of Him to instruct, warn, guide, and let me feel a little fear and a little pain. But when I was a child, I acted as a child, and now that I am a spiritual adult, I try to listen very carefully, because the time of lessons is past.

Now it is time to swerve, and then find out why later.

Brother John

The Three Voices

I *want to share with you a powerful tool to develop a* greater understanding of revelation and how to receive it. The idea of this tool just came to me one day as I was pondering these very things, and I have personally found it to be of great worth. I gave it as an assignment to my institute class several times, and as many people as actually did it found it to be amazingly illuminating.

In order to understand how to use this tool, we first need to consider how to distinguish revelation from other noise in our heads.

The Voice of Our Mind

There are three voices that a "healthy" mind hears. The first and loudest is the voice of our own mind. We hear ourselves think. We ask questions, debate, and doubt. We analyze the events of our lives and make decisions. This voice is almost always unsure. It wonders about everything and questions, "Why did that happen?", "What should I do now?", "What does that mean?", and "How could I be so dumb?" This is all our own thinking and reasoning. The easiest way to identify this voice is that it often references "me" and "I." For example, "I think I'm in trouble," is from your own mind. "I'm hungry" or "Why is this happening to me?" are similar ruminations of the human psyche.

The Holy Spirit

The next voice we hear is from the Holy Spirit. In its earliest stages, this voice is called our conscience. *The most important fact here is that it is revelation, and it is the voice of Christ.* Making this realization is the most important thing a soul can do to promote great righteousness.

The easiest way to identify this voice is that it always leads us to do something good and to believe in Christ. It rarely asks questions. It clearly distills a thought or pure concept into our minds or heart: "Don't do that." "Put it back." "Pick it up." "Go to church." "Help your wife with the dishes." "Be loving to your husband." "Play with your kids." These are all examples of the voice of the Holy Spirit. The Holy Spirit has a single purpose in our lives, which is to constantly inform us of what is right and wrong. Any time we must choose between good and evil, or right and wrong, the Holy Spirit will nudge us in the direction of truth and right.

Moroni 7 tells us that by learning to hear the voice of the Spirit, we can tell good from evil as clearly as the daylight from the dark night.

> 15 For behold, my brethren, it is given unto you to judge, that ye may know good from evil; and the way to judge is as plain, that ye may know with a perfect knowledge, as the daylight is from the dark night
>
> 16 For behold, the Spirit of Christ is given to every man, that he may know good from evil; wherefore, I show unto you the way to judge; for every thing which inviteth to do good, and to persuade to believe in Christ, is sent forth by the power and gift of Christ; wherefore ye may know with a perfect knowledge it is of God.
>
> 17 But whatsoever thing persuadeth men to do evil, and believe not in Christ, and deny him, and serve not God, then ye may know with a perfect knowledge it is of the devil; for after this manner doth the devil work, for he persuadeth no man to do good, no, not one; neither do his angels; neither do they who subject themselves unto him.
>
> 18 And now, my brethren, seeing that ye know the light by which ye may judge, which light is the light of Christ, see that ye do not judge wrongfully; for with that same judgment which ye judge ye shall also be judged.
>
> 19 Wherefore, I beseech of you, brethren, that ye should search diligently in the light of Christ that ye may know good from evil; and if ye will lay hold upon every good thing, and condemn it not, ye certainly will be a child of Christ. (Moroni 7: 15–19)

It is important to grasp the power of this concept, which is that *everything* that invites you to do good—including ideas for good that pop into your head—is inspired of God and *is* revelation. Choosing to be obedient to all such promptings will dramatically increase your spiritual strength and set you upon the ordained path to joy and upward spiritual mobility. Just as we continually hear the voice of temptation, we also continually hear the voice of Christ—at least, unless we shut it off through disobedience.

Such promptings are rarely actual voices. Promptings are most often just thoughts or impressions that come into the heart and mind, usually when you least expect it. To some they come as visual images or flashes of pictures or sudden insight. But we can tell without a doubt that they come from Christ when they lead us to do something good—even if that good thing is as mundane and annoying as a thought to drive the speed limit. As the scripture says, *all* good things are inspired of God.

The Voice of Evil

The final voice we hear is the voice of evil. We are all quite familiar with temptations. They are most often appealing to the flesh, our pride, or our vanity. They try to get us to go contrary to righteous promptings.

Someone asked me recently if the "devil" can hear the promptings we receive. I believe that the evil ones, *while not able to hear our thoughts,* are keenly aware of when we are receiving promptings from righteous spiritual sources. I believe it because when there is a prompting to do good, the evil ones immediately rant against it, railing with many reasons why we should do otherwise.

As well, the evil ones certainly know the behaviors and weaknesses of mankind, and eventually they come to know and recognize us. They have millennia of experience in discerning the mood, emotions, and likely intentions of their human prey. As they systematically gather information about us and learn who we are, who we were in premortality, and what our strengths and weaknesses are here, they intelligently and logically persuade, fight, reason, and rant against anything good that the Lord wants for us. I consider it unlikely that we interact with the actual prince of darkness. But we do hear from his minions, tempters, and messengers. My experiences have led me to believe that these beings are hateful and angry and have very real intent to destroy us. What seems like a vague scuffle to us is an all-out war to them, and they fully intend to win. Their goal is to get us to obey them, thus separating us from the voice of the Holy Spirit.

An example of these three voices operating in our lives probably happened to a lot of us just last Fast Sunday. The voice of the Holy Spirit might have prompted you to bear your testimony. The opposition, keenly aware of what is going on, and knowing you and your weaknesses, would immediately counter with a barrage of clever arguments tailor-made for you: "You won't know what to say. It will be embarrassing. You will just start crying. Leave the time for other people. Nobody really cares about what you think anyway," and similar lies. Your mind then says, "Oh, my goodness, what should I do?"

When we are able to identify these three voices correctly, then we don't need to ask ourselves what we "should" do, because we "should" bear our testimony. This is what Christ desires of us at that moment. The real question is, "Will I be obedient and bear my testimony?"

With this understanding embedded in our souls, we are ready to employ this great tool I mentioned earlier.

The Small Plates of John

Go get a small notebook, preferably one you can keep in your shirt pocket or purse.

Take a marker and write on the cover "The Small Plates of . . ." inserting your name. Every time you receive a prompting, and every time you hear a temptation, write it down in your small plates. Be as specific and detailed as you can.

Leave blank space after each entry.

Go back at the end of the day and record whether you hearkened to that which was good, or if you succumbed to that which was evil.

Record the result of your decision—how it worked out for you. When you were faithful, what happened? Whose lives were changed? Were you happier because of your obedience? When you failed to obey, what were the consequences?

What you will find is that you receive dozens of "revelations" every day. You will see that your life is literally submerged in promptings. You will see that with every decision you made, right or wrong, you knew what you "should have" done.

You will also find that the voice of opposition is very informed. It is specific and intelligent. It is your enemy and is giving you hundreds of reasons to disobey and satisfy some carnal desire or lust. You will know without a doubt the war that is being waged for your soul.

Keeping your small plates does not have to go on for a long period of time. It is an exercise designed to teach you the difference between the voices of revelation, evil, and your mind. Every person who tries this is flabbergasted by the volume of information received each day. You will be delighted at how clearly Christ is leading you and amazed and dismayed at how thoroughly evil opposes any truth and all light. You will soon see why Christ characterized us as walking in darkness at noonday and often lamented that He is a light shining in darkness, and the darkness comprehendeth it not.

49 The light shineth in darkness, and the darkness comprehendeth it not; nevertheless, the day shall come when you shall comprehend even God, being quickened in him and by him.

50 Then shall ye know that ye have seen me, that I am, and that I am the true light that is in you, and that you are in me; otherwise ye could not abound. (Doctrine & Covenants 88: 49–50)

For those of you who take the initiative to try this experiment, I applaud you. When you discover the truth and power of being able to discern between the "three voices," you will have found new wings for your spiritual flight.

Brother John

Stephanie, There Really Is a God

Dear Stephanie,

I have read your letter several times and pondered if there was anything I could say to help you. It sounds like your life has hit bottom, probably more than once. It sounds like you have lost your faith in God, possibly even your belief in God. You want a miracle to prove that God exists and that He loves you. Perhaps there are a lot of people aching just like you, so I decided to answer you publicly.

Stephanie, there really is a God, and He really does love you— and the odd thing is that I can prove it to you.

I want you to place yourself in this scenario in your mind's eye. Let's say you are driving down the road with a few wild friends, and you come upon a young mother pushing a baby stroller beside the road. Let's say your friends started taunting you and urging you to run over the cute baby in the stroller. They offer you money and call you a coward. Would you do it?

I know you wouldn't because as you just considered that scenario, you felt repelled and sickened by the idea, didn't you? You knew it was awful and wrong. I could pose a thousand other similar scenarios to you, and you would know if every one of them was right or wrong, all by yourself, without anyone helping. The amazing thing is that I could also pose the same scenarios to every person on the planet, and they would likewise know, exactly like you, the rightness or evilness of each.

Do you know why?

It is because you and every other living person were born with the Light of Christ within them. We call it our conscience. What you may not have realized is that your conscience comes from Jesus Christ, and it is actually revelation to you. This is where God *is* in your life. This is your connection to the divine. This is your proof that God actually exists, that He loves you, and that He is with you every moment of your day. You have never been alone—ever.

When you do those "despicable" things you mentioned, you wouldn't even know that they were despicable without your conscience to tell you. Did you realize that each time you choose to do something dark, there is a war inside of you? You have to fight hard against the feeling of doing right. You have to purposefully choose to do what is wrong in the face of knowing you shouldn't. The source of *all* your unhappiness is this war within your heart.

Each time you choose to do the right thing, the war ends and you feel proud of yourself, don't you, Stephanie? And each time you do the wrong thing, you feel awful, you hate yourself, you hate everyone else, and you hate God—because it feels as if God has been mean to put you through this awful dilemma of forcing you to choose between what He calls right, and what your wants, lusts, and addictions keep insisting that you must have.

You say you want to be a person of light, a positive example to your children, and a source of light for other people. Here is how to do that: Choose the light in every single decision you make. Choose to do what your conscience tells you is right. This is actually Jesus Christ giving you a perfect knowledge of what is right. He does this because He loves you, and because He knows that this is the *only* way you will be happy in this life and able to live with Him in the next. Choose those good things and you will become that person of light you want to be! Choose anything else and you will remain in darkness.

Stephanie, learning to obey one's conscience is the single greatest lesson people learn in their lifetime. For some, it seems easy to choose to do right. They learn quickly that happiness flows from obeying that guiding voice and doing good. Others must experience great pain to be motivated to choose the right. This is the merciful reason for your pain and discomfort: to guide you back into happiness.

What is interesting to me about you is that you admit that you have lived a hard and dark life—and yet there is a part of you that wants to be full of light—fearless and free. Your spirit must be very strong within you. You must be a person of extraordinary strength to even want light and truth after indulging yourself in darkness for so long.

Because of your inner strength, I have faith in your ability to choose the right and turn your life around. If you don't have that faith in yourself, decide here and now to have faith in Jesus Christ, and in His voice of revelation to your soul. Just choose to obey, and obey, and obey. As you do so, He will change you, and you will find that you no longer desire your former sins. The fear will depart, the darkness will lift, and you will feel satisfaction, then contentment, then self-worth, then happiness, and, in time, you will feel joy. Somewhere along that path you will also feel clean and worthy.

At some point, your inner sense of right and wrong is going to suggest that you go talk with your bishop to get the further help you need. Your bishop can guide you through the repentance process. He will be loving and understanding, and he'll see that you are trying, that you are willing to pay the price to become that person of light that you truly can be. Trust his counsel.

This is the only pathway back, Stephanie. You have the inner strength and empowerment through the Atonement of Christ to claim your life in the light. You also have the choice to remain where you are. You can't do both. You must walk the path of light completely, without reservation and without excuses, or you must forever (including beyond the grave) remain in darkness, trapped in a life of unhappiness and pain.

God bless you,

Brother John

Living Faith in Christ

*F*aith as an idea or tenet of religion is static. Having faith in Christ as a great teacher, or as a prophet, or even as the Son of God whose words and works are set and accomplished has its basis in truth and effects a positive upward push in our lives—but it is static. By that I mean that it does not change. This type of faith is that of adoring believers looking upward. On the other hand, *living* faith is knowing that Jesus Christ is looking downward, responding to our needs, answering our prayers, sending forth poignant and timely blessings, directing our lives and feet and hands. It is living because Jesus Christ is living. He is not an idea; He is our Savior, a living being, and He is intimately involved in our lives.

Last October, I had the opportunity to teach the high priests group in our ward. The subject was faith in Christ, with the second part of the discussion being the question, "How can we increase our faith in Christ?" The comments from the group were leaning toward "keep the commandments" and "repent of your sins," which are true faith builders, but suggest that Christ is only involved in our lives when we're relatively perfect. Christ isn't in our lives to just minister to the whole and the saved, but to those who are struggling and lost, who are at a loss as to how to proceed. "Keep the commandments" as a sole formula for faith reveals a less-than-intimate understanding of how faith works and why it is even present in our lives.

To have living faith in Christ, we must first understand who Christ is and where He is. I don't mean that He is in heaven. I mean *where* He is in the barren fields of our own lives—our day-to-day existence. We cannot have faith in something that is nonexistent or not active in our lives. If you don't know how Christ interacts with you, what His voice sounds like, how to receive answers to your prayers, or even how He answers them, then just having faith in the *concept* of Christ will not be profoundly life-changing, and you have very little upon which to make your faith operate.

When you realize that Christ is the literal source of all truth, and that you hear His voice constantly in your life—first as your conscience, then further on as the powerful workings of the Holy Spirit—then you suddenly know where Christ is, what He's doing, and how to become a disciple. When you become aware and accept that this little voice of truth that has been niggling at you all your life is actually your Savior attempting to direct you into salvation, then you have in a very real way "come unto Christ."

As you realize that all of these little urgings to do good, or perhaps to not do something wrong, have come from Christ, you can begin to sample obedience. As you do so, in a very short time you'll come to realize that this isn't just a bothersome voice of "stop, don't do that," but it is a loving voice of safety and peace—and it is never wrong. Safety follows obedience, experience produces confidence, and that confidence in the voice of Christ is in fact "living faith in Christ."

This then is powerful faith, because you soon come to realize, with great confidence, that the direction or prompting, truth or principle, words or acts you have just been directed to do will *always* bless your life and everyone around you. It is living because it comes from a living and loving Christ. It is living because it is the voice of heaven speaking in your ear for your benefit. It is living because it breathes life and hope into your soul. It is living because it is the very pathway to righteousness, peace, joy, and salvation.

It is such a simple concept that toddlers can learn it. It is such an impassable obstacle that the mighty and great ones stumble and stub their eternal welfare upon it. It is such a pure concept that the humble and meek of all the generations of mankind have used it to write their names in the books of the saved throughout all the generations of man.

Brother John

Preach My Gospel

When I was sent to the South African mission in 1971, we were told hundreds of times to "stick to the lesson plan." We memorized seven lessons in two languages, English and Afrikaans, and were commanded—I mean ordered—to adhere to the discussions. We were not to deviate even if the people asked us a question. We were to tell them that their questions would be answered as we went through the material, and then we were to just finish the lesson. We even practiced with actor investigators how to deflect questions and stick to the lessons as memorized.

I entered the mission field with a "testimony" of the missionary lessons. The mythical "Brother Brown" would listen politely, give the prescribed answers, and accept the challenge to be baptized; I was sure of it.

What I experienced was very different. We usually didn't make it past the first few statements before disagreement or even debates began. Brother Brown hadn't studied his part of the script and never gave the right answers. But, we pressed on and gave our cheerful next line no matter what. I had people throw me out of the house because they were insulted.

After about a year into my mission, and a miraculous experience where the Spirit led my companion and I to find a home of some investigators, I decided to change my tactic. With somewhat of a guilty conscience, I began teaching people according to what came into my heart—and we began getting return appointments and having wonderful missionary experiences. We directly answered people's questions and bore testimony out of sync with the lesson plan. I felt wretchedly disobedient, but I just couldn't help it.

I eventually got tattled on. The mission president sent an assistant to the president (AP) to our area with the instruction to get me back on track. I was the district leader at the time, and I wasn't towing the line. My companion and I split up and went to different appointments.

The AP and I drove to the home of a young couple who had been anxious to meet with us. We shook hands and sat opposite them. They sat close to each other and held hands. I started the first discussion, which was about the apostasy, the First Vision, and living prophets. I got maybe through the first concept (word perfect, I must say) and the brother stopped me.

"I would like to hear the rest of how your church started, but we have a specific question. You see, our baby died last week, and our pastor said she was going to hell because she hadn't been baptized. We really need to know—is our baby girl really in hell right now?" The young mother burst into tears, and his eyes filled.

I leaned forward and said, "No, absolutely not. Let me read to you what the prophet Moroni taught about baptizing infants—"

The AP took it from there, interrupted my answer and launched into the second concept. This brother and sister were amazed, and looked as if they had been slapped. They waited impatiently until the next concept turned the floor back to me.

I said, "The prophet Moroni taught us that little children are saved by the Atonement of Christ—"

"That's great, Elder," the AP said. "Why don't I finish up from here? From what I said earlier, you can see that the original church of Christ had completely apostatized, and—"

The brother we were teaching leaned forward and interrupted, "Excuse me, sir, but I am not interested in what you are saying. We are in agony here about our little girl, and I am asking you to be quiet and let Elder Pontius finish. After that, if I don't throw you out on the street, you can finish telling me about how your church came into being. Okay?"

The AP slid back in his chair and nodded. I was shocked and knew for a fact that my brief reign of terror as the DL had just ended. I knew they were going to chastise me, bust me back to junior companion, and probably send me home. Yet, after a moment of fear, I realized this was also one of the most wonderful teaching moments of my mission. I opened the scriptures and read Mormon's teaching to his son Moroni on infant baptism. I told them about my little brother, Timmy, who died when he was two, and how we were sealed into a forever family relationship in the temple. I told them that they would hold their baby girl again in the Resurrection, and I promised them in the name of Christ that their grief would be short-lived and that they would rejoice once again, all because of the Atonement of Christ.

They wept. I wept. The AP glared. They begged us to return as soon as possible and tell them why I was so sure this was true. They said they were anxious to join our church so they could share this faith too.

We drove home in silence. The AP didn't even shake my hand as we parted. I went to bed wondering where the mission kept its prison for disobedient DLs.

About a week later, I got a letter from the mission president. He had a distinctive southern twang in his speech, and as I read the first line I could practically hear him speaking the words, "Deeah Eldah Pontius, it has come to mah attention that you have been teachin' off the top of yoah head and not from the missionary lehssons."

I will have to paraphrase the rest of the letter; I just remember that opening line. He wrote that the assistant had come back and told him about the experience he had had teaching the first discussion with me. (I paused here a long time before reading on.)

He said that this was the finest example of teaching by the Spirit he had ever heard. He said that to give the first discussion in that setting would have been wrong, that I had sweetly met these investigators' needs, taught them the truth, and introduced our beliefs in a sweet and powerful way. He said he wished every missionary in Africa could do what I did that night.

The President continued, "Elder, this is instruction just for you alone, not for the other elders in your district. I give you explicit permission to teach any way you see fit. I am lifting the instruction on you to teach only from the missionary lessons. Please keep this to yourself. God bless and happy teaching."

I was so relieved! I didn't even know the term "teaching by the Spirit" at that time. Nobody had used it in my hearing as I went through the MTC. I just knew that when my heart burned and words came to my lips, joy always followed speaking them. I didn't know why; I just knew it was the right thing to say.

I later wrote *Following the Light of Christ into His Presence*, which is about this very thing—hearing the voice of the Spirit, recognizing it, obeying it, and teaching by it. I am certain that my president's letter was the beginning baby step in arriving at the principles I penned in that book.

Many years later in 2001, our son left on his mission to the Philippines. As he was walking to the boarding ramp, I handed him a copy of my book and said, "I don't know if your mission rules will let you read this book. But you can tell them it was written by your father, and they may allow it."

Our son hadn't read my book yet. I hadn't asked him to. I prefer to wait until the Spirit moves my children to seek light, just like everyone else in the world, and then they will read it with open eyes and ears. He read the book on the airplane—all of it. By the time he arrived in the Philippines, he had decided that this was how he was going to live not only his mission, but his life—by the Spirit.

So he stormed into Baguio, listened to the Holy Spirit, and began baptizing people. He was rejoicing in his labors, and the field was yielding much fruit for him and for the Lord. He ascribed every success to the Lord, and to having learned to listen to the Spirit.

He was made a DL, then an AP, and moved into the mission offices in Manilla. He began teaching others how to do missionary work by the Spirit, and their overall mission success took a surprising upswing. While he was serving as AP, a member of the Quorum of the Twelve became the Area General Authority and worked directly with the mission president and my son.

This apostle asked our son to write a training plan detailing how he had taught the missionaries under his leadership to teach by the Spirit. Together with an apostle of the Lord, he developed a teaching plan that they put to effective use. A few years later, this same apostle returned to the United States and assisted in the development of *Preach My Gospel*. I don't know how much of his work went into that inspired volume, but I do know that our son's example of success in teaching by the Spirit fit well into that model.

The single greatest teaching in *Preach My Gospel* is to first acquire the Spirit of the Lord and then to go out and say and do what the Lord inspires you to say and do. It teaches the very things that my kind mission president gave me permission to do, which was, above all other things, to teach by the Spirit. Because our missionary system is now based on the infallible and true principle of following the Spirit as we teach, and because the Holy Spirit is always present when we seek it, and because this *is* God's work, it is the most effective tool of conversion that has ever been created.

This method of teaching by the Spirit is also the same one that Adam and Eve, Enoch, Melchizedek, Abraham, Jesus Christ, Joseph Smith, and every other inspired soul has used to great success.

Words from Christ's lips to our ears: "Preach my gospel." And do it by the Spirit.

Brother John

The Law of the Celestial Kingdom

If I knew I were going to die tomorrow, and I could take one truth from my heart and plant it into my children and grandchildren's hearts and minds, this is what it would be: The law of the celestial kingdom. It has taken me half a lifetime to acquire this knowledge, and the other half to understand how powerful and invaluable this knowledge is. Besides the fact that Jesus is the Christ, this is quite literally the most important thing I know.

Speaking of Jesus Christ, the scriptures teach us: "He that ascended up on high, as also he descended below all things, in that he comprehended all things, that he might be in all and through all things, the light of truth; Which truth shineth. This is the light of Christ" (Doctrine & Covenants 88: 6–7).

From this scripture we learn that a great deal of the suffering and agony Christ experienced on our behalf was to prepare Him for His mission as the source of all truth. This, as the scripture states, is the Light of Christ. Or in other words, the Light of Christ is the source of all truth. Stating the same thing another way, there is no source of truth other than Christ.

What follows in section 88 is an enlightening discussion on what the Light of Christ means to us. It states that it is the power that gives and sustains life, keeps the stars and planets in their proper orbit, and gives order throughout all existence. Further, it is: "The light which is in all things, which giveth life to all things, which is the law by which all things are governed, even the power of God who sitteth upon his throne, who is in the bosom of eternity, who is in the midst of all things" (Doctrine & Covenants 88:13).

Consider the impact of these words. Not only is the Light of Christ the *source* of all truth and the origin of our conscience, but it is the *law* by which all things—including we ourselves—are governed.

When any divine command is sent forth, whether it be something as complex as creating a new world, as powerful as healing the sick, or as simple as a prompting to kneel and pray, it is done through the Light of Christ. When He commands the elements to form into a world, He speaks and He is obeyed. Presumably, His voice sounds the same to the elements as it does to us. When He whispers, all creation obeys. All, that is, except mankind.

"And they who are not sanctified through the law which I have given unto you, even the law of Christ, must inherit another kingdom, even that of a terrestrial kingdom, or that of a telestial kingdom. For he who is not able to abide the law of the celestial kingdom cannot abide a celestial glory" (Doctrine & Covenants 88:21–22).

This scripture is teaching us that the Light of Christ is not only the source of all truth but is also the *law* of the celestial kingdom. Not only is it the straight and narrow way—the only way—but it is literally the law against which we will be judged. As a direct result, we will be either welcomed into the celestial kingdom, or asked to dwell in another kingdom whose law we *are* willing to obey.

Notice the last sentence of the above verse. If we cannot abide the law, we cannot abide the glory. If we can't be obedient to the voice of revelation, we cannot attain unto the glory that such obedience would naturally bestow upon us. When we obey the celestial law, we are quickened by a portion of the celestial glory. This is the empowering element of the Atonement; it is what uplifts and sanctifies us. And if we are quickened by a portion of celestial glory in this life, when we are resurrected, we will receive a fulness of the same glory. "They who are of a celestial spirit shall receive the same body which was a natural body; even ye shall receive your bodies, and your glory shall be that glory by which your bodies are quickened. Ye who are quickened by a portion of the celestial glory shall then receive of the same, even a fulness" (Doctrine & Covenants 88:28–29).

The scripture further explains that when we choose to be governed by the voice of Christ, we will be preserved, perfected, and sanctified by the same. And when we rebel and seek to become a law unto ourselves, then the law cannot sanctify us, nor can anything else.

> And again, verily I say unto you, that which is governed by law is also preserved by law and perfected and sanctified by the same. That which breaketh a law and abideth not by law, but seeketh to become a law unto itself, and willeth to abide in sin, and altogether abideth in sin, cannot be sanctified by law, neither by mercy, justice nor judgment. Therefore, they must remain filthy still. (Doctrine & Covenants 88:34)

The course to eternal life may at times seem overwhelming. But it doesn't need to be! Even though your goals and aspirations are most lofty and at times may seem unreachable, the way to accomplish them is truly simple. Grab hold of the iron rod of personal revelation and obey the law of the celestial kingdom. The Lord will help and empower you every step of the way.

It sounds simple, and it is simple; however, simplicity does not mean it is easy. It is a life-long task.

Of the billions who have lived, you are among the most noble and valiant of God's children. You are capable of such obedience and can become worthy of all these blessings. When anyone sets his or her heart on a course of obedience and taps daily into the empowerment and grace available through the Atonement of Christ, they will soon accomplish all of this much more quickly than they ever thought possible.

A commitment to total obedience will blast you off so fast and high that it will be breathtaking, with a spiritual height that's unimaginable, and the promised blessings will be very near.

Brother John

Live Each Day

It seems that my weekly blog is slipping to Thursday. It's probably because I struggle somewhat to know what to share.

Most blogging is personal in nature, and being a rather private person, I can't seem to blog about the trivia of my life.

However, I think I want to share that these last few weeks have been a great trial for us. We have had some discouraging news about my health. This has forced many changes into our little world. One of them has been that I have suddenly realized that quite a few of the clichés about life are true. You know, "Live each day as if it were your last," "Live so that you can leave at any moment without regret," and on and on. When you're looking at the frayed end of your rope as you dangle from a great height, those things do matter—a lot. They matter best if you can say that you *did*, and that you *are*. They matter because they become sweet comforts, and the "could have been" clause of reckoning is rendered mute.

Another interesting change is that we value the sweet things more. We are more faith-filled, more complimentary, more patient, more compliant, easier to be convinced, quicker to serve, and more joyous to be loved and in love. We hold one another longer and seek ways to serve with greater urgency. We have more purity of purpose and a greater endowment of charity for all of our fellow pilgrims. These things I didn't expect—and I find them the sweetest.

With gratitude, with faith born of sight more than hope, with truth painted by the divine brush upon the canvas of my soul, I am grateful for my life and grateful for the blessing of learning these things now while there is time, so that I do not have to die ignorant of the things that matter most. I am grateful that I can see the flowers scattered across the landscape of my world, that I can gather them into a divine bouquet and cherish them while there is time. I realize what a gift it is to drink from the waters of life and to treasure the light of divine day.

No mortal knows when life will end. Death is an inevitable outcome of life, unless Zion happens to call you into a state of translation. In truth, I may live another twenty years. Nobody knows. They speak of odds and averages, with no view of divine will or of faith and priesthood. They look at their numbers and steeply stack the odds against the afternoon hours of my little day, and the road they describe is a rocky trail that dwindles into impassible obstacles. But it is a trail that leads to the face of God, to Zion, and to the destination that is my birthright. To this pilgrim's feet, it seems a path far more desirable than a speeding thoroughfare to nowhere that brings you to any destination, ignorant of the sweetest parts of living, which irony seems to teach us on the shadow side of life.

I know in whom I have trusted. My God hath been my support; He hath led me through mine afflictions in the wilderness; and He hath preserved me upon the waters of the great deep. Rejoice, O my heart, and cry unto the Lord, and say: O Lord, I will praise thee forever; yea, my soul will rejoice in thee, my God, and the rock of my salvation. (2 Nephi 4:19–20, 30)

Brother John

The Journey Home
Part II: Of Pain and Pills

I stayed with John in Providence Hospital every day and night, sleeping on the lumpy roll-in cot, watching him float in and out of morphine dreams, singing hymns by his bedside, and rubbing his feet and head. Hospital life for me became sweetly routine: I slept when he slept, and my usual crazy-busy life was reduced to tranquil simplicity. I never felt bored, only grateful for one more day with my husband. The grandkids sent precious little hand-made cards, and as John was in the bishopric at the time, the youth from our ward had all signed a gigantic get-well poster, which proudly graced the wall above his bed.

In mid-October 2006, John was finally released after two weeks of intensive treatment. Once home, he continued a six-month stint of IV antibiotics. Actually, it was I who administered them, with instruction from a homecare nurse. I marveled at John's resilience and absolute trust in the Lord, no matter what his body was going through. I had never seen him endure so much physical hardship, and now his steady faith was a true testimony to me of his innate character. Even when he was trying to get off the pain pills, which he characterized as the most difficult thing about the whole event, he absolutely trusted in his Lord and often told me that the refinement gained was much greater than the trial he was enduring. After months of taking the pills out of necessity, John realized with some horror that he was addicted to the things. He vowed that day to quit cold turkey and made me promise to take them away and never give him another pill, no matter how much he might beg.

I did, and he begged, and I didn't, and we made it through.

—Terri

Chapter Three

It's All True

It's True—It's All True!

My father passed away in May of 2008. He and I had a unique relationship. We disagreed on many things, but on gospel subjects, we were spiritual twins. Because we jointly owned several businesses, built houses together, and often worked side by side, we constantly discussed the gospel. We would ride to a job site or to the business talking of gospel principles—marveling, rejoicing, testifying. We would speak often during the day of such things, and on the drive home. For a few years, he was my bishop, and I served as his elder's quorum president. We counseled in private for many hours of deeply spiritual searching and planning our duties.

We often switched places as teacher and student. From my early teens, he taught me gospel truths, and I would ask questions, propose additional truths, and he treated me like a peer, even when I was not. It was our special relationship, and I still rejoice in it. When I became a spiritual adult, I often enjoyed sharing insights and truths I had gained. He would go home, study, search, and return to me with an additional or adjacent truth, which broadened my understanding and my soul. We leap-frogged each other for our entire lives together.

When Dad was a few days from death, I flew from Alaska to his home in Idaho to see him. Again, we spoke deeply of spiritual things. We talked of what it would be like to meet the Savior, as well as loved ones who had gone on before. I said, "Just think, Dad, in a few days you will meet and embrace Jesus Christ, and you will be able to ask Him every question you ever had and get answers that no mortal can possibly understand. Then you will know with your eyes, not just by faith. It will be a glorious experience!"

He replied, "I certainly hope so," and laughed nervously. His whole life had been a walk of faith. As far as I know, he never saw angels, watched the heavens opened, or had his faith confirmed in any concrete way. He just believed, received, and acted upon inspiration and lived his life walking the straight and narrow way. His nervousness came from the fact that he had never experienced anything *greater* than faith. His spiritual eyes and ears had not physically seen or heard the things he had yearned to experience all his life.

I was back in Alaska when he finally passed away a few days later. My sister called me to let me know. I stood up from that conversation and went to my bedroom to prepare for bed. As I was standing at the sink, I felt my father's presence, along with an indescribable joy, enter the room. I knew it was not coming from me because I was feeling sad and a little conflicted. I missed him terribly, but I was glad he was no longer suffering.

No, this feeling was coming directly from him. His joy was so intense that no mortal word can describe it. I imagine it would be something like having someone hand you a blank check worth a billion dollars, and in the same second to be crowned king of the world, and at the same time to find out that you had the power to heal any illness or disease, and that anything you wanted would become a reality. If you can imagine that kind of joy and multiply it by a million, this was the emotion that was radiating from him and into me. I don't believe a mortal is capable of feeling such powerful emotion in this sphere.

I heard his voice say, "John, it's all true, it's all true, it's all true!" repeated over and over and over. His voice finally tapered away into the distance, taking the feeling of ecstatic joy with him.

I consider it a tender mercy to myself and to my father to have had that brief glimpse into his joy. I knew exactly what he was talking about. He was confirming forty-five years of deep and intimate gospel discussions and eternal truths we both loved, both understood, and which by faith alone he had embraced fully throughout his life. He was also telling me that he had at last seen with his eyes, and felt with his hands, and knew in a most intimate and powerful way that the restored gospel and every truth associated with it is true.

I will never forget his joy and those ecstatic words ringing in my ears, "It's all true!"

Brother John

Choose Ye This Day

*M*y *Dear UnBlogospherians and Other* Famous People,

As I have been invited to speak, to visit, and to teach, it has come to my attention that there is among some folks a sense of dissatisfaction with the LDS Church. The point of conflict shifts with the group or individual involved, but it is generally something they feel is missing in their own life, which they blame on the Church for not providing.

Let me say as strongly as I possibly can: The Church of Jesus Christ of Latter-day Saints is the only true and living church on the earth. It is not the only place where truth or Christ or faith or hope is found. It is just the greatest of such places. It holds the authority and the priesthood keys and is the only place that does. It has within its doctrine, ordinances, and structure everything that is necessary for every blessing mankind can seek in mortality or in eternity. It has a prophet selected by the Savior Himself and apostles whom I joyfully sustain as prophets, seers, and revelators. From one inspired program and gospel principle to another, this church has it all.

At the risk of offending someone, let me add: if there is an empty place in someone's soul for which the Church is being held hostage for not filling, the fault lies with that individual, not with the Church.

Is the Church flawless? No, flaws come from flawed people who have yet to understand Doctrine & Covenants 121; but they do not come from the Lord or His gospel. Even those beloved brethren who sit in the red seats are still just people. And as Judas could not by his betrayal diminish the office of apostle nor the Church, so is the Lord's Latter-day Church still true, despite what flawed people may do within it.

This is the truth, and this will be true until Christ returns in glory: The gospel of Jesus Christ is not only true, but it works, it functions, it exalts, it binds the ordinances and seals the covenants. It calls down angels and ministering beings and lavishes blessings upon those who see past the gears, nuts and bolts, and happenings of the Church and who look heavenward at what this inspired church is successfully providing for us.

So I say, "Choose ye this day." As for me and my house, we choose to serve the Lord, as He reveals Himself through the latter-day kingdom.

Brother John

Peas Porridge Hot

Not long after the creation of the first Wasilla (Alaska) Ward, my father and I drove to the local feed store to get something. I was loading some bags into the back of the truck when my father jumped from the truck and almost ran up onto the dock. He walked up to a guy with a long black beard and shoulder-length black hair. This guy had a knife on his hip nearly a foot long. My dad shook his hand and said, "Hello, I'm your bishop."

The guy acted like his hand had been burned and yanked it back. His face clouded, and he put his hand on the hilt of his knife. "Not interested!" he muttered, and he turned his back on my dad.

I admit this happened almost forty years ago, but as I recall, Dad replied something like this: "The only reason I know you're a member is because there is a certain light in your eye. I don't know your name or your reasons for not coming to church, but I am cleaning up the membership of my ward. You can either come to church, or I'm going to have to excommunicate you and your family."

This guy turned around, and I thought he was going to slit my dad's throat. He said, "My wife would kill me if you did that!"

"We meet at 10:00 in Palmer," Dad said and turned away.

I was so stunned that I couldn't pick up another bag. I looked at Dad, and we both immediately jumped into the truck—for safety. My Dad's hands were trembling as he turned the ignition key.

"Dad, you can't say that!" I said incredulously.

He looked dazed. "I know. It just—seemed like the right thing to do."

We drove away with both of us kind of in shock.

The next Sunday, a battered old Suburban pulled up with this guy, his wife, and four teenage daughters. He wore leather pants and a jacket that I actually think said "Hell's Angels" on the back. His wife wore a tight red miniskirt and two pounds of makeup. His daughters walked in a cluster, holding onto one another as if they were prisoners being led to execution. Everyone—I mean every person in the chapel—shook their hands. His name was Clyde Peas. His grip was like an alpha-male baboon's. The ward swirled around them and lavished so much love on them that they were visibly stunned. The sisters gaggled around Sister Peas and treated her like a visiting dignitary. The young women swooped in on the girls, and soon they were actually giggling and smiling. The brethren enfolded Brother Peas in pure fellowship and acceptance.

We found out they lived three hours' drive from the church. We organized a dinner calendar so they were invited every Sunday to someone's home. Each Sunday, Brother Peas's beard grew a little shorter and his wife's dresses a little longer. It took months, but the girls became bouncy and happy.

After about six months, I asked Brother Peas to teach the elders quorum lesson. He came back to church with an armload of books. He had shaved his beard and pulled his hair into a ponytail. He walked up to the front and from the first word out of his mouth began teaching false doctrine. The brethren in the quorum began to resist, and I stood up.

"Brethren," I said, "Sometimes the lesson gets taught from the pulpit, and sometimes from the congregation. Brother Peas has worked hard on this lesson, and we love him, and he wants us to help him give a good lesson."

The feeling changed, and nobody challenged him. When he said something wrong, some brother would say, "That's a wonderful way to look at it, Brother Peas. I've always understood it to mean . . ." Brother Peas would laugh and say, "I'm sure you're right. Thanks for bringing that up," and then away he would go with another false concept. But he felt safe, and he felt loved. The lesson he taught us that day was how to care more about the teacher than what he was teaching.

One Sunday, Brother Peas showed up in a suit and tie, clean shaven with short hair. He literally looked handsome. I said, "Peas porridge hot, Peas porridge cold."

He replied, "Peas porridge is always hot."

They moved out of Alaska a few years later, and the last I heard they had been sealed in the temple, and he was serving in an elders quorum presidency.

Peas porridge is hot indeed.

Brother John

Fellow Christians

One of the dark lies that have been invented to hinder us is that Mormons are not Christians. We must overcome this lie with the walk of our lives and the words we speak when defending our faith. This is a true story:

A few years ago in Alaska, my wife Terri and I were out in the yard raking leaves on a crisp autumn Saturday when three people walked down our drive. They were obviously proselyting. I greeted them, and they introduced themselves as "Christian missionaries." I thanked them for coming and told them how grateful I was that they were out spreading the message of Christ. The older gentleman, who introduced himself as the pastor of a local congregation, said, "You must be a Christian."

I replied, "I am! I love my Savior."

He said, "You must have been saved then."

I said, "I have taken Jesus Christ as my Savior and Redeemer."

He replied, "You really are a Christian then. Do you believe that one is saved by grace?"

I replied, "I rely upon His grace and mercy every day of my life. He is my rod and my staff. I try every day to walk in the path He shows me."

He asked, "Is there any other way or name whereby a person can be saved?"

I answered with reverence, "Only through Jesus Christ, and Him alone."

He replied, "Well, it is wonderful to meet a fellow Christian. Most people we meet don't want to talk to us."

My answer was, "I am so grateful that you have the courage to go out and take the message of Christ to anyone who will listen. In this world of darkness, any light is of great worth, and for those who will listen to you and upgrade their lives, you have done a great service for God. I thank you too, for you have done a personal service to me and my family by improving the world we live in."

He said, "I feel the same way. May I ask what church you attend?"

I said, "I am a member of The Church of Jesus Christ of Latter-day Saints."

His face darkened, and he said, "You're a Mormon. Well, then you can't be a Christian."

I smiled and said, "We have been talking for a half-hour here, and you have affirmed many times that I am a Christian. How did you feel when I told you sincerely that I love Jesus Christ? Did you believe me?"

He pondered this and then said, "I did feel that you truly love Jesus."

I bowed my head and said, "I would do anything for Him."

He replied, "But Mormons aren't Christians."

I answered, "Obviously, you have found that statement to be untrue. You, your friends here, and Christ Himself all consider me to be a Christian."

He said with some force, "Well then, you must be different from other Mormons!"

I answered him, "I don't think so. Every member of the LDS Church I know feels the same way I do. They may not use the same language I do, or they may be intimidated by three ministers walking down their driveway and are not able to express themselves when faced with the accusation of being a non-Christian. But if they could truly tell you what is in their hearts, they would say what you have heard me say now."

He said, "I am confused and a little stunned by your words. But I am grateful I met you today."

I said, "May I pray with you before you go?"

He nodded and bowed his head. I prayed for them and their

ministry's continuing success. I didn't mention the LDS church, myself, or anything we had discussed. I prayed with faith and with great hope for his endeavors to spread Christianity, and the Spirit testified to them that I spoke truly.

They left, and I have not seen them again. But a year later, this same minister approached my bishop and said, "My congregation is having a workshop on Mormons. In the past we have invited various ministers who specialize in revealing what Mormons believe. I don't think that that approach has been fair or even honest. I was hoping you would come to our meeting. I will give you an hour to express your beliefs. If you are willing, we will then have a question-and-answer period. I promise that it will be courteous and positive. We have no intention of attacking your beliefs. We just hope to be able to ask about points you may not cover in your talk."

My bishop was dumbfounded but agreed. He later told me that he took a member of the mission presidency with him, and they both spoke at the workshop. He said he mostly went through the first article of faith and emphasized our faith in and worship of Jesus Christ. He said they were very agreeable and non-confrontational. He also said the minister introduced him with an apology for speaking negatively of Mormons from the pulpit in the past, and he asked the people to listen and try to understand his message.

My point in rehearsing this event is merely this: Our Christian friends, if they are spiritually honest, will judge you, all of us, to be Christians when they find out that we truly believe these three things:

We have taken Christ as our personal Savior.

We are ultimately and literally saved by His grace, and not by our own merit or works. (We understand that works follow faith, and so do they.) (See Moroni 10:33.)

We accept that there is no other name or means whereby man can be saved. (See Mosiah 3:17.)

By their own criteria, anyone who embraces these principles is a fellow Christian. It sometimes requires repeating these things many times, but because in the very fabric of our souls we *are* Christians, they will in time embrace us as such. There's no real hurry. We don't have anything to prove, but we do have something to proclaim—and it is our greatest truth: Jesus *is* the Christ, and in the most intimate way possible, we *are* His disciples.

Brother John

Humble Followers of Christ

Second Nephi 28 is a blistering commentary on the latter days. Reading it with the Holy Spirit convinces the humble soul that it is speaking of our times, of our day, of our situation. We live in a wicked world, one ruled by those who are corrupt in the most vile ways. They have killed the innocent (v. 10) and have become fully lifted up in pride such that they rob the poor to build grand buildings and to array themselves in fine clothing. They persecute the meek and poor in heart (v. 13) by outlawing that which is good, making war on religious freedom, mocking moral values, and making it politically incorrect to be a Christian.

They are swilling in pride, wickedness, abominations, and whoredoms. According to the holy word, they have all gone astray save it be a few, who are the "humble followers of Christ" (v. 14).

It is tempting for us to step into self-adulation of pride, and point out that "they" whose crimes are listed above, are everybody else, and "we" are the humble followers of Christ. To think such a simplistic thing is surely part of what the divine word means when it accuses: "Others will he pacify, and lull them away into carnal security, that they will say: All is well in Zion; yea, Zion prospereth, all is well—and thus the devil cheateth their souls and leadeth them away carefully down to hell" (v. 21).

I believe there are three great indicators of those who are "humble followers of Christ":

First, Jesus Christ is their shepherd. He leads them. They follow Him. They hear His voice and are counted among His sheep (Mosiah 26:21, Alma 5:37–38, Alma 5:57, Helaman 7:18). They have taken Him and His voice as their guide and have dedicated themselves to obedience. They will do anything for Him—anything.

Second, they have received the truth. "And at that day, when I shall come in my glory, shall the parable be fulfilled which I spake concerning the ten virgins. For they that are wise and have received

47

the truth, and have taken the Holy Spirit for their guide . . . shall not be hewn down and cast into the fire, but shall abide the day" (Doctrine & Covenants 45:56–57). Lest we prematurely pat ourselves on the back, we must continually remind ourselves that truth is eternal in scope, and the Lord reveals truth line upon line as He deems necessary for the completion of our life's work. The truth the Founding Fathers knew was different from yours and mine, but it was ordained to their mission, and they received it and gave their lives for it, thus accomplishing their mortal journey. Many people—millions of people—live in the light they are given. The point isn't that they have received "the whole truth and nothing but the truth" but that they have received (embraced, loved, and lived) the degree of light and truth that they have been given. Those who do not live by the truth they receive live in darkness.

The third criterion is that they have not been deceived. The full quote of Doctrine & Covenants 45:56–57 is:

> And at that day, when I shall come in my glory, shall the parable be fulfilled which I spake concerning the ten virgins. For they that are wise and have received the truth, and have taken the Holy Spirit for their guide, *and have not been deceived*—verily I say unto you, they shall not be hewn down and cast into the fire, but shall abide the day.

Since we are speaking of humble followers both inside and outside of the Church, it is probable that the range of possible deceptions is vast. But deceptions can all be summarized into a single sentence. *A deception is when you persist in believing something after the Holy Spirit has taught you otherwise.*

A common deception outside of the Church is that Mormons are not Christians. When our Christian brethren take the Holy Spirit to be their guide (and they do; many of them are marvelously dedicated to Christ)—their discipleship exceeds our own in many cases. Then, when the Holy Spirit whispers to them the truth about Mormon Christianity, they will either hearken to the voice of the Spirit and embrace and believe that truth, or they will not, and endure in a deception.

A common deception inside the Church is that being an active member alone will save and exalt us. Why will it not? Because the formula is more exacting than that: We must take Christ as our shepherd, take the Holy Spirit as our guide, receive the truth, and not be deceived.

Membership alone doesn't make us disciples of Christ, nor does it compel us to take Him as our shepherd. Discipleship is a personal quest and relationship with Jesus Christ and the Father developed through desire, obedience, and hungering and thirsting after them. Membership surrounds us with truths, but it doesn't make us receive them or even believe every truth we possess. To actually "receive the truth" we must seek it out through diligent study, prayer, and obedience.

Membership also doesn't mean we have not been deceived. The greatest evidence of this is the verse noted above in 2 Nephi 28, warning that those in "Zion" will be pacified into feeling falsely secure. But membership does spread the glorious restored truths as a banquet before us. It gives us the greatest opportunity the world has ever known to become "humble followers of Christ." We have the fulness of the gospel, living prophets, the priesthood, temples, and the privilege of seeking and building Zion. All of these things empower us, but they also have the potential to condemn us if we fail to live up to our privileges.

I am convinced that the "humble followers of Christ" consist not only of those souls within the restored gospel but also many of our brethren and sisters outside of the Church. I am also convinced that we cannot rest upon our membership to be counted as a humble follower, but we must dedicate our lives, our hands, and our hearts to Christ, partaking fully of the feast of restored truth laid generously before us.

Brother John

The Flames of Faith

My mind seems to be stuck in the beginning days of the Wasilla Ward in 1978. There were so many miracles of faith and manifestations of the Spirit. There still are—everywhere around us—but these were my first experiences with such things, and like the first time someone tells you "I love you" and means it forever, or like that first kiss, they seem to linger in the mind.

Because there were so few of us LDS faithful in the beginning, fast and testimony meeting generally consisted of the stalwart half-dozen bearing testimony and long stretches of silence. I really hate protracted silence during fast and testimony meeting because it makes it all the harder for someone to get up who is struggling to respond to the prompting. Most of my elders quorum presidency were only recently very active, and part of the bishopric, most of the Relief Society, and many others in the ward were attending church for the first few times in years. The dreaded "fast and testimony silence" seemed to be inescapable.

Besides being the elders quorum president at that time, I was also organist for nearly every meeting, which meant that I sat on the stand a lot—which also meant I was close to the pulpit during fast meeting. This particular Sunday I waited until the Spirit was warm in my soul and then stood up to bear my testimony after another long silence. I hadn't rehearsed in my mind what to say—as I usually did back then—and something unexpected came out of my mouth.

I briefly bore my testimony and then said, "I am your elders quorum president, and I have stewardship over almost every male member of this ward and your families. I am asking Brother Jones, Brother Smith, and Brother Brown to come up and bear their testimonies. When they're done, during the next long silence, I will call on a few more of our quorum members. In the name of Jesus Christ, amen."

I sat down hardly able to believe I had just said that. The bishop (my father) looked at me as if I had just proposed we all take our clothes off.

Brother Jones stood reluctantly and appeared to be deciding whether to come to the podium or run to the door. Brother Jones had never borne his testimony in his life. His face was white and his movements, jerky. He walked very slowly to the podium, stood facing me for a few seconds and then turned to the microphone.

He said, "I stood intending to walk out of the meeting because I have never been to the pulpit in my life. Something made me walk up here. As I came I was praying so hard, because when I started this long trip up here I wasn't even sure God lived, let alone that this Church is true. Somewhere near the sacrament table, I felt a warm feeling come over me, and I suddenly knew God lives. Somewhere near the organ, I came to know that this Church is true, and when I stood at this pulpit I realized that this had been the most important journey of my life. You other brethren whose names got read, don't be afraid. Just listen to my words. I now know that God lives, and that God loves me enough to embarrass the dickens out of me so that I will get on with taking care of my duty to teach my family and get us all back to heaven one day. In the name of Jesus Christ, amen."

He turned away as Brother Smith stood and made the very long walk to the pulpit. Brother Smith wept as he said that for years he had wanted to come up and bear his testimony but had never thought it was big enough or eloquent enough to share, even with his family. He was so grateful that he had been jolted from his apathy and that he was here now.

The next brother and the next stood and wept at the pulpit. When they were finished, another brother bolted to his feet and came to the pulpit. "I don't want Brother Pontius to stand up and call my name, so here I am. I'm one of those who hasn't ever borne my testimony, and I want to say that for me too, it got way stronger as I walked up to the stand today. . . ."

When the meeting was over, it had been such a spiritual high that I can't remember a fast meeting since that has equaled that one.

Part of the miracle was these brethren needing, pleading, and begging for a testimony as they walked slowly to the stand. But I think there was another principle working that Sabbath morning. It was simply this: I was too innocent to edit my words. I was too inexperienced to fear saying something that would embarrass or offend. It was just what the Lord moved me to say. And when the words came from my lips, almost without my permission, they lit the flames of faith, because when the Lord commands His servants to speak—even His small and immature ones—and they do, then He sends angels to work the miracles that make those words true.

It is a lesson I have found to be powerfully true from that day to this.

Brother John

Called to Serve

I consider it a sublime privilege to have lived this long—to have seen and known so many truths and so many powerful events, and to have felt so many loving hands upon the clay that has become uniquely me. It has been a glorious and painful journey. But it is one in which I rejoice.

As I have considered and prayed about what to UnBlog today, I realize that there is a lush supply of events that were powered by God's hand in my life that have literally resulted in a mortal glass through which I mercifully no longer see darkly, but brightly to an eternal vista illuminated by faith.

About twenty years ago, I witnessed an event that dramatically demonstrated what faith really is. It is something that few people of this generation have ever seen.

It occurred during an adult session of stake conference. The meeting began normally, which meant I was playing the organ (a common theme throughout my life). The first speaker was the first counselor in the stake presidency. He stood and opened an envelope and withdrew multiple pages. He unfolded them and flattened them against the pulpit. I will attempt to capture what happened next in my own words.

"Brothers and sisters, in the early years of the Church, the Prophet Joseph and his successors called faithful members from the pulpit to serve missions. The records of the Church indicate that the vast majority of those calls were faithfully fulfilled. People left their homes, most often their wives and families, almost always in great financial difficulty, sometimes knowing they likely would not see loved ones again. Yet they left to willingly serve the Lord."

He drew a measured breath and continued.

"The present world condition, combined with the accelerated pace of missionary work and the extraordinary need for missionary couples, has moved our prophet to reinstate that system of calling missionaries. I am going to read a list of names of couples and individuals who are being called to foreign missions tonight. If you accept this call, please stand and come up to the podium. You will have one week to sell your homes or whatever you need to do to finance your mission. If for any reason you cannot accept, no explanation will be needed. Just remain in your seats. It won't affect anyone's respect for you. We will all understand."

There was a powerful sense of stunned amazement in the room. I have never felt anything like it. It was a little bit of fear, but mostly it was astonishment mingled with anticipation. He read the list very slowly. With each name, someone gasped. Many cried out. Sisters wept openly. A few people shouted for joy. They all stood when their names were called and went to the stand. It was the most tension I have ever felt in a church meeting.

When there were ten or so couples on the stand, he explained a few more details of their calls and asked a few of them to bear their testimonies in preparation for leaving on their missions. They came to the podium slowly. Their words were few, their emotions powerful, and their message was of stunned willingness to lay everything on the altar for the Lord. A few sisters walked to the pulpit, wept, said nothing and sat back down. One brother bounded to the pulpit and exulted in the call and then very softly said he and his wife would have to liquidate everything they owned, but that it was a joy to be able to do so.

I listened with a growing sense of watching history being made. I marveled at the faith of these good Saints. Not a single one of them failed to come to the stand and accept the call. They were ready, their heads were high, and their faith burning so brightly that it illuminated their faces. They were like twenty angels sitting there, glowing with divine power. Had I been blessed with eyes that could see beyond the veil, I probably would have seen pillars of fire over each of them.

The stake presidency member stood and folded the pages and put them back in the envelope. "It has been a privilege to hear your words and to feel your faith and your willingness to accept this call."

He paused a long time, and when he spoke again his voice was husky with emotion.

"I only regret that it is not true. None of you are actually being called to foreign missions. We, your stake presidency, just wanted you to experience your own faith, and to feel your own commitment to the Lord, and to realize that we are not much different in our willingness to sacrifice for our Savior than those who took up this cause before us. Brothers and sisters, you may return to your seats, and to your lives as you were before. In the name of Jesus Christ, amen."

As astonishing as his words were, what happened next was even more astonishing. Every man and woman on the stand began to weep openly and deeply. They were so enveloped in this moment that not a single person stood to return to their seats. They just sat there and wept.

At first I thought it was relief that made them so emotional. Then, when they still did not return to their seats, I realized that it was regret; they were sorely reluctant to lay down what had moments before been a joy. They had made a sudden, life-altering decision to serve God at great expense, and now that privilege had been snatched away. They were weeping out of loss. Every person present realized this, and it was so deeply stunning that I and nearly everyone there began to weep. Slowly, a couple stood and returned to the congregation. One sister ran from the chapel, then another and her husband. They didn't leave to go home, they just needed time to recover. All the rest of them walked to their seats with their heads upon their chests, suffering from a sense of loss one generally experiences only at funerals.

I don't remember the rest of the meeting. I recall initially feeling that it was unfair that they had been subjected to this experience. But, when I grew a little wiser, I realized that those faithful few had done what Abraham had done. They had raised their knives above their own lives, and when the moment came, they plunged the knife with perfect intent to follow through; and then the angel delivered them, and they walked off of the mountain with their lives returned to them.

What a privilege those angelic souls enjoyed that night, to have their faith and righteous obedience permanently recorded in the record of heaven. What an exceedingly rare thing to witness! By their example and faith I learned that night what it means to say, "I'll go where you want me to go."

Brother John

And Then I Knew

*A*mid the tumble and tinsel of Christmases past I have sung in a local performance of Handel's *Messiah* for nineteen years. It has been an amazing journey—all that worship, sound, and inspired music that changes lives. I experienced it for nearly two decades.

For the last nine years before we moved from Alaska, my very talented wife was stake music chairman and organizer of the *Messiah* performance. She developed it from a local, good-enough performance to a professional-quality performance, with soloists from around the state and orchestral members from symphonies with broad experience and remarkable talent. In a word, it was a delight to perform with them. Conducting them was like driving a Ferrari—responsive, powerful, and instantly gratifying. The musical and spiritual G-force was life-changing.

When Terri first began to invite community members to perform with us, there was a lot of blunt resistance. The local churches refused to contribute to anything even loosely associated with "Mormons." She persisted, campaigned, and encouraged; mostly she testified again and again that Mormons really are Christians.

The first few non-LDS performers came because we begged them as friends. When they felt the Spirit of God that was abundantly present and perceived the quality of the performance, they invited their friends to participate and to attend. We didn't proselyte anyone, hand out literature, or mention any specific religion. It was a "community performance" only.

What happened was astonishing. People came from all over the Mat-Su Valley and from Anchorage to perform with us, and they invited their families and friends to attend the performances. They worshiped Christ with us in our chapel and went home with two truths in their hearts: Jesus really *is* the Christ, and Mormons actually *are* Christians. No amount of public relations, missionary work, or open houses could have accomplished as much. There was no duplicity in our hearts; this was a time to worship Jesus Christ as a community. The worship just also happened to be in an LDS chapel.

At the last performance I conducted in 2009, more than half of the chorus and 75 percent of the orchestra came from the community at large. These people became our dear friends, our brothers and sisters in Christ, and our faithful colleagues in the Mat-Su Community Handel's *Messiah* performance.

In 2007 I realized I was too sick to conduct *Messiah*. I attended one rehearsal and couldn't get all the way through it. As Terri was busy with another Christmas project that year, I prayerfully considered who else in the church or community could take over. Conducting this oratorio is not a small task; the technical, musical, and spiritual requirements are significant, not to mention the time involved. I usually began rehearsing the orchestra in early October, with multiple choral and soloist rehearsals every week until the performances in December.

A name came forcefully to my mind: a Russian conductor I'll call Natasha. She had a master's degree in choral conducting and violin performance and was the conductor of the community choir and several other musical groups. Terri had asked her to be involved in various ways in the past, and she had declined. While I was pondering this, the phone rang, and it was Natasha. In her heavy accent, she said that she had been thinking about the community *Messiah* performance and felt that she would like to be involved this year, even if all we needed her to do was to make phone calls or hand out music.

I was astonished but not surprised—if you understand the contradiction. The Lord has intervened in my life so many times that I was not surprised; miracles are ubiquitous in my life, but I was nonetheless delighted and astonished because *she* had called *me*.

I invited Natasha to conduct the *Messiah*. Her response further astonished me. "I have never conducted Handel's *Messiah*," she said in her heavy Russian accent. "In Russia we don't sing the religious music. We sing about spring and flowers and birds singing. So, I very much like Handel's *Messiah*, but it is difficult music, and I don't know it."

I assured her that she was up to the task, that her musical prowess was formidable. Then she said something that astonished me once again. "There is just one more thing. I am a Catholic by upbringing, but I don't think I'm a Christian."

I would have choked and reconsidered my invitation to have her conduct, except that the Holy Spirit suddenly flooded my heart. I replied, "If you conduct this performance of Handel's *Messiah*, you will be a Christian before it is over."

Silence from Natasha.

I continued. "This music is about the life, death, Resurrection, and triumph of Jesus Christ. It is a master work of inspired music. I believe Jesus Christ actually loves this music and sends His angels to assist those who perform it. Every time I've been privileged to conduct it, I have felt the Spirit of God in great abundance. I have often heard angels singing with us and have been further convinced each time that Jesus is the Christ."

Protracted silence from Natasha. Then she said, "I would like to try. But, would you come to the rehearsals and help me bring the right Spirit? I will do the music, and you can make it a spiritual experience for everyone. I don't think I can do that part."

"For a few times I will come if you need me," I consented. "But, quite honestly, Natasha, God will inspire you and lift you up, and you won't need my help. You will experience miracles for the first time in your life, perhaps."

"When would you like me to begin?" she asked.

"How about next Sunday evening at 6:00 p.m.?" I asked her.

I faded back into the chorus to sing bass, and Natasha picked up the baton. I had sung under her many times before and knew exactly what her talents and strengths were. From the first rehearsal she was brilliant, but she was also different—humble, gracious, and inspired. She didn't bring her usual Russian "when I pick up this baton, I am god" persona. There was no need. The performers loved and respected her, and she poured her heart and soul into her new task.

Natasha called me occasionally to tell me her feelings and to make sure she was doing things right. She reported that she heard Handel's *Messiah* in her mind all day and all night; such a thing had never happened to her before! She said she often would awaken from dreaming about conducting the *Messiah* with full knowledge of the meaning of the words and how to embellish, beautify, and perfect the music. This was a wonder to her.

The performance was glorious. The angels came, and they sang with us. Natasha was inspiring, powerful, and beautiful. She actually glowed.

A few days later she called me. After congratulations for all, she paused and then said, "You know, when you said that this performance would change me, that I would hear the angels sing, and that I would come to know that Christ is my Savior, I thought you were just trying to encourage me. I knew you felt that way, but I just assumed I would not. I have sung and conducted music all my life, and I have never been moved that way by music or anything else. So, I just doubted what you said."

I let silence be my reply. She waited. I could hear her breathing deeply.

"I just wanted to tell you that you were right. I now know that Jesus Christ is my Savior," Natasha whispered, and her voice caught in her throat.

"I am not surprised," I said softly.

"Well, I am! It happened during the Hallelujah Chorus," she told me. "I just felt this power move through me. I felt joy and peace, and this wonderful warmth in my chest. My eyes filled with tears, and I couldn't see my music! And then I knew that Jesus really is my Savior."

"I am so happy for you, Natasha! Do you know why it works that way?"

"Not really," she admitted.

"It happens because Jesus really *is* the Christ, and He loves you. And when people of faith, who love Him, sing praises to Him the way they did as you conducted, the Spirit of God testifies that Jesus is the Christ. Anyone who experiences such a powerful outpouring will be changed. You were standing there in the epicenter of all that praise and worship! It's no wonder that you gained a testimony of Him."

She struggled to control her emotions. "I am so grateful. Thank you for asking me to do this."

"Thank *you*," I replied, "and Merry Christmas."

Brother John

The Journey Home
Part III: Good News

Cancer is a scary word. In fact, in this telestial world, there seems to be no physical diagnosis quite so chilling. When the doctors whispered this word to us, John and I wrestled with how to deal with it. We read many books and talked to doctors and specialists, friends, and health nuts and quacks, folks who had been healed and folks who had not. We had long, struggling conversations with the Lord and fasted and prayed for a miraculous healing. We went to the temple and pleaded for the Lord's intervention. Surely there was so much more for John to accomplish in this life, and surely the Lord would not require his life so prematurely!

As for me, the whole thing seemed surreal. I just could not imagine life without my best friend. We were intertwined. We were one.

With his doctor's tentative approval, in January 2007, John postponed surgery to begin an oral regimen of Viruxcan, which is a natural product that we knew from experience destroys cancerous cells topically, and which (we hoped) could destroy cancer internally. After twelve months of Viruxcan, John was given a clean bill of health. The tests showed that his cancer was completely gone, and all he needed to do was to come for a check-up in six months.

We were ecstatic! We fell to our knees in gratitude to the Lord, called all the kids, and went out for a fancy Italian dinner at Evangelo's to celebrate. We then resumed our blissful life in Alaska with great hopes for the future. In our annual New Year update to friends and family in January 2008, John wrote, "I am personally excited for the new year. I have a great feeling about it. I am looking for great spiritual growth and the opening of the heavens over us. . . . You all know now that my health is no longer threatening. That is a great blessing to us, as well as the opportunity to complete my life's work (as soon as I figure out what that actually is!)"

Ahhh, but there's the rub. What really is our life's work, and where are we to do it? How do we actually receive the spiritual growth and further opening of the heavens we so desire? The answer was unexpected, totally unwanted, but (we knew later) essential to the Lord's plan for us.

—Terri

59

Chapter Four

Believing in Miracles

Just Believe!

I believe we constantly underestimate our potential in this life.

We all seem to believe we have the potential to one day enter into the celestial kingdom, but we have strict belief limits on what we think we can accomplish in this life while yet mortal. Yet, the scriptures bear testimony that some among us have achieved a spiritual stature that has allowed them to conquer death, raise the dead, move mountains, reverse the rotation of the earth, conquer armies, and walk and talk with God. In the very same scriptures, we are taught that we may do the same things if we believe and are willing to pay the price to obtain them.

Why then do we not believe? Why would any sane persons chose to *not* act upon such a promise when the opportunity was laid before them! We can, like our spiritual forebearers, walk a path that will take us into the very presence of God, and it can happen while still in this mortal world. There truly is no limit to what miracles may occur and no limit to what we may obtain in this life.

Brother John

The Year of Belief

I was speaking to a friend a few days ago, and he made an enlightening observation. He said that when a baby is in the womb, the womb is reality to him. Every sound the baby can hear seems like the most beautiful sound that exists. The light that he can perceive is the brightest and most beautiful in the world. Yet, the womb is only a tiny fraction of our mortal existence. There is so much more, but one must pass through the struggle of birth to experience it.

As adults, we tend to view our present experiences as being the whole world. To us, this is reality. We rarely conceive of more than what we can see, touch, or taste. When we are presented with the idea of a whole new world existing at our fingertips that we cannot see, we reject the idea because it seems impossible. Or we think that if it *were* possible everybody would know about it, so we dismiss the idea and return to our old comfortable world.

Jesus Christ used this very metaphor of being born to teach us of the world that He offers, into which we must be born—again. It is the world of spiritual truth, which the soul receives from Him and from the Holy Ghost. It is the world of scripture and restored truths, and of priesthood and purpose. It is the world in which most everyone I know in the embrace of the Latter-day Church lives and rejoices.

Yet, it was never intended that we should live our lives as spiritual infants. Just as there was another world we could not see prior to being born again in Christ, when we mature into spiritual adults, there is yet another world beyond this one into which we have been invited. While still requiring sustained fellowship in the Latter-day Church, this new world is the spiritual world of priesthood power, of miracles, of divine visitation, and of privileges the human mind can't even perceive without the aid of the Holy Ghost. This is the world of Zion, of society with translated beings, and of our Savior. It is the world we will inevitably build before Christ will return to cleanse the earth. And it is at our fingertips.

It takes prolonged exposure to truth; persistent obedience to laws presently understood; and a great deal of seeking, asking, and knocking to open the doors into Zion. Let us not, like the immature child in the womb, trick ourselves into the foolish belief that what we see, feel, and know is the totality of all that there is available in the gospel. There is so much more! And that which lies beyond our immediate perception is not invisible; it is merely guarded by law. In quiet moments, when the Holy Ghost is streaming through the window panes of your soul, one can at times perceive the greater vistas and feel the yearning to part the veil and wander amid the misty meadows and joy-dappled flowers of divine places.

As this year draws to a thundering conclusion and we prepare to walk away from the struggles and strains of 2010, I want to have the record show that I have seen and I do know that there are greater things, glorious things, divine gifts, and heavenly manifestations that are ours to claim. I am not guessing or hoping. These are things that I know. The Lord of Salvation stands ready, delighting in our importuning pleas to part the veil and invite Him to dwell with us.

Just as beginning tomorrow we must train our fingers to write "2011," let us begin tomorrow to train our hearts to believe. Let us make this year our year of knowing, of parting the veil, and of kneeling at His feet. Let us make this the greatest year in our history, because it is the year when we invited Christ to return—not so much to cleanse the whole world, but to cleanse our souls, and to redeem us back into His presence, into that very real world of divine things seen presently by faith alone.

That will make it the greatest year indeed.

Brother John

The Gift of Tongues and Ears

I want to tell you about the time a bumbling mission- ary spoke in tongues.

It was about 1972, and I was on my mission in South Africa. I had returned from Rhodesia and was about a year old in missionary terms. Rhodesia had been an exclusively English-speaking area, so my Afrikaans had not grown or improved for eight months. I was given a junior companion and assigned to an Afrikaans area. I was scared.

The first few weeks were a struggle. I didn't know Afrikaans well enough, and my junior companion not at all. The only thing that kept me going was faith—faith that the Lord would put the words into my mouth when they were needed. Mostly I stumbled, but we worked hard.

My junior companion was a very interesting fellow. He was a senior at Berkeley when he decided to go on a mission. He had an

IQ about double mine. The first full day we were together, we got up to do morning scripture study. New missionaries were supposed to spend most of their study time learning the discussions—you know, the ones we did by rote. That morning, he was thumbing through the pages with his eyes half closed, and then casually picked up the scriptures. I suggested he go back to memorizing the discussions.

"I've memorized them," he replied.

"You know them all?" I countered in disbelief.

"Yes."

I didn't believe him and opened my discussions to some random place. I started a concept, and he finished it, word for word. We did this in two or three different places until I was certain he really did know them. I was amazed because it had taken me months to know them as well as he did on his first day.

"How could you know them so soon?" I demanded.

He looked at his lap. "I don't want to say."

"Why not?"

"Because it's embarrassing. I've been teased all my life because of it."

I pondered this and finally said, "Whatever it is, I consider it a gift. It took me months to memorize these discussions."

Finally he said, "I have a photographic memory. I literally can't forget. Sometimes I wish I could. When people find this out they either avoid me, or treat me like a side show."

Something occurred to me. "Repeat the very first concept for me."

He did it flawlessly. I helped him with pronunciation on a few words.

I asked. "What does it mean?"

He smiled sheepishly, "I have no idea."

He had memorized seven discussions in a foreign language as a sequence of sounds, with no comprehension of what he was saying!

I laughed, and we spent the next several days translating the discussions back into English. When he had the translation, he could do it frontward and backward in either language. I found him to be delightful, and to this day he was my favorite companion. We did a lot of laughing, and he did a lot of correcting; when I would start singing a hymn, he would correct every other word I sang. Finally, I told him to just keep the words of hymns to himself. We both laughed.

I'm telling you this so you will understand what happened next.

Afrikaans people are very hardheaded, and we had almost zero success until one day we knocked on a door, and an attractive lady met us pleasantly. She listened to our introduction and invited us back that evening when her husband was home. We happily agreed. Not only was she interested, but she was young and pleasant—and best of all, she spoke English.

We returned at the appointed hour to find her husband to be an intelligent and interesting fellow as well. He was an electrical engineer and was excited to speak to us. We sat in their small living room and I asked if we could begin with prayer.

He nodded, and then he switched to Afrikaans and began to pray—mostly that we would come to know the error of our ways. I'm sure you have never heard someone pray in Afrikaans, so let me explain. There are two Afrikaans languages: one is the common language they all use, the other is a form of the language that only ministers use when they are preaching and praying. It is very dramatic—almost shouting at times—and it uses old forms of words, kind of like "thee" and "thy" in our language. It isn't hard to understand after you get used to it, but when someone uses it, you know they have been to ministry school, and you're in for a bumpy ride.

After the prayer, he started arguing right away. He dragged out his scriptures and began quoting verse after verse, in Afrikaans. I couldn't follow it. I asked if we could speak English, because they spoke it as well as I did. He said that the scriptures and true religion should be preached in Afrikaans. I felt my heart sinking.

Then, something odd happened.

He quoted a scripture, and I understood both him and his explanation. I suggested (under inspiration) that if he would read the next verse, he would find that his interpretation was not correct. (I still don't know what reference he read, or what the next verse said. It was just the right thing to say.) He looked down again, and his face blanched. He quickly turned to another verse and read it even louder.

To my ears, it sounded like he had switched back to English, though spoken with a heavy accent. I replied in Afrikaans, but it seemed like English to me as well. It's hard to explain. The right words were just there for me to speak. We verbally sparred like this for nearly two hours. With each exchange, he became more angry and convicted by the words I was given to speak.

Then in frustration he started shouting, sending us to a fiery damnation. I replied with words that came to my heart. His face grew red, and then white. He told us that we were the devil's missionaries.

I don't remember the words I said, but the content was that he had just spent two hours listening to servants of God and feeling the Holy Ghost as we discussed the scriptures, and that he knew what we had told him was true. I said that if he rejected the truth, a judgment would come upon him and his home, and that he would know it was from God.

You can well guess what happened next. He stood, and I thought he was going to become violent. We left immediately without even saying goodbye. As I was standing on his front porch, the thought came to me to dust off my feet. We were instructed to never dust off our feet about anyone we didn't want to have to accuse on judgment day. I hesitated and had another confirmation to dust off my feet.

My companion saw that I had stopped just on their doormat. "Are you sure?" he said to me. (He was unusually perceptive, as you can imagine.) I nodded and wiped my feet on their doormat. We got into our car and left.

As we were leaving, my companion said, "Elder, that was the most amazing and eloquent teaching I have ever heard in any language. I could just barely follow the conversation, but you were quoting scriptures that I know you have never memorized, and all in Afrikaans."

I replied, "No, we switched to English, lucky for me."

He shook his head. "No, Elder, it was entirely in Afrikaans."

"What? Are you sure? It all sounded like English to me."

"Elder, believe me when I say I know the difference between English and Afrikaans. From his prayer onward, the entire discussion was in Afrikaans."

I was speechless. Then I realized what a miracle it had been. "I guess it was the gift of tongues."

He chuckled, "And for me, it was the gift of ears, because I understood most of it." We both laughed.

About two weeks later, we found ourselves on their street looking for a different address. We both commented about our previous experience there and drove toward their home. When we came to their driveway, only a blackened hulk of a house was standing.

It had burned to the ground.

Brother John

Miracle of the Curry

It seems to be hard to start an UnBlog without using the word "I," which is not the focal point of anything being recorded here. Still, the only life I have intimate knowledge of is my own. Please forgive me....

I served my mission in South Africa from 1971 to 1973. It was a vastly eye-opening experience for such a quiet and inexperienced spirit as mine was at that time of my life. I remember being surprised when I still had to use the restroom! I had idealized a mission so thoroughly that I hadn't ever considered that life would just go on. A little crazy, but it gives you an insight into the deep personal hole I started to climb out of while a missionary in Africa.

Every day was an education. People were a mystery to me. Religion was a mystery to me, at least other people's. Money was a mystery; I had always had enough, and to my childish brain everything seemed like it should be free. The first time I sat down at a table in Africa I was shocked to find the food meager and barely edible; and then to stand up hungry and graciously thank your host was beyond comprehensible. I lost over thirty pounds before returning home.

We also found the people very hardheaded. They called themselves Die Steinkopies—the stone heads, because they were so stubborn. We had very little success and tracted day after day with almost universal rejection. We began to consider a door that didn't slam, or threaten our lives, to be a good contact.

In time, I was transferred to serve in the little town of Germiston. They had a cute little chapel built in an A-frame style with a large stained glass window over the pulpit. It felt more Catholic than

67

Mormon, but the building was new and fresh and housed a gentle and loving spirit. In the midst of swirling ineffectiveness, we hatched the idea of hosting an open house and inviting community members to come into this very lovely building and feel the Spirit. We decided not to preach or press, just entertain and rub shoulders. My companion and I did most of the planning, organizing, and advertising.

The farm boy in me was surprised to learn that I have a natural ken for promotion. I proposed that we have a men's cake baking contest. They loved it. I talked a professional pastry chef from a nearby Hilton Hotel into being the judge. I procured a local magician to do magic tricks and talked the Relief Society into preparing a nice meal. Knowing the small portions of their normal meals, I asked them to cook twice as much as they thought they might need, and they agreed. I also talked the ward into printing fliers (remember this was way before Brother Xerox). We made posters, wrote scripts for people, planned a cute floor show, and arranged for real glass plates instead of paper. It took us weeks—and was a welcome, welcome change from tracting (at least tracting so much).

The evening came, and people began walking through the door. We had planned on 150 at most, probably less. The active membership of the branch was about seventy-five, and we hoped and pushed for every member to bring one person. They came, and came, and came, and came. We stopped counting at three hundred because that was all the chairs in the whole building. We hurriedly set up additional tables. As we were slinging chairs around, the Relief Society president grabbed my arm. "Come into the kitchen," she whispered.

I followed her into the sparkling new kitchen to see two kettles on the stove. One had about four gallons of curried chicken, and the other about the same amount of steamed rice. I looked around for something like vegetables, salad, or bread. That was it. She was frightened and panicked. "We don't have enough food!" she said urgently.

I remember feeling a stab of terror and then almost immediately, peace. I wasn't experienced enough then to realize the Lord had just sent His Spirit into my soul. "Let's ask a blessing on the food," I said.

"You better make it a darn good one," quipped one of the brothers wearing a cook's apron.

I bowed my head and asked a blessing on the food. I remember specifically praying that there would be more than enough to feed everyone present to their satisfaction.

We went ahead and started the program. There were two tables full of amazing cakes that people from all over the community had entered into the contest. I had saved and saved and purchased a few plastic trophies to give away. There was excitement in the air. I introduced the chef who would judge. The people lined up, and the serving began. While they ate, a magician told dirty jokes and did poor magic tricks. (I'm not kidding!) The people laughed their faces off and probably thought Mormons weren't as stuffy as they had imagined. I hope they thought something like that!

The judge chose some winners. I handed out trophies after the floor show. We ate all those cakes, had a closing prayer, and people began leaving. The Relief Society president came up and took my arm again. "I want to show you something."

I followed her into the kitchen. She lifted the lid on the pot of curry. There was still a gallon or so left. She lifted the lid on the rice, and about the same remained. Her eyes teared up. "We served normal sized portions, Elder," she said. "Many people came back for seconds. We just kept dishing them up, and when we were done serving, we were astonished to see that there was still some left. It was a miracle, Elder!" she cried.

It was indeed. Four gallons of curried chicken will feed about fifty people. We fed three hundred or more and had leftovers to spare. It has astonished me as many times as I have thought about it over the last forty years. I was so grateful then, but it has taken many years of miracles and rending my own veil of unbelief to realize that this wasn't a manifestation of food—it was a manifestation of our Savior's love. He cared that the guests at a wedding feast in Cana had fine wine, and He cared that His little struggling branch in Germiston, South Africa, served a fine curry.

Brother John

Entertaining Angels

I have been pondering how to write about this next experience. It is sacred to me and not the type of thing I feel comfortable "posting" on the Internet for the world to read. But it was very formative in my life, and since I'm "un-blogging" my soul, this happening is going to come out—one way or another. I pray that those who read it will take it in the spirit in which it is given, which is reverence and wonder.

This event occurred in 1993 during a period of great upset and upheaval in my life. Almost everything that could go wrong did. I was losing my battle to avoid a divorce for reasons I didn't even comprehend at the time. I was dealing with a one-year closure of the main road to my business, which was almost bankrupting me. I was being audited by you-know-who for my personal and business taxes. I eventually came out squeaky clean, but it took two years of blood, sweat, and accountants to pull it off. I had just been released from the High Council and was between church jobs, needing one badly. I was fasting two or three times a week for spiritual strength and growing tremendously but still losing almost every other war I was fighting. There was another major upset I choose not to detail, but that's not what this story is really about, anyway.

I was asked one Sunday to conduct our high priests group meeting and to teach the lesson. It just happened to be on the subject of "personal revelation." This was the subject of a book I had just published, so that topic was (and is) dear to my heart. I watched the brethren file into the Family History Center for the lesson. These were good brethren I had known for over twenty years. Then, two gentlemen I had never seen before came in. There was a tall, thin fellow, and a short man with gray hair who walked with a cane. He didn't seem to need it; he just had one and seemed to use it as a matter of style or habit.

They introduced themselves to the group. I asked them what they were doing in Alaska. The tall fellow gave an answer something like this: "In our line of business, we travel all over the world representing the interests of our employer. We have traveled to many places, including to Alaska a few times. When we end up in a place where the Church is established, we like to meet with the Saints to see if the Spirit is present and if truth is being taught, and to determine how the work is progressing in that area."

I thought it was an odd, almost evasive answer, so I asked them if they were in Alaska on business or pleasure, and they said business.

I proceeded to teach the lesson, and the Spirit was unusually strong. The tall man offered many comments, while the shorter one said nothing. He just listened. When the lesson and closing prayer were over, everyone stood and left except for the short brother. When he and I were the only ones in the room, he walked around the far side of the table and approached me. I was putting books in my briefcase when he stopped by me. The following dialogue is paraphrased from my memory of seventeen years ago, but it is the sort of experience from which one clearly remembers the message, if not the exact words.

"Brother Pontius," he said. I looked up and shook his hand. He continued, "I just want to tell you that the Lord is pleased with what you taught today, and with what you have been doing in your life."

He did not say this as if he were giving his opinion. He stated it as a fact, as if he had authority to speak for the Lord. I felt the Holy Spirit nudge me and insist that I give him my full attention. I turned to face him. "Thank you," I said.

He continued with several statements of fact that indicated that he understood my recent struggles. This was somewhat startling to me, and I didn't know what to think.

He then said, "I just have one question."

"What's that?"

"I just want to know if in twenty years you'll be as good a man as you are now."

I thought about this question and about how odd it was to be asked such a thing by a total stranger. I finally replied, "If I have my way about it, I will be a much better man in twenty years."

His eyes seemed to focus on the distance as he looked slightly over my left shoulder and then back at my face. "Yes, you will," he stated matter-of-factly and then held out his hand.

I shook his hand, and he said, "That's all I needed to say," smiled, and turned to the door. He hooked his cane on his arm and walked away with no hint of a limp. I thought, "Wait, I need to talk to you! Who are you, really?" So, I snapped my briefcase closed and looked back up. He should have been near the classroom door, but he was not there.

The halls going in both directions were thronged with people getting out of church. I took three steps to the door and looked up one hall and then the other. I couldn't see him in either direction. I walked to the nearest exit and then around the entire outside of the building. He was not to be found.

I went home and wrote all of this in my journal, wishing so badly that I had not looked down at my briefcase for all of those five seconds it took for me to look up again. I filed this in my brain as "I don't know" and pondered it.

Nearly a month later, on Mother's Day 1993, I was startled to see him sitting in sacrament meeting. He was on the left side of the chapel on the second row. My family generally sat in the middle, on the third row. We ended up on the second row, right in front of the pulpit. I made up my mind that as soon as the meeting ended, I was going to jump up and ask him questions. I watched him out of the corner of my eye the whole meeting.

The sacrament meeting speaker was a friend of mine. I'll call her Sister Wilson. She spoke about her mother, who was not a member of our church, but who had taught her children to read the Bible, to pray, and to trust in God. Sister Wilson spoke of her mother's courage and of the fact that all of her children had later joined the Church, but her mother had died before joining herself. Sister Wilson spoke of her joy in doing her mother's temple work. It was one of the most beautiful Mother's Day addresses I have experienced.

After the meeting, I stood and watched my gray-haired stranger. He did not stand, but just sat there listening to the organ music. I was waiting for someone to let me out into the aisle, seriously considering stepping over the pew to get out, when Sister Wilson came into the pew behind me. She asked me a question about something, and I responded. For just a minute, I forgot about my gray-haired friend, until he walked up beside Sister Wilson. She turned to him and shook his hand.

"Sister Wilson," he said, "I want to thank you for that Mother's Day address. It was one of the sweetest and most moving I have ever heard. It reminded me of my own mother, and believe me when I say, that was a long, long, *long* time ago. Thank you very much for bringing such a sweet spirit into our lives."

She smiled broadly. "Well, thank you very much. You know my name obviously, but I don't believe we have ever met, so I don't know yours."

He laughed and smiled. "Oh! I don't have a name," he said. "I'm just one of the Three Nephites going around visiting the Saints!" He said this quite loudly, with joy in his voice. He didn't even glance at me.

He turned to leave the same way he had come. Sister Wilson and I both watched him in amazement as he made his way to the aisle. I was just about to jump over the pew to catch him when Sister Wilson asked, "What do you think he meant by that?"

I remember thinking that it would take him a few seconds to get into the aisle, so I would have time to answer her question. I reluctantly took my eyes off him to reply, "I think he's telling the truth!"

We both quickly looked back to where he should have been, but he was gone. We looked both directions, up and down the main aisle of the chapel. He was simply gone. There were people everywhere, and he would have had to run, knocking people over to get out of the chapel in the two seconds or so it had taken me to answer Sister Wilson's question. We both were amazed and confused by his sudden disappearance.

I went home and wrote this all in my journal, and I have pondered his message often. I've written this event as a story in one of my novels, and in several other documents, but it actually happened, and it still causes me to wonder.

His question was whether I would be a better man in twenty years, and I have counted the years, trying to make his words prophetic that I would be a much better man, but also wondering if his timetable was a random period of time, or a specific period of time. I have often wondered if something special, or joyful even, was scheduled for me in May of 2013. I don't know, and given my present state of health, I might not find out as a mortal. Perhaps that is a date bracketing my mortal experience; I have no way of telling.

But of this I *am* certain: He was who he said he was.

Brother John

Faith and Belief

*F*aith is a result of exposure to the Spirit of the Lord, and it is a gift of God. Faith does not naturally reside in man. When we obey some principle of truth, or a commandment of God, or any whispering of the Spirit, the Spirit of the Lord touches our souls with a tiny increase of faith regarding that principle.

One can have faith only in things that are true (Alma 32:21). We can't have faith in a falsehood. Only to the extent that a principle contains truth can we exercise faith in it. For this reason, faith is always centered in Christ, because all truth flows from Christ.

Unlike faith, which is always pure, our belief structure includes both pure elements of truth, and impurities of human assumption, tradition, false conclusions, and out-and-out lies. Most of what we believe comes from the experiences of our lifetime, all of which occur in the natural world, and most of which are in some way tainted. Such false beliefs are hostile to our progress unless overridden by revealed truth.

By so noting the difference between faith and belief, we are not assigning to belief second-class citizenship. Belief, while very different from faith, is the sum total of what we think, both good and bad, true and false. Belief is extremely powerful and has a greater pull upon our lives than any other single force, because our belief literally defines our universe. Life is what we believe it to be. People are what we believe them to be. Our perception of our world, our belief structure, imposes so much distortion upon our vision that, in many ways, creates the world we view.

Our every act is driven by a belief. Whether that belief is based upon truth or upon a misconception determines whether that act is righteous or evil.

Often, our faith can be profound, while our belief about how that faith applies to us can limit—or even eliminate—our enjoyment of the fruits of our faith. Such faith-opposing believing is called "unbelief" in the scriptures. It is not necessarily an absence of faith and can coexist with faith quite companionably. But it is nevertheless an effective, and often long-lived, damnation of our faith.

An example of this might be: We may have faith that Heavenly Father loves us and has the power to heal an illness or disease we may have. But we may simultaneously believe (or assume because of what others have taught us) that Heavenly Father wants us to learn some lesson through our suffering, or that we must seek a medical solution first, turning to Him only as a last resort. Or we may conclude that since we haven't personally seen this magnitude of healing with our own eyes, He may just not be doing healings of this degree nowadays, and thus, we doubt the will of God to heal us— not His power—but His intention to do so. In other words, we have great faith He can, we just don't believe He will, and thus uninspired belief (unbelief) smothers our faith.

Another example may be: We read the scriptures and have complete faith that the Brother of Jared (or any other righteous figure) truly experienced the profound blessings, visions, revelations, and angelic visitations he recorded. And, even though the same prophet records that God is no respecter of persons, and liberally grants the same blessings to all who righteously seek them, we believe that the scriptures are largely for our education and not a prototype of our personal spiritual potential. We may conclude that such things do not happen in this day, or if they do, they would happen to someone more highly placed, or more obedient. We thereby doubt—not God's power, which is a by-product of our faith—but we doubt His will to grant us a place within His promises. Such doubt is, by definition, unbelief.

In other words, we extinguish the fire of faith with the cold rains of unbelief.

The Lord told Moroni:

> 7 And in that day that they [the latter-day Gentiles] shall exercise faith in me, saith the Lord, even as the brother of Jared did, that they may become sanctified in me, then will I manifest unto them the things which the brother of Jared saw, even to the unfolding unto them all my revelations, saith Jesus Christ, the Son of God, the Father of the heavens and of the earth, and all things that in them are. (Ether 4:7, comment added)

This verse contains one of the most incredible pronouncements of promise this dispensation has ever been given. It is saying that when—notice it doesn't say "if," it implies *when*—we rend the veil of unbelief and develop faith like unto the Brother of Jared's, God will unfold unto us all of His revelations, which means that we will know all things, which would enable us to part the veil in many places and to lay hold upon all promised blessings. This promise isn't being made just to the Quorum of the Twelve. This is a promise that is held out to every person who chooses to seek and obtain it. In other words, we have access to the same gifts in this day, in this priesthood, in this church, as the Brother of Jared used to rend the heavens in his day, which lit up his sixteen stones and his eternity.

So why aren't we doing so? The Lord's explanation of why we fail to lay hold upon these vast things is illuminating: "Come unto me, O ye Gentiles, and I will show unto you the greater things, the knowledge which is hid up because of unbelief" (Ether 4:13).

So it is unbelief, not necessarily a lack of faith, but unbelief, which keeps us captive in a state of wickedness. Does it seem harsh to characterize unbelief as wickedness? What is wickedness, if not something that destroys our faith? False beliefs always send us off in pursuit of some path other than one that leads to exaltation. And pursuing a forbidden path is always the result of failure to heed His voice.

> 52 And whoso receiveth not my voice is not acquainted with my voice, and is not of me.
>
> 53 And by this [that they receive not my voice] you may know the righteous from the wicked, and that the whole world groaneth under sin and darkness even now.
>
> 54 And your minds in times past have been darkened because of unbelief, and because you have treated lightly the things you have received—
>
> 55 Which vanity and unbelief have brought the whole church under condemnation. (Doctrine & Covenants 84:52–54, comment added)

The Lord here defines not receiving (hearing and obeying) His voice, unbelief, and wickedness as the same spiritual malady. Furthermore, He explains that our minds have been darkened because of unbelief, not sin or a lack of faith, but unbelief! Darkened implies a prior, or even continuing, presence of light that is being ignored or dimmed because of unbelief. Our minds are robbed of the light of our own faith through our inability to believe the truths that surround us. Further, we stand in darkness because we have treated lightly the things we have received.

If our goal is to lay hold upon great things in this gospel, then these scriptural accusations of unbelief are profoundly important. If unbelief truly is the obstacle we face, then we have laid hold upon a great tool to change our spiritual lives because we alone can change what we believe. There are two ways to change what you believe: One is to wait until something glorious and profound happens before your eyes and then believe what you saw, and the other is to let our faith that this same event happened exactly as recorded in the scriptures reshape our belief to include ourselves in the heavenly gifts.

The first way places us in a holding pattern we can't control. It is somewhat faithless, because we are waiting for signs and evidences. It is almost evidence of a lackluster desire to actually participate in these super-mortal blessings.

But we do have the ability to take those things we know by faith and simply believe them. The scriptures promise us that these same blessings are ours to claim, so believe in your right to claim them. Tell yourself you believe them. Tell God in prayer that you believe them. Remind yourself hourly, if necessary, that you believe these promises apply to you personally. Herein lies a key. If you do this, something astonishing will happen—you will find that once you believe, nothing doubting, the heavens do not have the ability to withhold them from your sight.

Brother John

An Angel Turning the Pages

*There have been some wonderful and terrify-*ing moments for me sitting at the piano. I started studying piano when I was eight and continued without interruption until I left on my mission. Since that time, I have played for many of the meetings I have attended and for hundreds of soloists and choirs. At one time, I was fairly talented—never actually brilliant, but good enough to play most anything with some practice.

I was invited during my late teens to play for an intermission of a Regional Road Show. I showed up on time and stood in the wings of the stage waiting for my turn. There was an upright piano in the front of the stage. I was standing there trying to decide what to play. I had several classical pieces memorized. When the time came, I walked out on stage and found myself facing about 4,000 people. It scared me so badly that I couldn't remember my name, let alone what I was going to play.

I plunked down numbly at the piano, and the only thing I could remember was "Dizzy Fingers," which is a very fast, rag-jazz piece. I hammered through that in record time and then escaped stage right. I heard later that there was a lot of applause, but I didn't stick around to hear it. By that time, I was in my car halfway home.

That was the uninspired pianist in me at work.

My most inspirational moment occurred a dozen years ago when President Hinckley came to Alaska for a regional conference. Besides the sessions of conference, he announced that he was going to give a four-hour priesthood meeting. He would be the only speaker and wanted to have a question-and-answer period in the last hour. Everyone was so excited. In the outer-Mongolian regions of Alaska (just kidding), we had never heard of such a wonderful opportunity! I arrived an hour early for the meeting and found the stake center packed. I'm estimating there were a thousand or more priesthood holders present.

The meeting opened with a men's choir. I had never heard the piece before. It was beautiful, and I could tell that the piano accompaniment was incredibly complex. The chorus was powerful and polished. The sister that accompanied them was excellent, and the music was technically and spiritually stunning.

President Hinckley spoke for two wonderful hours and then announced a thirty-minute recess. We were about halfway through that break when a brother approached me. "President Hinckley would like to have the men's chorus sing that song again. The sister who played can't be reached. Someone suggested you might be willing to do it?"

I was shocked and explained that it was a very difficult piece, and I had never seen it before. He asked me if I could maybe play just one hand—which is actually harder to do with complex music than two hands. I asked to review the music and went to the piano in the Relief Society room. It was way, way too hard to sight read. I was just standing up to tell them it was too hard when President Hinckley's personal secretary walked into the room with three other brethren, including the conductor of the choir. I said it was too hard for me to play without some practice. I asked if it could be performed as a closing song instead of now, which would give me a little time to rehearse.

"President Hinckley asked for it after the recess," he said, which in his mind seemed to settle the matter forever. He then offered to say a prayer. I decided to do whatever I could and bowed my head more in submission than prayer. I don't remember the prayer because I couldn't hear it over my pounding heart.

We walked from the prayer onto the stand. I sat at the big Kawai grand and opened the music. It looked like black ink spilled on paper. I was panicked.

At the very second that I was trying figure out how I was even going to begin, a middle-aged man with dark hair and kind eyes came and sat beside me on the bench. I didn't know who he was. He hadn't been in the prayer meeting or on the stand, and I hadn't ever seen him before in other stake meetings. He just sat beside me.

"You're going to do just fine," he assured me with a smile, and for some reason I believed him. My heart slowed down. "I'll turn the pages for you," he said and reached for the music.

The conductor raised his baton, and suddenly the notes on the page seemed to spread out, as if there were fewer of them to play. The piece started with an elaborate introduction, which my brain did not comprehend, but which my fingers played easily. Then I more or less watched my fingers as they went on to play the whole piece without a single error, including difficult runs, key changes, and variations in tempo and dynamics. My page turner followed along easily, even flipping back for a repeat, which he pointed to; I would have missed it otherwise. When it was all over, this performance had been as beautiful as the original one. It was a miracle.

I returned to my seat a little dazed. What I had just done was absolutely beyond me. My father leaned over and said, "That was beautiful. How did you ever pull it off? I know that was much harder than you usually sight read."

I shrugged my shoulders and said, "It was just a miracle."

He smiled and said, "I believe you."

I looked around for my page turner. He wasn't on the stand or in the pews, and in all the intervening years I lived in that stake, I never saw him again.

At the time I attributed this miracle entirely to the fact that it was requested by a living prophet, and to the fact that I was willing to sit down and do whatever part of it I could, even with the certainty that I was going to fail—and to the apparent fact that I had an angel turning the pages.

I still do.

Brother John

I'm a Pepper

In the late '70s, I moved to Alaska with most of my family. We settled in the Matanuska Valley, about an hour northwest of Anchorage. It is a beautiful place, very unspoiled, nestled between majestic mountains in a sprawling valley dominated by birch forests and salmon-rich streams.

The Church in that area was strong but tiny. The only ward met in a little LDS chapel in Palmer. Soon, construction began on a new building a few miles away. My father was called as the first bishop of the newly made Wasilla Ward. A few months later, I was called as the elders quorum president. Our first sacrament meeting was attended by only about twenty-five people. Meeting in that big new chapel, we felt very small indeed.

My father was a great bishop who wore his priesthood mantle well. He was inspired and inspiring. He immediately got everyone who had even part of a testimony to work, and missionary work was the call and command for all.

I was recently home from my mission, newly married, and had never served in a quorum presidency. My counselors and I began looking for our lost members. We had pages and pages of names with no addresses and no telephone numbers. I remember as a presidency praying diligently that we could find these people.

Not long after I was called, the mantle settled upon us, and miracles began to happen. We began finding people in amazing ways. The following true story is just an example of many similar events.

I was driving home from work, tired and hungry, when I heard the Spirit direct me to turn left onto a lane that opened up into a new subdivision. I had had no idea it was even there, buried out of sight in the birch forest. I slowed, and the Spirit nudged me to turn left again, which I did. I was led through a right turn, another left, and past three houses on the left, where the Spirit lit up this new house as if a spotlight was on it. I drove into the drive, past kids' toys scattered on a dirt front yard.

My heart was pounding as I banged on the door. I had no idea what to say. How do you say, "The Lord just led me to your house— umm, who are you?" I waited, and the door opened rather quickly. This attractive lady was in gym shorts and a tight red T-shirt that said, "I'm a Pepper."

I said, "Good afternoon, my name is John Pontius; I'm your elders quorum president."

Her expression didn't even change. She looked over her right shoulder and shouted, "Joe, the Mormons are here!" I thought, "Oh dang."

This big guy came to the door with no shirt on, sweat running down his face. He was physically buff. I learned later he was a semi-professional body builder. Put a black bag on his head and he would have looked like a medieval executioner. He looked at me and then opened the door. "Come in," he said. I thought in my head, ". . . said the spider to the fly."

They led me to a living room filled with exercise equipment. We exchanged names and sat. He was silent for a long time. I didn't know what to say, so I kept quiet. Finally he said, "I knew you were coming. You see, we're Mormons, but we have been kind of hiding from the Church. This morning I had a dream that you would come to our home; I actually saw your face. The dream said that if I wanted God's blessings for my family, we had to become active again in the Church. So, my only question is: where's the church and when do we meet?"

As I said, this was not a terribly unique experience. A year later, we had gathered a couple hundred people into sacrament meeting, nearly ten times our first day's attendance. It is now almost forty years later, and there is a large stake in Wasilla with thirteen wards and branches. A split in the stake is imminent. Most of the people in bishoprics and in the stake council are unaware that their fathers and mothers and sometimes their grandparents were the ones we went out and miraculously gathered into God's fold. Almost all the active members of the Church in that area can trace their spiritual heritage back to the Lord's work through my father and that sad little first Wasilla Ward.

It was a glorious time, a time of good old-fashioned inspired sacrifice. Miracles were the bread we ate every day.

Brother John

Today *Is* Eternity

Over the years of writing, speaking, and answering the questions and criticisms that always follow a public stance on anything true, I have learned one important thing: No matter what the doubters attempt to say, not only is the gospel of Jesus Christ true, as is the Church He has established wherein to house it, but it works.

It works the same today as in any dispensation of the gospel. Every blessing that has been available throughout time—every vision and miracle and priesthood power that they enjoyed—is available in this dispensation today, now. I have added to that profound part of my testimony the even deeper understanding that I, and anyone else who is willing to learn the way, walk the path, and endure the process, can obtain those blessings too.

Today *is* eternity. Eternity doesn't start after the Second Coming or some other future event. The very word *eternity* establishes that it has always existed. It predates the counting of time and will continue everlastingly beyond any future event we can consider.

Since we believe in eternal progression, there is no endpoint defined by death, or even by translation. The heavens keep opening before our eyes, revealing heavenly vistas newly within our grasp.

Who can even guess what glories await the eyes and ears and souls of those who are invited into that great General Assembly and Church of the Firstborn, who company with translated souls, angels, the notable and profound of past generations, and our Savior? Who can imagine being a part of the 144,000 who reap the earth by miracles and openly manifest power, who receive their assignments from Christ's lips, and who move mountains at His command? What mortal mind can even conceive of the wonders of such a life: sacrament meetings where John the Beloved might be the concluding speaker, where angels sing in choirs, and testimonies are illustrated by visions shared by all present? What mortal imagination can reach beyond the finite mind and understand the joy of living without fear, without opposition, and without possibility of failure; of being sent forth to do the impossible with prophetic visions of success?

None can, and yet we do believe; and by faith we see through the glass of mortality dimly, to these profound blessings that surely await us.

Brother John

The Journey Home
Part IV: Off to the Tropics

Okay, so we waited almost a year for John's next check-up. What's the big deal? A clean bill of health is a clean bill of health, right? In December 2008 (eleven months after the cancer was proclaimed gone) John decided it was time for him to get a check-up; what he didn't share with me is that he was starting to feel a bit weak and sometimes queasy. The check-up revealed another cancerous mass, this time attached near his liver, which was quite large. Immediate surgery was required.

We didn't have health insurance. John had long owned his own business, and private health insurance was a huge monthly expense to someone who had never needed medical treatment much before. And once John got the liver abscess, private health insurance was not available for us to purchase at any price. I felt completely overwhelmed thinking about the $75,000 out-of-pocket bill for his needed surgery. But although shaken, John remained calm and unruffled. "The Lord has an answer for us, and we'll find it," he would tell me.

Then we thought we found the answer. We discovered something previously unknown to us called "medical tourism," where we could go to a foreign hospital that was Joint Commission-accredited and staffed with American-trained doctors and there receive a comparable surgery for a fraction of the money required in the U.S. After prayer, we settled upon Costa Rica as our destination, as it is only a few hours' flight from Houston, a progressive and relatively safe country, and, to our thinking, a tropical paradise.

Our surgeon in Alaska was fully on board with this decision and sent tests and medical charts with us for the doctors in Costa Rica. I was actually excited; after all, it would be a quick laparoscopic operation, and then there were white beaches and cool volcanos to explore as soon as Johnnie felt better! By the end of February, we had procured passports, packed our beach clothing, and were off to the tropics for a holiday.

But things didn't exactly work out that way.

—Terri

Chapter Five

Unlocking the Mysteries

The Greater Portion of the Word

To those who will not harden their hearts is given the "greater portion of the word," until they know the mysteries in full. This greater portion of the word constitutes those things that are vast and true, which are not commonly taught within the standard programming of the Church, but which are essential to exaltation nonetheless. As a point of fact, those who obtain mysteries for themselves, by obedience and revelation, are generally not permitted to openly discuss what they have learned.

> 9 And now Alma began to expound these things unto him, saying: It is given unto many to know the mysteries of God; nevertheless they are laid under a strict command that they shall not impart only according to the portion of his word which he doth grant unto the children of men, according to the heed and diligence which they give unto him. (Alma 12:9)

These are not just interesting principles and doctrines we receive during some divine bonus round; these are the very truths that have catapulted the righteous of every dispensation into the great blessings that they record in scripture.

These mysteries unveil the "rights of the priesthood" in the sense that they open our view to the greater blessings and privileges that flow from the priesthood. These rights, as we observed earlier, are "inseparably connected with the powers of heaven" (Doctrine & Covenants 121:36). In other words, the fulness of the rights of the priesthood are only to be found within the "greater portion of the word," which are called "mysteries," because so "few are chosen" (Doctrine & Covenants 121:34) to receive them.

It may be more accurate to say, "because so few choose to *receive* them." Additionally, the mysteries are that which "bringeth joy, that which bringeth life eternal" (Doctrine & Covenants 42:61). For those who obtain these "hidden mysteries of my kingdom" in full, their "wisdom shall be great, and their understanding reach to heaven."

> 7 And to them will I reveal all mysteries, yea, all the hidden mysteries of my kingdom from days of old, and for ages to come, will I make known unto them the good pleasure of my will concerning all things pertaining to my kingdom.
>
> 8 Yea, even the wonders of eternity shall they know, and things to come will I show them, even the things of many generations.
>
> 9 And their wisdom shall be great, and their understanding reach to heaven; and before them the wisdom of the wise shall perish, and the understanding of the prudent shall come to naught.
>
> 10 For by my Spirit will I enlighten them, and by my power will I make known unto them the secrets of my will—yea, even those things which eye has not seen, nor ear heard, nor yet entered into the heart of man. (Doctrine & Covenants 76:7–10)

Why will their understanding reach to heaven? Because they will see into heaven. "The wonders of eternity shall they know, and things to come will I show them, even the things of many generations" (Doctrine & Covenants 76:8). These mysteries are by very definition the "greater portion of the word" (Alma 12:10). These are the things of the Spirit and cannot be known any other way than by revelation. For one who refuses to reach beyond sight into faith and into the grand mysteries, the mysteries of godliness are the things that "eye hath not seen, nor ear heard, nor yet entered into the heart of man" (Doctrine & Covenants 76:10).

Tragically, this defines the vast majority of us, whose hearts are so set upon our worldly labors.

But should we even be trying to rise above the norm? Isn't the revealed portion that we all love and embrace enough? Why press into something that isn't commonly known? Isn't that shooting beyond the mark? Aren't we supposed to adhere to the basics and leave the mysteries alone?

Elder McConkie had this to say:

There is a true doctrine on these points, a doctrine unknown to many and unbelieved by more, a doctrine that is spelled out as specifically and extensively in the revealed word as are any of the other great revealed truths. There is no need for uncertainty or misunderstanding; and surely, if the Lord reveals a doctrine, we should seek to learn its principles and strive to apply them in our lives. This doctrine is that mortal man, while in the flesh, has it in his power to see the Lord, to stand in his presence, to feel the nail marks in his hands and feet, and to receive from him such blessings as are reserved for those only who keep all his commandments and who are qualified for that eternal life which includes being in his presence forever. (Bruce R. McConkie, *New Witness for the Articles of Faith*, 492)

Elder McConkie clearly states what one of the greater mysteries is. There are many others, the more pertinent ones having to do with the establishment of Zion in this dispensation.

Because of the open nature of the Internet and this UnBlog, these mysteries must remain unlabeled. But, in the course of time, if the heavens concur, we will discuss most of them without much fanfare. Those who have ears to hear and eyes to see will understand.

Brother John

The Miracle of Obedience

I *received a comment from Juli asking about my* experiences after I decided to be completely obedient. After thinking about it for a while, confessing that it has taken me multiple recommitments to this principle, and admitting that flawless obedience is still before me, I would like to tell you of the first time I humbly committed myself to flawless obedience to anything I could identify as the Lord's voice, or His will or commandments.

The time period was about 1991. I was serving on the high council and working very hard. It was a time of blessings and happiness, but I realized that something was missing. I didn't seem to be experiencing *joy* in my labors. I was happy and willing, but I was not experiencing joy.

After quite a bit of prayer and study, I began to realize that I was picking and choosing among the promptings I was receiving. I had felt perfectly comfortable at that time in rejecting a prompting that was inconvenient or hard to hear, because I had yet to identify promptings as coming from Jesus Christ personally. I still had thought these were just good ideas my own mind was generating. The realization that finally came to me by spiritual confirmation was that these promptings were coming from my Savior through the Holy Ghost, and that the reason I had yet to experience joy was because I was not being fully and flawlessly obedient.

During my evening prayers that night, I felt that familiar quickening, that opening of the heavens and warming of the chest, which, for me at least, signifies a special power is present in that prayer. I'm not sure what makes this happen, as I have tried to call upon it many times without success; and then at other times when I am not particularly trying, it just comes. So I was excited to feel the veil parting this little bit, and while in this state, I committed myself to this new level of "flawless" obedience.

I got up from my knees and had the feeling that I should fast the next day. I was a little shocked, because I usually prefer to prepare spiritually (and by eating extra) for a fast. I knelt back down and opened that fast and asked for help, because the next day was a regular work day.

I struggled very hard that next day but kept my fasting, and I kept the spirit of the fast. I returned home and gratefully ate dinner, interacted with the family, and prepared for bed. As I was brushing my teeth, I heard a distinct prompting: "Fast tomorrow."

This came as a greater shock, as I still felt depleted from that day's fast. I knelt down by my bed and began another fast. When I returned home, I ate and drank like a starving person, and while I was brushing my teeth, again, a warm presence, and the prompting, "Fast tomorrow."

This pattern continued for weeks. I fasted three to four times a week for several months. It didn't get easier; it just became powerful. My prayers expanded, my soul grew, my heart reached into the heavens, and I felt joy approaching from some distant place.

Then, one morning as I was preparing for work—and fasting— the Spirit prompted me to break my fast. I complied, ate a bit, and went to work. I realized later that what was happening wasn't about fasting—it was about obedience. I had covenanted to be obedient in all things, and this was my testing ground. My body, my needs, and my natural urge to avoid hunger were being presented as tests to my determination to be obedient.

Praise the Lord—I persisted. I listened as carefully as I could, and the promptings became more than just "Fast tomorrow." I began to be taught principles, doctrine, and truths about myself and my spouse. I was so grateful! I began to rejoice when the Spirit prompted me to fast again. I had little regard for my body; I just knew that something wonderful was going to flow into my mind and heart that day.

One particular morning, I had not heard a prompting to fast, but I was so grateful for the blessings I had been receiving that I decided on my own to fast. It was an awful experience. My blood sugar crashed at work. I grew sick and dizzy and could not function. I stumbled to the cafeteria to find food. I arrived at home a physical wreck. As I was brushing my teeth that evening, I heard the now-familiar prompting to fast. I wavered and waffled. I reminded God how hard my day had been. Finally, I bowed my head, and in the tiniest voice my soul could produce, I began another fast.

As I knelt by my bed that evening, the heavens again opened. The Spirit swept over me. I felt my soul rising, seeking, asking, knocking. I began to understand things, hear things, see things. That experience lasted all through the night. It was the most grand and glorious experience I have ever had. It repeated three times, each one exactly the same. When it ended, I got out of bed, dressed, and prepared for work. As I looked in the mirror that morning, I realized that the predominant emotion in my soul was joy. That feeling has persisted these intervening years and still floods my soul. As I was brushing my teeth before work that morning (I have no idea why the Spirit chose to speak at that moment so many times!), I was prompted to end my fast. I simply obeyed.

That was almost eighteen years ago. I never again was prompted to fast so often, because the test was about obedience, not about fasting. I have been prompted on many other things, and I still endeavor to remain flawlessly obedient, though my mortal weakness has made it difficult even while I understand very clearly the blessings of that obedience.

Still I try, and still the voice of my Savior guides when I return from the wastelands of mortality and recommit to listening.

And still the joy resides in my soul.

Brother John

Reaching for Mighty Prayer

There are several powerful tools we must develop in order to walk the true path to all of the available blessings of the gospel. I hope to UnBlog about a few of them.

The first and the most powerful is to learn to hear the voice of Jesus Christ. I have UnBlogged about this so often that I am actually reluctant to belabor it once again. The key is to realize that your conscience is actually the voice of Jesus Christ and that it comes from Christ via the Light of Christ. By covenanting and dedicating ourselves to obeying every single prompting from Christ, we place ourselves on a powerful rocket, blasting into the skies of righteousness.

The second principle of which we must fully avail ourselves is mighty prayer.

The only way to learn how to really pray is to find the motivation to spend lots of time doing it. This becomes easy when we have attuned our hearts to His voice, because we soon begin to see His grace and love being manifest in our lives, and swelling gratitude begins to motivate every thought and word we direct heavenward.

During times of greatest and fastest growth, I have often prayed many hours a day. This isn't only formal kneeling prayer but also prayer while driving, while reading, while eating, and even just before going to sleep. Most of these prayers do not adhere to the strict formula, but often begin as an outpouring of gratitude and love and may also end with something other than "amen." A grateful glance at a beautiful sunset, a few seconds of worshipful wonder at a spiritual gift given, joy in a sweet grandchild, or inward thanks for divine interventional grace—all approach mighty prayer.

Here is the magic: It is that when we have learned to hear the voice of Christ by listening to and obeying our conscience, then that same voice of revelation attends us during prayer—both in teaching us how to pray and for what to pray.

These are the divine answers, which by prayer we learn to wrap around our needs. Obedience to the revelatory voice trains us to hear truths revealed during prayer more clearly and with greater power. This very act of attuning our spiritual ears to Christ is what makes powerful and mighty prayer possible. It is obedience and acting fearlessly on the voice of revelation that make the revelation continue, and in time, will amplify our little prayers into mighty ones.

Brother John

She Still Lights Up the Room

Some years ago, the Church Education System had an adult institute program in Alaska. I was called as the teacher and handed a manual and a list of names of people whom local bishops had encouraged to attend.

I have always loved teaching, and I read and prepared happily. The subject was the Book of Mormon, which is a topic I love. When I arrived, I found a room full of people who mostly would have preferred to be somewhere else. They were laughing loudly, talking about hunting and fishing, arguing about sports, and telling jokes. There was so little Spirit in the room that it was like walking into a chill.

After an opening prayer, I didn't open the manual but stood and said something like this: "I have found over the years that how much a class like this blesses the lives of the students has to do with two things, the least important being what the teacher does to prepare, and the Spirit that he brings into the class. The most important factor is what the class members bring to the class. If even one person comes to class seeking, or with an empty cup he or she is hoping to fill, then the Holy Spirit will come to teach that one person, and everyone else will benefit. If nobody comes ready to be fed, then nothing the teacher can do will bring the Holy Spirit into a room of unwilling students."

There were a little uncomfortable shifting and glances at the floor.

I then related an experience I had had with teaching a priesthood advancement seminar a dozen years earlier. Every person attending that seminar had been inactive or was married to an inactive or non-member spouse. The bishop had asked every one of them to attend, and few of them were happy to be there. We had met in the home of an inactive member, which happened to be a single-wide trailer. It was winter, and the trailer was freezing inside. I had begun the lesson, and the chill seemed to transfer from our skin to our hearts.

Continuing my story, I said, "About ten minutes into the lesson, the door opened, and a flood of cold swept through the little room. A young woman came in. I didn't see her face because she was wrapped up in a scarf. There were no chairs left, so she sat on the floor in the corner farthest away from me. The odd thing was that she came to learn and to change her life. Her bucket was empty, and she realized it and was seeking light. I couldn't see her sitting there, but the whole corner of the room lit up. The Spirit descended upon us like a warm blanket. A feeling of humble faith fell upon everyone present, and the teaching began."

I concluded my story by saying that every person in that room made a decision to continue to try to change their lives, because they felt the Holy Spirit that night because of one young woman who came into the room hungering and humble.

Back to the present, my newest class looked a bit more attentive now. I told them that I was going to give them three assignments, one each week. I promised them that if they would do these three simple things, their lives would change for the better, and, like that young woman, when they came to class, they would light up the room. I said, "Not only will *you* be uplifted and fed, but so will everyone else here."

Several of them got out their note pads.

"Assignment #1: Go home and get out your scriptures. Open them to any place in the Book of Mormon and put them on your bed stand beside your bed. You cannot read them; just leave them open there."

They laughed. I made them bring their arms to the square and promise me that they would complete this assignment. They all promised they would. It was very simple.

The following week, I asked them to report on their experience with their first assignment. Many of them commented on how they had had a very hard time *not* reading the scriptures while they were sitting there open. They asked if it was okay to read them. I told them not yet.

"Assignment #2: Find or buy a framed picture of Jesus Christ. Hang it in your bedroom where it is the first thing you see each morning, and the last thing you see before going to sleep." I again made them solemnly promise. They chuckled and promised that they would.

When they returned the next week, I asked them about their experiences with having the picture of their Savior in their bedrooms. They all said it brought peace to them and made them think of Him more often throughout the day—which is actually fulfilling one of the promises we make in the sacrament prayers.

"Assignment #3: Kneel by your bed just before climbing in. Look at the scriptures without picking them up, and read one verse. Pray for at least ten seconds, and get into bed." Again, I made them promise.

As the year progressed, I slowly added time to the prayers until we were praying twenty minutes daily (a good goal to shoot for) and reading a full page of scripture. I'm sure I lost a few along the way, but most of them said they were trying very hard to be faithful. The result was magical. They began to change. The conversation before class was more reverent. They were genuinely happy to be there. I knew this because they enthusiastically brought their friends and spouses. They also brought their scriptures to class, made notes, and volunteered readily to pray. Comments were reverent and uplifting. They became a joy to teach.

Each week it was evident that the Holy Spirit entered their lives more and more, and the God of love blessed them for their small obediences. Over the period of a year they began to read because they loved the effect in their lives, and they prayed more fervently because their faith had greatly increased.

I watched them light up—I mean, their faces became brighter with spiritual light each week! I watched husbands and wives that I knew had been struggling hold hands during class. I watched them slowly be reborn as they brought Christ into their bedrooms and into their lives by simple compliance with powerful laws.

No person can do these three things for any period of time and *not* be changed. The angels who guard us watch, and they anxiously wait to pour out blessings at the smallest blooming of our faith, and they rejoice when we do the simple things that quite literally part the veil.

And, as for the young woman who had come into that chilly trailer and sat in the corner out of sight, I found out later she was not even a member, though she had been. She is presently married in the temple to a wonderful priesthood holder. They raised five kids, sent three sons on missions, and saw all of their children married in the temple. When we meet now, as we occasionally do, she gives me a hug and reminds me with tears in her eyes of those joyful, struggling days as she began her journey back. She told me not long ago that she still has her scriptures open on her bed stand, and a picture of the Savior on her bedroom wall.

She's a grandma now, and she still lights up the room.

Brother John

Matriculation into Eternity

We came to earth at least in part to acquire a physical body, and one of the greatest consequences God has ever given was to deny a third part of the rebellious hosts of heaven the chance to ever have a body. The scriptures tell us that our bodies are how the devil tempts us and are a source of evil. Yet, God the Father has a perfected body, which I am sure is a source of infinite joy and perfection to Him, and which does not act as a source of evil but of light and truth.

So we came to earth to obtain a body and, through that body and the world it lives in, to be tested to our utmost.

It seems apparent from all this that conquering our body of flesh is essential to our spiritual journey. We must baptize it in water, and in the Spirit, and teach it to serve our spiritual desires without complaint, rather than forcing our spirit to serve our bodies unto our own destruction. Most of the evil we experience comes to us as an urging of the flesh, or as a desire to please, show off, or play with our bodies.

One of the very powerful tools we are given to help us place our spirits in charge of our bodies (rather than the other way around) is fasting. Fasting gives our spirit temporary dominance over our body. It places our spirit in perfect control and places our bodies in submission to our righteous will. This is the reason we feel "spiritual" when fasting, because the normal balance of control and command between our eternal spirit and our mortal bodies has been shifted slightly toward our spirit.

Repeated fasting, as directed by the Holy Spirit, can permanently alter this relationship. One of you very wisely commented that fasting helped you conquer an addiction. What is an addiction, other than the body of flesh demanding something with a screaming voice that we allowed it to experience once in a moment of spiritual weakness? What is sin, if not something we allow the flesh to do in a moment of spiritual weakness? What is the natural man, but someone whose primary motivation in life is to release control to the flesh to do anything it wants?

Fasting thus becomes one of the few tools we have to quickly and powerfully reassert spiritual control over the body.

Fasting is most powerfully done in obedience to a prompting by the Holy Spirit. I am very reluctant to establish a routine fast programmed into the week. Our body adapts, and it ceases to be an exercise in spiritual control, but one of habit.

I went through a period of rapid growth many years ago when the Spirit instructed me to fast every other day for months. After that prolonged period of sacrifice, I could sense my body as a separate entity from me. My spirit was the governing entity. Rather than seeing in my mind's eye that my body was a container for my spirit, and I was more or less "riding" in it like a passenger in a car, I began to view my spirit as the larger, more powerful, and more permanent entity, and my body as being smaller and within my spirit, under my spirit's control, completely subject to my spirit's will.

I discovered that visually having my spirit extending beyond my body was a powerful experience. Touch became revelatory; sight was enhanced to see things spiritually as well as physically. Hearing included words and intent, as well as the truth or error of the words. Priesthood blessings were easy to give and quickly followed by miraculous outcomes. Things of the Spirit, the scriptures, writings, mighty prayer, and profound revelation were everyday happenings.

The demands of the flesh were still heard, but as if from a distance, and more like a whine than a screaming demand.

Such a relationship of spirit over body does not last easily. The telestial forces of mortality tenaciously try to reassert control of body over spirit. But by effort and lasting obedience—by hearkening without fail to the voice of the Holy Spirit, and by calling upon the Lord's mighty empowerment to change us into spiritually-controlled creatures—our eternal spirit can remain dominant throughout our matriculation into immortality.

Brother John

Have I Been Born Again?

I *want to discuss today how to tell whether one has* been born again. The scriptures use various names to describe this grand spiritual upgrade. It is interesting and wonderful that it takes so many names to describe it. One of the factors bringing forth so many names is that there is not just one rebirth or mighty change we enjoy, but there is a continuum of them.

Each name describes being born again at some level, and since there are many levels, there are many names.

Let's also note that there is not one format for being born again. Different people experience each level differently and with more or less emphasis. For some it is one long process that ends in a serene righteousness. For others, it is many events which immerse them in spiritual fire. It is even true that some people experience much of it without realizing it, as did the Lamanites in 3 Nephi 9:20.

My guess is that most people don't realize they have been born again until later. So, the question is, how can you tell if you've already experienced being born again, and on what level?

One can tell by the spiritual attributes that you possess.

If you have developed, or have been given by a powerful experience, some of these attributes in some degree—not all and not perfectly, but in some degree—then you have been born again on some level. If you have all of them, then you have been born again in the greatest sense possible:

- Faith in Jesus Christ
- Testimony of Jesus Christ
- Love of God
- Love of fellow man
- Humble
- Meek
- Obedient to counsel
- Willing to submit to all things
- Patient in suffering
- Teachable
- Love of the Scriptures
- Delight in prayer
- Become as a little child
- Full of faith, hope, and charity
- Possess some of the gifts of the Spirit: faith, testimony of Jesus Christ, belief, discernment, wisdom, knowledge, faith to be healed, faith to heal, miracles, prophecy, discerning spirits, speaking or interpretation of tongues—and many others.
- Have a perfect knowledge of Christ
- Possess the fulness of the Priesthood

If you possess some of these gifts, and if they flow forth from you in the things you do and say, then you have been born again on some level. If you felt it once, but no longer do, then you were once born again and have allowed yourself to step back.

Now, let me state the not-so-obvious. There are many stages and many degrees of being born again. There is the moment when someone knows by the power of the Holy Ghost that Jesus is the Christ. This is a very real moment when the Holy Ghost changes us. It is a necessary step for every mortal and is the nativity of a Christ-filled life. On the far end of that same journey is the moment the heavens open, the veil parts, and we step into the presence of Jesus

Christ; when we no longer have faith in Christ but a personal and perfect knowledge of Him; when we have become like Him and have His image and perfections in our countenances. This is not just a "mighty change" but the mightiest change mankind may enjoy and still remain upon the earth.

So, between these two glorious bookends of the "born again" continuum, there are many milestone upgrades to our souls that change us by grace and prepare us for the "perfect day" when Christ shall appear to us personally. Each of these incrementally greater changes is a rebirth, an awakening, and a mighty change. Each of them happens because we acted upon and fully embraced the light where we were; at that level, we were perfect in obedience and ready to progress onto the next step along the straight and narrow path to another grace-empowered rebirth.

Let me illustrate this process in over-simplified terms.

Someone studies the scriptures or embraces the testimony of another, and in an inspired moment that person's heart burns for the first time with a testimony that Jesus is the Christ. Most probably, this happens in the Christian universe, not within the relatively tiny orbit of the LDS Church.

That person's life will change dramatically. Suddenly, there is a whole world of things to learn and to do. There is action required, commandments to live, a commitment to make, possibly a baptism to submit to, scriptures to study, and service to render. The voice of the Holy Spirit becomes more audible, urging obedience and compliance with the law of Christ.

If such newly minted Christians will submit, obey, and act, then another dispensation of grace will bring them to a greater rebirth. If they do not act upon the things their testimony of Christ is urging them to do, then they remain at this level or decline. But they do not advance spiritually.

At some point, they will receive the opportunity to hear the truths of the restored gospel, and the Holy Spirit will urge them to listen and to comply. When they do, further and greater opportunities open before them. They receive marvelous ordinances empowered by true priesthood power. The blessings of the temple become available, and covenants begin to operate in their lives.

If they live true and faithful to these greater things, angels, seen and unseen, work in their lives. Miracles happen, and profound opportunities for service and sacrifice appear. Grace flows like a river, and covenants define a more narrow and exacting course of life.

If they obey, embrace, and covenant, then they are born again and again and again. Calling and Election occurs, splitting the night sky with spiritual lightning. The doctrine of the priesthood distills upon the soul; visions, miracles, and angelic ministrations bless and protect. Each change is a mighty one, and each is a rebirth.

As they progress, in the furthest reaches of human believing, they begin to see the veil before them and the blessings of a personal experience with Jesus Christ beckoning them into His light.

Every step requires obedience to truths known and promptings heard. Each step is unavoidable and cannot be skipped or zoomed over. Each step is in itself a rebirth, an awakening, and a mighty change. Each occurs by the grace of Christ, and each is a baptism of fire in some degree, until we actually enter the fire of divine presence.

Brother John

The Way of Growth

I was speaking to a great friend the other day who was discouraged. He had worked and fasted and prayed very hard and had achieved a new spiritual stature over many months. Some profound blessings had come; he had felt the Spirit night and day, and he received glorious spiritual insights and revelation moment by moment. And then, the spiritual high began to dissipate. New opposition arose. He tried harder—and it still slipped away. He worked even harder still and found he couldn't stop it from slipping away. He wasn't doing anything wrong; as a matter of fact, he was doing more things right than ever before in his life.

He sat down in my office very discouraged. After a few minutes of hearing his tale, I knew exactly what was happening, and it had nothing to do with any error or sin on his part, but just the opposite. It was happening because he was seeking and obtaining great spiritual growth.

Here's what happens: When we pay the price for some new

spiritual growth, we arrive at a spiritual high, or a type of honeymoon period where we bask in the new blessings, the powerful prayers, the peace, and constant revelation. Obedience is easy there because everything is so wonderful! We can easily see the path before us, and hearkening to the voice of revelation and to any commandment is a joy. But alas, we are living on borrowed light—the Lord's light. We are glowing with spiritual power that is not our own.

This always happens. Following periods of growth, new opposition always arises that challenges our new gifts. The Spirit begins to withdraw to give us the opportunity to continue in this level of obedience through the darkness, simply because we know it is correct, not because we are lit up with a trillion volts of spiritual light.

It may seem, and actually does seem, that something has gone dramatically wrong. The adversary whispers, "If what you experienced were actually true, then it wouldn't be slipping away." Or, "See, you're not good enough. You're too weak to maintain any great blessings."

The truth is that the rise of this additional opposition and loss of spiritual power is part of the plan. It gives us a chance to be tested at this new level of spiritual growth. The test is to continue doing those things we learned to do to get there, even when we no longer feel like doing them.

On my mission, we had hundreds of mission rules. Because I had a great trainer and first companion, I learned to keep the rules from day one. We worked hard and studied hard, prayed hard and testified hard. And we lit up spiritually and had wonderful experiences. We knew where to go, what to say, what to teach. We just loved it. Then, after a few months, there was a spiritual tapering off. We lost some investigators. We got yelled at and threatened by the local ministers. It became hard. We didn't feel the Spirit as often. We didn't know who to find or what to say once we found them.

My companion looked at me and said, "It happens. We just keep working and doing the Lord's will even when it's hard." So we trudged along for another few months in the hot African sun, doing everything we knew to do—fasting, praying, studying, keeping the mission rules. Sure enough, in a few months, the Spirit returned with greater power, new spiritual gifts, and new investigators. We were thrilled.

My wise companion looked at me and said, "It happens. We just keep working and doing the Lord's will even when it's easy."

He was right on.

In other words, keep doing everything right—because it is right—even while standing in darkness or in light. This is the test. This is where we prove that we are "willing to serve Him at all hazards." This is the magic of obedience. This is the test that guards the way to the next greater thing you are seeking. Then, when the Spirit returns—and it will return—it does so with greater power, with new spiritual gifts, and with new levels of obedience for us to navigate. Then we bask in the new honeymoon period and prepare for the test that will surely come.

This is the way of growth: Struggle, grow, receive blessings, bask in the blessings (honeymoon period), greater opposition, lessening of the Spirit, remain faithful, climb to new spiritual heights, start all over again.

The blessing of knowing this process is operating in our lives is that it empowers us to forge onward, to know that it is merely the law of opposition at work, which is for our ultimate good, and not some unfair and unholy obstacle. It will end, and we will regain our blessings, and more, as we endure. We are not lost in some spiritual wilderness but are climbing upward upon the ordained path that leads to eternal vistas.

It is the way of growth.

Brother John

Grace like a River

When people are born again, they generally don't realize it, don't really know why it happened, and have a tendency to falter and yoyo in and out. Rather than being an indictment against humankind, it is a fact of tender mercy on our Savior's part. He is willing to let us learn, let us fall down, forgive us, teach us, and then hold us up while we reach further again and again.

I don't know how to write about this topic without using personal examples. Please understand that I am sounding the Lord's horn, not my own. I am surely the least among any of you.

I can remember three times that I experienced being born again.

The first time was on my mission. I had the mission rules to guide me. These included prayer three times a day, studying the scriptures twice a day, memorizing three scriptures a day, and teaching, testifying, tracting, and listening to the Spirit seven days a week. In this divinely orchestrated situation, I blossomed spiritually. I felt the Spirit almost every moment of those two years. It made me willing and courageous. It also took me many years afterward to realize that what I had experienced was the rebirth of the Spirit. When I returned home, I got sucked up into mortal life—school, getting married, having kids, moving to Alaska—and the spiritual power faded. I recognized it was waning but didn't know why, and I felt powerless to stop it from slipping away.

The second time was when I was called to be the elders quorum president in the newly formed Wasilla Ward. I felt the mantle of the priesthood descend upon me, and I went to work. I re-enthroned listening to the Spirit. I worked every day to do my duty. I taught classes, held seminars, gave blessings, spoke in church, and loved and served my quorum. Before long, I felt the wonderful power of righteous living again. My prayers soared to new heights. Once again, I didn't know why exactly, except that I was working hard and rejoicing in the Lord. About five years later, we moved to a new city for work, and I got caught up in life again, starting a new job, building our first house, having more babies, building a new business, dealing with life on a different scale. And the spiritual power slipped.

The third time I was born again was about ten years later. I found myself on the high council and began to really work hard and to seek the guidance of the Spirit more fully. I renewed my dedication to flawless obedience and righteousness in Christ, in the midst of debilitating challenges that threatened to destroy my world.

One evening in deeply striving mighty prayer, the words came, and I covenanted to obey unconditionally. What followed was the greatest spiritual experience of my life until then. It kept me awake all through the night. I got up the next morning and went to work without having slept. I was not tired and felt no physical or emotional exhaustion. I was just elated and terribly confused. That next evening, I prayed diligently to know why this had happened to me, as unworthy as I felt. I was well aware of my faults, and this experience seemed too wonderful given what I realized were my imperfections. As I prayed, the Spirit whispered, "Yes, you are imperfect, but you are obedient."

The next morning, I was walking down the hall of my home when I suddenly saw myself in a split-second vision. It was sort of like what I thought one might experience after death. I saw my life from beginning to end, except that I was watching myself as if from about ten feet above and behind myself. I saw my decisions and realized that in every single situation, I had been prompted by the Holy Spirit with the correct action. In my vision, I actually heard the promptings, and then I heard the opposition argue against it, and I witnessed my decision and where it had taken me. I saw me wander a little off, and return, and wander again, all as I learned by experience to obey the Spirit. I saw my path travel many miles, with only a little forward progress. Finally, I was shown the previous evening, and how my entire life had been preparing me to consecrate myself to total obedience. I saw how this one act of consecration worked this amazing miracle of grace. When the vision closed, I was midstride in the hallway of my house. No actual time had passed, but I had seen almost forty years of my life.

It was then that I finally understood the power and might of obedience. It was then that I realized that our Savior didn't care about perfection, works, position, power, or money. He didn't care about how learned or wise or clever or rich I was. He didn't care how many scriptures I could quote or how many times I had read the Book of Mormon or the Bible. He only cared about obedience. Through complete consecration of my pitiful offering of unconditional obedience, which was the only thing that I had to offer, a key turned in the celestial door, eternal gears were engaged, and the heavens opened. I then understood perfectly what "grace like a river" truly is.

After that, I began to have daily revelation and instant answers to my prayers, and miracles and tender mercies seemed unending. I was completely changed in that instant. I had no more desire to see or even know about anything evil. I honestly couldn't stand the appearance or smell of evil. I was now born again on a new and higher level, and I knew why, and I finally understood how to retain it.

I haven't been perfect since that time. Far from it. I haven't even managed to keep the world from sucking the spiritual air from my lungs. I have been on the razor's edge of death when I couldn't feel anything but pain. But I have come back time and again, quickly returning to that grace, which is in Christ, which is everything the human soul yearns for and has no idea how to embrace, until one learns the sweeping power of consecrated obedience to His voice.

Brother John

The Heavenly Gift

Having one's Calling and Election made sure is a natural progression in the quest for righteousness of all forms, including seeking Zion. It is not an obscure doctrine, nor is it mysterious—though it is rightly a "mystery" until we seek and obtain it.

The way to experience this high and holy blessing is to walk the straight course to Calling and Election as we have discussed so far:

- Obedience to the voice of Christ / Holy Spirit
- Sacrifice
- Prayer
- Faith
- Repentance
- Baptism
- Gift of the Holy Ghost
- Being born again
- Becoming perfect in Christ
- Personal revelation
- Temple endowment
- Taught by angels
- Power in the priesthood
- Becoming pure in heart

- Calling and Election made sure
- Personal visitation with Christ

Like all of these potential steps, "Calling and Election" is not something that one can obtain out of context. It isn't possible to skip being baptized, for example, and yet seek the blessings of the temple. It also isn't reasonable to skip the rebirth, or the temple, or obtaining greater power in the priesthood and yet yearn for and seek after the higher blessings, including Calling and Election. The only way to walk the course is line upon line, precept upon precept, until the brighter day dawns incrementally upon us.

It is important to observe here that this list we are developing is a theoretical outline of the journey to these high and holy blessings. Different seekers may experience them in a somewhat different order, or perhaps with different emphasis. Some events will occur quietly, unnoticed for years, until the Spirit of the Lord highlights them in our thinking. A possible postscript to this is that some steps may occur so personally and without fanfare that they may appear to have been skipped until greater light is shown upon our past.

The astonishing truth regarding this pathway as noted above is that we are *already* upon it. Most of us, even by casual measurement, are at least halfway through the process. When one considers the state of the world today and throughout history, this is an astonishing, one-in-a-million accomplishment.

So see, don't you feel encouraged already?

Here is the key to going beyond where you are today. This is so precious that most who read this will miss it or misunderstand it, or it will be hidden from their understanding until they are ready. The key lies in Moroni's explanation of why the Brother of Jared had sufficient faith to part the veil.

Moroni states in Ether 12:

> 19 And there were many whose faith was so exceedingly strong, even before Christ came, who could not be kept from within the veil, but truly saw with their eyes the things which they had beheld with an eye of faith, and they were glad.
>
> 20 And behold, we have seen in this record that one of these was the brother of Jared; for so great was his faith in God, that when God put forth his finger he could not hide it from the sight of the brother

of Jared, because of his word which he had spoken unto him, which word he had obtained by faith. (Ether 12:19–20)

We often marvel at the faith of the brother of Jared, but what we miss is *why* he had that faith. Notice in the next verse:

21 And after the brother of Jared had beheld the finger of the Lord, *because of the promise which the brother of Jared had obtained by faith,* the Lord could not withhold anything from his sight; wherefore he showed him all things, for he could no longer be kept without the veil. (Ether 12:21)

In other words, the brother of Jared had obtained a promise from the Lord that he *could* part the veil and enter into the divine presence, which entering-in is the "heavenly gift" spoken of in that same chapter. This is the "great and last promise" we seek.

Given the very powerful truth that the gospel of Christ is the same in each dispensation, and that we *do* have the same gifts and privileges as the brother of Jared, then *we have the same promise!* The difference may only be that we don't recognize it, or that we don't believe the promise actually applies to us.

Where and when did you receive this promise? It was the last time you went to the temple. The ceremony of the endowment is teaching us, with painstaking repetition, that by the process defined in the temple we can arrive at the veil, knock, and be allowed to converse, receive additional promises that are unspeakable, and then enter into the divine presence.

This is the same promise the brother of Jared obtained by faith. The difference is that he believed so completely that the Lord "could not withhold anything from his sight; wherefore he showed him all things." This is the promise that you also have obtained by faith—and is your calling card at the veil.

Moroni then teaches over and over how every miracle of the divine presence was brought to pass by faith. He is not speaking solely of faith in Christ. He is also speaking directly of faith in the promises we have obtained. What remains for us to do is to recognize the vastness of the promises we have been given, believe with trembling joy that they truly do apply to us, and take that great faith to the veil.

Then, like the brother of Jared, when we are fully prepared and the Lord's timing is correct, we will also lay hold upon the heavenly gift.

Brother John

Our Journey to the Veil

*I*t occurred to me as I was reading *Moses* that he had a similar experience at the veil as we are taught in the temple. The brother of Jared records a similar experience, as do others. Since there is only one gospel process that takes a person to the veil, and since the Lord's path is "one eternal round," that process repeats over and over again. And so it will with us as well. Let us briefly study how this process works so that we too may apply it.

- Moses first spoke with God without seeing Him in the burning bush (Moses 1:17). At that time, Moses was taught his future delivering labor for Israel. When God finally appeared to Moses, the pattern of coming into the presence of the Lord was unveiled.
- Moses is confronted by Satan (Moses 1:1–22).
- Moses speaks with the Lord through the veil (Moses 1:25–27).
- Moses learns that the waters will obey his command as if he were God (Moses 1:25).
- Moses beholds every particle of the earth (Moses 1:27).
- Moses is transfigured and beholds the glory of God face-to-face (Moses 1:11, 31).
- Moses learns of the seven creative days and of Adam and Eve (Moses 2–4).
- Moses was translated, delivered the children of Israel, worked many miracles, received the law of God, and delivered his people to the outskirts of their promised land.

Compare now the brother of Jared's very similar experience:

- The brother of Jared spoke with the Lord in a cloud (through the veil) but did not see him (Ether 2:4).
- The brother of Jared learns of their journey to the promised

land and receives a promise that if he would believe, the Lord would show him all things (Ether 2:5–7, 3:26, 12:21).

- The brother of Jared goes through a period of trial and forgets to call upon the Lord.
- The brother of Jared has great faith in the promises he had received while initially speaking with the Lord and returns many years later to claim the fulfillment of those promises. He sees Christ's finger, and then His whole person (Ether 3:6, 13).
- The brother of Jared sees the vision of all things (Ether 3:26).
- The brother of Jared worked miracles in delivering his people to the new land. He was commanded to write the things which he had seen.

Now here is the life-altering realization: the temple teaches us this same process.

- We are given the gospel and taught that by keeping covenants we can speak with the Lord face-to-face.
- When we believe the promises and keep the covenants, we are privileged to speak with the Lord through the veil. We do not see Him.
- The Lord gives us a marvelous promise at the veil which, when understood, gives us a powerful desire to qualify and return to the veil for one great purpose: to petition the Lord for the unspeakable thing we have been promised.
- We leave the veil and go through a period of trial and testing, which may actually take many years to complete.
- We are at last reintroduced at the veil for the purpose of claiming the fulfillment of the earlier promises. Like the brother of Jared, if we have allowed this former promise to create veil-rending faith in the promise, the veil parts and we enter the presence of the Lord.
- We are then shown the vision of all. This is also a reason that the experience in holy places begins over and over with the depiction of the creation—because the actual "endowment" begins this way.

- We are given instruction and taught of our future service for the Lord.
- We enter into a new life in the presence of the Lord. This new life, if in accordance with the will and timing of the Lord, can be a life as a living mortal who is immune to death and mortal pain.

The key to parting the veil is thus: By a process of inspired inquiry and obedience to the Holy Spirit, we come to believe the promises we have already received. If you think upon the temple, especially the first event with the Lord "through" the veil, you will realize that we have been promised vast blessings. We make ourselves worthy of those blessings through obedience and faithfulness. Once we have a revealed knowledge that we are worthy and ready, with a firm faith in the promises received before, then we go back to the veil in mighty prayer and importune the Lord to allow us into His presence to ask for this gift.

This trip into the presence of the Lord isn't for the purpose of worshiping Him or because we miss Him or even because we love Him. Surely it embodies all those things; but the veil-rending faith that is required comes from our believing in and desiring the fulfillment of the promises received before. This principle of asking with complete faith for those things that we have already been promised is of such transcendent and magnificent power in parting the veil that Moroni actually says it twice.

> 19 And there were many whose faith was so exceedingly strong, even before Christ came, who could not be kept from within the veil, but truly saw with their eyes the things which they had beheld with an eye of faith, [not seen in vision, but envisioned through faith and inspired believing] and they were glad.
>
> 20 And behold, we have seen in this record that one of these was the brother of Jared; for so great was his faith in God, that when God put forth his finger he could not hide it from the sight of the brother of Jared, because of his word which he had spoken unto him [the promises at the first trip to the veil], which word he had obtained by faith [which faith is the by-product of obedience].
>
> 21 And after the brother of Jared had beheld the finger of the Lord, because of the promise which the brother of Jared had obtained

by faith [at the first interview at the veil], the Lord could not with-hold anything from his sight; wherefore he showed him all things, for he could no longer be kept without the veil. (Ether 12:19–21)

These grand eternity-altering events are foreshadowed by the temple but do not necessarily occur in the temple. We take the teachings we receive there and live them in our lives. We take the process we learn there and apply it diligently for most of a lifetime. Then in the privacy of our private chambers and personal holy places, or in the temple if directed, we petition the Lord in mighty, mighty, mighty prayer—and we receive the promises. This is speaking with the Lord through the veil—typified by the first veil experience.

After we actually understand and believe the promises we received during that first experience with Him, the Lord will guide us through further purification. Then we return in mighty prayer, and having been obedient and faithful in all things, we courageously petition the Lord with perfect faith because He, the God of salvation, promised us that we could.

And the veil opens to admit us.

Brother John

A Loving Word

Each day as I sit down to UnBlog, I wonder if I am using words that bring the message into your hearts. I also wonder if folks are seeing the overall picture that is being painted, or if they're lost in the nouns and verbs of the moment. When I speak to people in firesides or small groups, they ask questions, and I have the privilege of saying the same things in different ways—to help everyone understand. When I am UnBlogging, I don't get to see your faces clouded with confusion or glowing with understanding, and it is harder to know when to move to the next point.

So, when you have questions or observations or relevant experiences, I hope you will share them. Submit them as comments on the UnBlog. I read every comment. Even though I don't respond to them all, I do ponder every one of them.

I am happy to answer doctrinal questions if I can, but not personal ones. You should probably ask your bishop any such questions. When it comes to personal advice, that really should come from your priesthood line of authority, which I am not within.

Last, I want to again express my love to you. Each day I feel the Holy Spirit as I sit down to UnBlog. Even when my mind is blank, my heart is full. Even when my body is weak and unpleasant to inhabit, my spirit is soaring. I love that it happens every day, and that it is sweet, often powerful, and always uplifting.

The magic isn't about what I am doing at all. The Lord isn't infusing me with UnBloggable words for my own enjoyment. The power of the UnBlog is that you—you—read it with open hearts, growing faith, and towering hope. When you feel the powers of heaven coursing through your soul, the heavens rejoice—and then they pump up Brother John in spite of his flaws one more time. That's the miracle. If the time ever comes that nobody is blessed and brought to Christ by these words, then the magic will cease.

Hurrah for Israel!

Brother John

The Journey Home
Part V: On the Edge

One month of hell. That is all I can say about our visit to the paradise of Costa Rica. The only thing that saved our (especially my) sanity was the ever-present intervention from the Lord. The initial surgery went very wrong; John's cancer mass had grown unexpectedly quickly, and two days later, he was rushed into a second surgery to save his life. During the next month of intensive care and intubation, John nearly died several times, as he explains in his blogs "Gethsemane" and "Let Go and Let God." As I was not allowed to stay overnight with him in the ICU, I moved to a dilapidated old hotel downtown and commuted to the hospital by taxi.

I didn't know much Spanish, but I had my laptop with me, and I would type my concerns and questions in English, and it would come out on the screen in Spanish. I felt alone, totally isolated, and sometimes terrified at what was happening to my husband. It was especially trying when John became "loco," as the doctor put it: he had a bad reaction to the drugs they had given him and started having delusions that were totally real to him. Besides the medical issues, two men in black suits followed me around the hospital every day, hitting me up for more and more money. I didn't have a choice but to charge every credit card to the limit and borrow money from my generous brother. The final cost made the initial quote of $75,000 for a U.S. surgery pale in comparison.

But he wasn't improving. Finally after three weeks, I realized that John was not going to get better in this foreign hospital. I told the doctor that I was taking him out on April 1, and that was that! The doctor told me firmly that if I did, John would die before he got to Houston. He said that if John were not well enough to get into the airport van all by himself, he would not be allowed to leave the hospital. I prayed mightily for the Lord to help us to go home, but I was not at liberty to advise John of the doctor's ultimatum.

Finally the day for discharge came. I gave John a sitz bath that morning, and he was utterly exhausted afterward. I realized that if the staff saw him like this, he would not be allowed to go home. I silently pleaded for the Lord's mercy that a miracle would allow my husband to get on the plane. The nurses came, placed John shakily into his wheelchair, and wheeled him to the front entrance where the airport van was waiting. When it came time for John to get out of the wheelchair and into the van, everyone—even I—stepped back and did not assist him.

To the astonishment of us all, John rose smoothly from the wheelchair and almost effortlessly climbed the big step into the van. My heart was beating fast, but I tried to appear confident as I looked back at the doctor. He shrugged in disbelief and walked away. Quickly I climbed in beside John, and we sped off crazily down the streets of San Jose toward the airport and home.

John later told me that he felt two sets of hands on either side of him, lifting him up into the van and his seat. He had initially thought it was the two orderlies who had helped him, but when he looked down after climbing in, he saw everyone standing away from him, staring incredulously. This surprised him, and he didn't understand until we were on the plane, and I explained the miracle.

We were both grateful to tears. I do not believe I would have survived another week there. I know John wouldn't have.

—Terri

Chapter Six

Trials, Tests, and Tribulation

The Fist of God

In 1977 I was working on a large wheat ranch in Idaho that my father had recently purchased. I needed a break from college and decided to help on this farm and then return to BYU. We had worked very hard to make this farm work. It consisted of 720 acres of sprinkler-irrigated land. We had installed new irrigation equipment, drilled new wells, replaced and rebuilt most of the original farm equipment, and worked like slaves day and night.

Normally you move the sprinklers every twelve hours. We decided to put a larger nozzle into the sprinklers and move the water every eight hours. This put the same amount of water on the field but let us cover more acreage. It took about three hours to move the pipes each time. We moved them at 6:00 a.m., 2:00 p.m., 10:00 p.m., and then started over, sleeping between sets.

I promise there is a spiritual message coming. . . .

The effect of this was that we couldn't attend all our church meetings. We were too busy moving water and trying to catch up on sleep. When we realized this, we fasted and prayed, and my father decided to turn off the sprinklers on Sunday. His reasoning was that if we did the Lord's work and kept His Sabbath holy, then He would work whatever miracle it took to make the crops grow.

This is a huge mistake normally. You can lose a million dollar's worth of crops by turning off the sprinklers just one day. Still, that Sunday morning we shut off the water and went to church. Our neighbors urgently whispered to us that they had noticed that our water was off when they drove to church. When we told them why, they just shook their heads and walked away.

During this time, the ward was building a new chapel. We had small pieces of time between water sets, and we spent most of them working on the church. We paid a full tithe, fasted often, served and served, and held prayers together at the beginning of each work day and before leaving to go home. We were on the most spiritual high I had ever experienced in the "real world" up to then.

The crops prospered. They were lush and full. People stopped, got out of their cars, and took pictures of our fields, because nobody had ever seen such an amazing stand of wheat in that area. Our neighbors incredulously asked us how we had done it.

It had been early fall when we shut off the water. Now the fields were golden, within a few days of being ready to harvest. We estimated we had seventy-five bushels of wheat to the acre. The average for that area was fifteen to twenty. We rejoiced and praised God all day long. It was such a wonderful feeling to know that we had been obedient and that the Lord had rewarded that obedience with such an abundant crop, in spite of the apparent stupidity of turning off the water on Sunday.

I was sitting in the cab of a large John Deere combine. I had just repaired and greased it up. It was running, with the front beater bar spinning in front of me. It sounded perfect. I was happy as I looked up, and being about twelve feet in the air, I could see across the valley. At the northwest end, there appeared a small black cloud. I watched it as it came our way. I turned off the noisy machine and shouted for my Dad and brother to look.

We stood there and watched as this black cloud approached. It was about a mile across; the rest of the valley was sunny. This little cloud hit the end of our first fields and began to hail. The stones were about one-half inch in size. Our farm was "L" shaped. The cloud went east across our fields, turned abruptly left, and traveled up the other leg of the farm. Just beyond our fields, the cloud broke up and dissipated. No other farmer's fields were affected.

It was the fist of God. In shock, we staggered out into the fields, and every head of wheat was empty. The ground was a golden carpet of ruined grain. There was no way to pick it up off the ground fast enough before it would decay. We were devastated—financially, emotionally, and spiritually. We could not fathom why God would allow such a thing to happen.

I went home. There was nothing else to do. We were bankrupt. I went to bed and prayed and prayed, and I admit, I moaned and complained. It didn't seem fair. It actually wasn't fair.

During the night, I had a vivid dream. It was so real that I could feel the breeze on my face, smell the smells, and hear the world I was viewing. It was as Paul said, "Whether in the body, or out of the body, I cannot tell." It was that real.

I was looking at a large farm. The fields were lush and perfect. The roads were lined with flowering bushes and ornamental trees. It was like a farm planted in the middle of a Disneyland park. I saw a large yellow machine in the distance and walked toward it. They were harvesting the wheat, and the hopper was rapidly filling with a golden stream of grain. The driver was hardly paying attention to the machine; he was singing and dancing on his platform. There was no dust and very little noise. On the ground, there were a half-dozen women and as many men dressed in white. They were laughing and dancing right in front of the machine. Some of them were mere inches from the big threshing wheel.

I began to fear for their lives when I suddenly understood. The machine could not hurt them. It was against the laws of "nature" as they existed in this world. The machine never broke down or needed repairs. It just worked flawlessly.

I began learning things—more like remembering them, as if I had always known this place. Their world existed without opposition. The rains came exactly on time. There were no weeds, no insects, and everything they tried to do was successful. These people had grouped together to own and operate this farm. They were very wealthy because of the abundance of their harvests. They were dancing to praise God and to rejoice in their continual good fortune.

I realized that the beautiful park-like plants and flowers grew there spontaneously, just because the people enjoyed them. In my mind's eye, I saw them moving a house-sized boulder so they could farm there. One man put his hand on the rock, and it slid across the ground with a great noise. He expended no more effort than pushing a child on a toy trike. By divine decree, the stone could not resist him.

I became aware of every other aspect of their world. They could do anything—or nothing. They could not get hungry or cold or become sick. If they wanted to sit by a pool and sip syrupy drinks, they could do that forever. If they wanted to build an empire of factories and become obscenely wealthy, they could do that too, and they would succeed—by divine decree, they would succeed. Nothing would oppose them. There were no taxes and no laws except one: they could not harm, injure, cheat, or hurt anyone or anything.

I was thinking this was the celestial kingdom and was beginning to ache to be there. A voice interrupted my thoughts and said, "No, this is the telestial kingdom."

I was flabbergasted, but more information flooded into my mind. These people had lost their ability to sin, to hurt, to injure, or to even disobey the law. They were free to do anything else, but they couldn't disobey. I mean, it was impossible. If they attempted, they would find it impossible, just like the big machine couldn't injure the girls dancing right in front of it. They had lost this part of their agency.

I then realized that these people weren't living as couples. They didn't marry. They had friends and lived with them as they chose, but they were not able to be sexual, and these associations of friends were both large and small, but they were not intimate.

They could not participate in governing because there was no government. Their leaders weren't even from this world, and their decisions were not subject to disobedience. It was simply impossible. They could not vote. They had vast choices in what they could do, but zero agency to disobey the law. There was no punishment, because there was no ability to disobey. I realized then that this was similar to what Satan had promised to do just before the war in heaven.

I noted that there were no children, anywhere. There was no priesthood, no authority, and nothing that resembled faith, because they could plainly see the miracles of God every day of their lives.

At this point I was thinking that if this were the telestial kingdom, it wasn't too bad at all; as a matter of fact, it sounded quite wonderful, especially after the catastrophic loss of our farm just hours before. I remember thinking this would be an acceptable outcome for my life—but then something inside me rebelled. "No! I want to make it to the celestial kingdom."

Then the same voice returned to my mind. "In order to enter the celestial kingdom, you must be willing to submit to My will, and to endure whatever experiences you need in order to qualify for that kingdom." I suddenly realized that the loss of our farm was one of those experiences. It wasn't random, and it wasn't a punishment. I couldn't imagine why, but God knew we needed that experience, as unjust and unfair as it seemed at the time; if I wanted the greater reward from life, I needed to stop complaining and murmuring and just submit. Somehow this harsh pathway was the right one, and it led to the celestial kingdom, not just to a nice farm where it never hails or snows.

Shortly after those events, we lost the farm. I helped my father and mother pack up and move off the farm. They had to sell everything they owned but a few personal possessions.

In a few months, my parents decided to move to Alaska. I had relocated my family to Rexburg and was working to earn tuition to return to college. My wife and I had almost nothing; it was three years lost. One morning, I awoke and "knew" we had to go with Mom and Dad to Alaska. I hated the idea. I had other plans. My wife had had a dream that night as well, and she also "knew" we had to go. We both cried as we packed our few belongings and turned north.

Alaska has been a fertile field for me. You have read my blogs about my father being the first Wasilla bishop. He rose to every occasion, activated and baptized hundreds of people, and sealed his own eternal joy.

As for me, moving to Alaska gave me a chance to write, publish a few worthwhile things, raise a family, make too much money, and cleanse my soul. It also was the only path that could have filled my soul with the fire-hardened faith that now illuminates my way and has gifted me with such sweet and eternal assurances. I "know" it was where I needed to be. It was harsh, and it was far more challenging than I could have ever imagined, but I thrived.

I marvel that it all began sitting in a threshing machine, watching the fist of God change the direction of my life.

Praise the Lord.

Brother John

In the Arms of Christ's Love

They say that there are two things that are inescapable: death and taxes. There is one additional inescapable in life: spiritual ups and downs.

When I was a boy scout, which was shortly after Noah's flood, we went on a camping trip in the Uinta Mountains. After setting up camp, we decided to climb a nearby mountain. The mountain was composed of loose pieces of shale ranging in size from popcorn to pianos. Every step we took, we slid back almost the same amount. Being young and full of energy, we took to running up the mountain. It was steep, and the stones remained flat as they slid beneath our feet, so we started an avalanche of sorts as we ran up the mountain. We found that the bigger rocks—the piano-sized rocks—did not slide, and if we could get to them, we could rest until the mountain quit sliding past us, and we could begin again.

When we finally arrived at the top, we had climbed the equivalent of ten mountains. We sat, exhausted, for a long time at the top, looking out across other mountains far taller than the one we had just climbed.

In my life's experience, everything has been like this mountain, where I take three steps forward, and then slide back two—sometimes more. Every gain has been opposed. Every spiritual gift has been challenged, and every truth I have learned has met its equal and opposite lie.

I consider that this constant opposition, and the grace of Christ to find those rocks that do not slide, are responsible for every spiritual muscle I have. I have learned my greatest lessons when struggling mightily to climb out of the darkest moments of life.

I have never met a person who is not involved in this struggle, even those who seem to have everything going their way. If you really get them to tell it like it is, you will find that they struggle just the same as you, sometimes even more. This is true of everyone—General Authorities, bishops, our heroes, and our children.

The point I would like to make is that we can certainly knock ourselves into a spiritual power dive by disobeying a commandment or the voice of the Lord, but most of our dramatic struggles upward are not a result of disobedience—they are the result of the loose rocks on the mountain God has given us to climb. We should cease to chastise and punish ourselves because we are struggling. We should cease to berate ourselves because we have not yet conquered every obstacle. We should cease to shame ourselves because we seem to lack the strength to climb out of the current hole we find ourselves in.

What we should perhaps do instead is to stop struggling for a moment and listen to the voice of the Holy Spirit, because God knows where those few stones are that will not slide: the stone of faith in Christ, the stone of personal revelation, the stone of eternal truth. These we can stand upon with sure footing until the mountainside stops moving once again.

I believe Mormons and Catholics have something unusual in common—guilt. I've heard that Catholics are good at feeling guilty. Mormons certainly are. We think we should be doing everything—all the time—by our own genius and strength. And when the mountainside moves beneath us, we feel guilty, unworthy, and weak.

Instead of guilt, let us feel gratitude—gratitude for this earthly experience of tumbling rocks, for the humility it generates, and for the power it is building within us. More than anything else, let us be grateful for the fact—the rock-solid fact—that when we obey Christ's voice, He lovingly empowers us to climb to the next safe rock with legs that are no longer weary. This is when the fatigue dissipates, and the journey no longer feels too long and hard.

This is how we arrive at the top, renewed and reborn.

When was the last time you were carried safely in the arms of Christ's love? What say you?

Brother John

The Right Thing to Do

When I was about twelve years old, my father was a practicing veterinarian. He had a busy practice in Roy, Utah. During the summers, I often spent the day there to help feed the animals or hold dogs for their shots or watch surgery. It was fun. I got to wear a white lab coat, and I felt very important. My dad encouraged my feelings of being needed.

One day, a middle-aged woman brought in a dog near closing time for shots or something minor like that. Her husband dropped her off and drove away. She paid for the service and waited for her husband. At 5:00, our closing time, he was still not there, and she became agitated. At 5:30 she was upset, and by 5:45 she was furious. My dad declined to close and leave her standing on the road, so we waited as she became more and more angry. She began rehearsing all of the nasty things she was going to tell "that man" when he finally picked her up. Finally, my dad asked if he could offer her some advice. She nodded, probably feeling like she owed him something for having to wait on her.

He said, "When your husband returns, thank him for picking you up and for his willingness to go out of his way for you. Say nothing about being angry or about him making you late or inconvenienced or embarrassed. Just thank him and be kind."

She nearly choked on her tongue. She refused, saying how he was going to get the dressing-down of his life! Then she asked, "Why should I?"

Dad said, "Because it's the right thing to do. Whenever we respond with love and patience and kindness, it is the right thing to do, and doing the right thing always brings happiness and peace. If you want to turn this unpleasant experience into a good experience, be kind when he returns."

I listened to this with more interest in when we would finally get to go home than in his advice to her. Finally, the husband arrived, the lady got into the car with her dog, and they left.

Several days later, this same lady returned with a little thank-you card for my dad. She came right at closing, just like before. She waited until she was the only person in the waiting room and then asked for my father. When she spoke to him, her voice was choked with emotion. "How did you know?" she demanded. "How did you know?"

My dad was perplexed and asked her to explain. She said there were problems in their marriage, and she was considering asking him for a divorce. When he left her hanging at the vet office, she had decided to demand a divorce that evening. After listening to my dad's advice, when she got into the car, she held her anger and eventually thanked her husband for driving her to and from the vet office. When they arrived home, she found the house filled with flowers, and there was a special dinner fixed. The kids had been sent to friends' homes for this special evening. She had entirely forgotten that this night was their wedding anniversary. Her husband's thoughtfulness and loving gesture touched her. Her kindness to him on the way home made the night magical.

She asked again, "How did you know? Are you a prophet or something?"

He replied, "I didn't know anything about your life, of course. All I know is that when you do the right thing, no matter how hard it might be, your life is always better. Doing the wrong or harsh or angry thing always destroys."

She shed a few more tears and then said, "I think you just saved our marriage."

My dad smiled and replied, "No, you just saved your own marriage."

The principle is true and undeviating. Our lives are always most blessed when we simply "choose the right."

It was a lesson I will never forget.

Brother John

Deliver Us from Evil

I am grateful for your comments and for your personal stories of faith and challenges. Sometimes the Lord gives me words of support and love that flow in a moment, and other times I ponder what to UnBlog. It always humbles and amazes me when these words help you, and I am so grateful.

I used to consider spirituality to be the ability to feel, hear, and occasionally see the unseen things of the Holy Spirit. Over the years, I have observed that spirituality is a sensitivity to *everything* spiritual—some of which comes of darkness.

You often send in comments about your struggles with great trials, evil things, great temptations, evil thoughts, and even occasionally with seeing bad spirits. My message for you is to relax—this is a normal process. I believe Heavenly Father lets us experience these things so that we know how intense the battle is. By these things we learn to be aware, to be cautious and vigilant, to depend upon the Savior completely. It is also important to recognize the flavor of these dark things, so that when they come more covertly, with intent to confuse and beguile, we reject them just as quickly as if they were screaming vile things in our faces.

When you experience these unwanted things, consider the following:

Don't give up. We must pass through these trials with valiant actions, not just inhibit them by refusing to grow further because we are afraid of more trials.

Don't give in. By recognizing that these things originate from outside our souls and are contrary to our desires, we can endure. They may bog you down and temporarily frighten you, but they can't harm you. Don't entertain them. Don't indulge in dark fantasy. Endure as Christ endured. Trust in Him as never before.

Get a priesthood blessing. Ask someone who understands the process of righteousness to give you a priesthood blessing to strengthen you and cast out any messengers of darkness.

Pray mightily. Explain what is happening to Heavenly Father in prayer, and sincerely beg for His relief. This may sound like odd advice, but in times of need, I have found that sincerely asking over and over has merit. I'm not proposing vain repetition, but I am proposing heartfelt, reverent, and respectful repetition—lots of it.

Ask for clarity. When it is over, ask Heavenly Father for the reason you were allowed to experience, see, and feel these things. These things don't happen randomly. There is always a reason. Heavenly Father may not reveal it in words, but eventually you will view these events as blessings that He allowed to occur to enlighten and empower you.

Don't ask for trials. I've heard some people say things like, "I think I'm ready for my Abrahamic test." My answer is—no you're not. You can't be ready, or get ready. No mortal ever gets that strong. What prepares us is increasing our dependence on Christ and recognizing our own nothingness. Don't think things like, "I'm strong enough to handle anything Satan can dish out." My answer is—you obviously have never been in the boxing ring with darkness, for you would realize by the end of the first bell that no mortal is "ready." The only reason we survive our encounters with darkness is because Christ governs with great tenderness what "they" can do and when. If you invite a battle because of a childish view of your own strength, Christ may step aside and let you have your moment in the ring. You will find yourself beaten unmercifully until all you can do is cry out for deliverance. Christ *will* deliver you, but you will not escape without deep scars. Experiencing all alone your own helplessness and utter reliance upon Christ is not a lesson you purposefully want to unleash upon your own head.

<u>Don't invite evil</u>. Don't do things that invite evil into your circle of protection. Don't view, read, listen to, entertain yourself with, or toy with anything inspired of evil. Don't watch movies that trivialize satanic things, acts of evil, or cruelty. Above all, reject pornography in all its forms. Banish immorality with great prejudice. These things push us outside of Christ's force field of protection.

<u>Don't be afraid</u>. Trust that Christ places limits on what can afflict us. Trust Him. Rely upon Him. Pray for His protection. "Deliver us from evil," Christ Himself prayed.

When bad things happen—because they will happen—just trust that they will also end, and you will be delivered and again be filled with light.

"Be faithful, be fearless, be patient."

Brother John

Gethsemane

I hope you will forgive me for this next UnBlog. It involves a very painful experience, yet it taught me something of supreme value. If you will allow me, I would like to share with you how I began to understand just a little of what happened in Gethsemane.

In 2009, I learned that I needed surgery. It was expensive, and I didn't have medical insurance at the time. We contacted local hospitals and were quoted $100,000 dollars as a starting point, with no ceiling at all. We searched and prayed and found something unknown to us at the time called "medical tourism." This involves traveling to a foreign country where surgery and medical treatment are far less expensive. The hospitals are all Joint Commission-certified, as are the doctors, many of whom are trained in the United States. The medical treatment is supposedly on par with that in the United States.

We selected Costa Rica because it wasn't far away, found an experienced surgeon, checked everything we could think of, prayed and felt good about it, and booked the trip. The surgery was going to cost $13,000 total, including airfare for two. We were relieved and felt very blessed.

When we arrived, we found that the hospital was state-of-the-art. The equipment was all made in the United States. The doctors and nurses were kind and knowledgeable, although there were very few of them who spoke English well. Still, we felt good about our decision, and I was admitted.

The first surgery went wrong. Although I had been told by doctors in Alaska that my surgery was routine and should be an easy one, an error in the surgery caused my sutures to fail and spill fecal matter into my body. I was all sewn up and in recovery for twenty-four hours before they figured this out. By that time, I was in critical condition. I was rushed back into emergency surgery, where they reopened the wound to clean it out and to flood the area with antibiotics. They put me into a medically induced coma and continued to irrigate the unclosed wound for several days. However, I was allergic to the medicine they used; I broke out into boils, and my heart began to fail. My internal organs were shutting down rapidly. They told Terri that I would probably die. When the antibiotic was changed, however, I started to improve. Finally, my fever began to drop, and they sutured me closed, although I remained in a coma for several more days.

When I finally awoke, I couldn't believe a body could be in that much pain and that sick and still be alive. For some reason, this hospital did not believe in pain medication. They gave me just a little to take the edge off, but I was in agony. I was astonished at the mess I was in. My wife was exhausted and overwhelmed, in a foreign country, with skyrocketing medical costs. It was a terrible time for us.

Soon after I awoke, I began hallucinating. I'm sure this was because of all of the drugs and the challenges to my body. I saw things. At first they were just silly things and then they became scary things. I saw people getting hurt. In my hallucinations, I witnessed innocent folks get killed for almost no reason. Cute little nurses were murdered because they didn't show enough obedience. I saw guns and fighting and torture and awful, awful things. They did horrendous things to me for reasons they never did explain. These delusions were never truly real, but they were very real to me. To this day, I could pass a lie detector test, because they literally happened to me. I saw them—I felt them.

Another time, I saw Terri try to get me out of the hospital, and they killed her three times in heinous ways. Of course, you can't kill someone three times, but I wasn't able to figure that out. Family members came to try to save me, and they were tortured and killed. I will forbear and spare you the X-rated details. But it is important to repeat that this was absolutely real to me. I lived it, over and over and over again.

As I finally began to come out of the delusions, I was completely traumatized—emotionally, physically, and spiritually. When I first saw Terri, I was convinced that she was really a spirit, because she was dead and I knew it. What was most interesting to me is that even though my delusions lasted only a day at most, to me they seemed to go on for weeks. It took Terri two days to convince me that she was truly alive, and that she was going to get me out of there in one piece. It was a miracle that I did get out of there—but that is another story in itself.

After we arrived back in Alaska and I began to get my health back, I thought again and again about that experience. I hope you will forgive me for saying that I don't believe I have done anything in my life to deserve a trip to hell. I couldn't imagine why the Holy Spirit would desert me and why the gates of hell would be opened so wide beneath me. If it had merely been a bad medical experience, I would have just felt lucky to be alive, but this was extended torture and torment of the type that I could not countenance as a punishment for even the most vile of the vile.

One evening, I was praying earnestly about this, and the Spirit swept over me and gave me this impression: When Christ was suffering in Gethsemane, He did not just look at or watch the pains and torment of mankind. He experienced them. He was there. He felt the searing pains of all our sins in His own flesh. He felt the anguish, the fear, the terror. He truly did descend below all things, and the reason He comprehended them all was because He was there. In the same way that my few hours had seemed to extend into weeks, His few hours had extended into an eternity of suffering on our behalf.

When I realized this, I was stunned and horrified. It changed my reverence, my worship, my eternal gratitude for what Christ did for me in Gethsemane. When I now read that by His stripes we are healed, I shudder, and my flesh grows cold. It was a far greater price than any of us could imagine. And when the day comes that we stand to be judged, and we do comprehend—when we finally know what it *truly* cost Him so that we might not suffer—then every knee will bow, and all of creation will worship in stunned silence and acknowledge that He *is* the Christ.

Brother John

Then Begins the Fire

Dear UnBlog Family,

Thank you so much for all of your warm wishes. What a privilege it is to feel your love and kindness—and to have a little more time to do so.

All of my life, I have been praying to understand God's will in my life. I'm still not very good at understanding it. I keep getting hit by freight trains I should have seen coming and then realizing, after the fact, that the freight train was the only way God could fully answer my prayer.

I used to pray most earnestly that if there was some way for me to learn the lessons Father wanted me to learn without pain, bloodshed, and suffering, to please, please send me down that path first! I would beg Him to give me a chance to humble myself and learn, rather than being driven into the ground head-first in order to be taught. Nevertheless, I always promised that if I just don't "get it," I would submit to anything the Lord saw fit to use to teach me. (That was the "fine print" I kept trying to insert into my mortal contract with Him.)

These days I think back on my life, and I can see that many things I did learn the easy way—but everything of grand eternal value I learned by freight trains crashing into me. I look at every spiritual refinement I may possess now, and it all came as a result of walking the fiery path, not flying over it.

I no longer look for the easy way. I know my Savior well enough to know that if there is an easy way to learn, He will kindly bless me with it first. And He knows me perfectly, so He understands that now I want the refining process to have its full and eternal effect upon me, more than I want to avoid pain in its many forms.

I used to think that the easy blessings, the "Oh, here let me just bless you with that attribute" gifts were the open doors—and they are, and they continue to be. Becoming perfect can only be obtained by grace and by being changed by Christ to become like Him. But I am learning that many of the things we suffer are also open doors to the great, greater, and greatest blessings to which we may aspire. These are the painful things that truly refine us into godly gold, which Christ lovingly allows us to suffer, all the while holding us tightly as we feel the heat.

This life is a test—but at some point we pass the preliminary exams, and then begins the fire.

Brother John

Let Go and Let God

In March of 2009, I was in Costa Rica struggling to stay alive. I related some of those experiences previously in "Gethsemane." Something I did not relate yet was that because of the trauma and stress of those events, I had real difficulty breathing. When the doctors checked, they said a lung had collapsed, and I literally had less than an hour to live. They wanted to intubate me immediately, drain the fluid from my chest, and see if they could reinflate my lung.

When I awoke after that procedure, I had a tube down my throat. I was at first surprised because I was under the impression that I would be asleep for the duration. Then I immediately realized that I wasn't getting enough air. It felt like I was suffocating. In fact, I actually was suffocating. The machine seemed as if it were set for an infant. It would giving me a little puff of air, pause a long time, exhale a little puff, pause again, and then start over. It was excruciating. At first, I tried to breathe past the machine but found this was impossible.

Terri came into the ICU room at that moment. From the look on my face, she discerned that something was wrong. I tried to write on a tablet, but my hands were both partly paralyzed from the previous anesthesia and lack of oxygen. She started asking me questions, and I was nodding and shaking my head, although I could not talk because of the tube. She could understand that I was terribly distressed but couldn't tell exactly why.

She confronted a nurse who didn't speak English but went to get a doctor. The doctor assured Terri that everything was perfect, and that it was normal for patients to fight intubation at first. He told her I just needed to relax and let the machine do its job.

Terri came back to me and said, "I tried to tell them that something is wrong. They said everything is fine, and so I don't know what to do. They say you will get used to being intubated."

I shook my head, more panicked than ever. Terri stroked my cheek and tried to soothe me. "I don't know what is wrong. I'm sorry, John! Whatever it is, you're going to have to turn this over to Jesus Christ and trust Him. If you can, this too will pass."

I knew she didn't understand, but I knew she was right. I pondered how I could turn the life-and-death burden of being suffocated over to my Savior. I was zapped on drugs, and my mind was operating slowly. I prayed and prayed and tried to understand how He was going to make me have more air. Finally, I realized that if I turned this awful struggle to breathe over to Jesus Christ, it meant that I was no longer in control, that I no longer needed control, and whatever the outcome of this struggle, it would be His plan, and everything would be perfect—even if I died of suffocation in the next few minutes.

Looking back, I believe it was the hardest decision of my life. If I turned being suffocated over to Jesus Christ, then I wasn't going to complain to the doctors or Terri about my struggle. I wasn't going to feel or look like I was in trouble. I wasn't going to try to make them understand, or appear to be in a struggle for survival. I was going to give up the fear and desire for control and trust my Savior to save me—or let me die—even according to His will. In prayer, and with great relief, I laid this struggle at the foot of the cross and walked away. I was free. It didn't change how much air I had, only that I was now trusting Him to take care of me.

The thought immediately came into my mind that I was under water, and this little tube (about the size of a pencil) was my only source of air. I felt grateful for each little puff. I began to pray and express gratitude for this little bit of air, and I relaxed. I learned to wait for the air and to be grateful when it came. The excruciating feeling of suffocation never abated, but I was no longer afraid.

I remained awake on that tube for five awful days. On the fifth day, a different doctor came into the room. Terri told him that she felt sure I wasn't getting enough air. He assured her that everything was fine. Terri objected strenuously, with tears. He walked over to the machine breathing for me and looked closely at the controls. Then, and after a moment, I heard a click.

"I'm so sorry, but someone set the machine wrong. John really *wasn't* getting enough air!" He turned to me. "Try taking a deep breath." Incredibly, for the first time in five days, I was able to draw as much air as I wanted into my lungs by sucking very hard on that little tube. It was hard work, but it was such a relief that I began to weep. I was profoundly grateful—not only for the air, but for Jesus Christ, who had been with me, comforting me, and giving me peace so that I could survive.

From that moment on, I didn't have to imagine myself under water, and I was grateful for that. I could get as much air as I needed, and I was so grateful for that. Later that same day, they removed the tube, and after some choking and gagging, I was grateful for that too.

I could talk to Terri again! She constantly showered me with love and assurances, and for that I was grateful. More than anything, I was grateful to my Savior for picking up my burden when I laid it at His feet. He really did deliver me. The doctors told Terri that it was amazing I didn't have brain damage from suffocation. They said the fact that I was able to relax and not struggle made what air I did get enough.

Over the course of my life, I have consecrated my "all" in different ways many times. But this was my first experience with giving away something I desperately needed to live. When I finally did, I was willing to accept any outcome because it wasn't my battle any more. For me this was a spiritual trial, and it changed my life.

This experience wasn't about breathing. It was about trusting— about being willing to consecrate my last and most precious possession—and then to let go, and let God.

Brother John

Evil Intent and Great Malice

*T*oday as I was sitting in the infusion center being basted in chemo, it occurred to me that we haven't yet discussed one of the worst inspired-by-evil things in our world: anti-Mormon literature. There is so much malicious intent from this evil source that it almost glows darkness. I was handed a lot of anti-literature while on my mission, and it always disturbed me. I mean, just touching it disturbed me. I read a little bit of it, and even while my mind was logically rejecting the arguments, my soul was struggling to hang onto faith. I don't know of very many people who have seriously read such literature whose testimony or even faith in God survived.

On my mission, the first family I tracted out, taught, and baptized was the Knott family. The day after they were baptized, we met to teach them the new member lessons. They listened with much interest. They had lots of questions and happily received our answers.

As I was telling them about the importance of faithful attendance at sacrament meeting, I had a fully developed idea enter my mind. I instantly knew it was a true principle. (This is one of the ways I recognize pure revelation: it comes in a sudden, fully developed thought from outside of my mind. It is simply there in its entirety and accompanied by the warmth of the Spirit.)

I said, "Three things are going to happen to you to try to make you lose your faith and testimony. The first is that someone inside the Church will accidentally offend you."

"But why?" they demanded. "Why would they do that to us?"

"They won't do it on purpose. It is just the way Satan always tries to get new members to stop attending church. They feel offended by something someone says. But the truth is, it isn't that person, it is Satan using his time-tested plan to get you to lose your testimony. Just watch for it, and when it happens, come talk to us and we'll help straighten it right out."

They nodded and took a deep breath.

"The next thing will be that it will become inconvenient to come to church. Many things will happen to keep you from coming."

"But why?" they wanted to know.

"It is because this is Satan's method. I've seen it in every investigator we have taught or baptized. Apparently, when Satan has a working plan, he just keeps using it. I am certain this will happen to you too."

"What will we do?" they wondered.

"Come to church no matter what. You will know that you're actually fighting back against Satan, not against the circumstances of your life."

Alfred smiled. "We intend to win this fight," he said.

"You will. Lots of people do win. But the fight is real, and only about one-half of new members make it into full activity."

"That's frightening! What will happen next, do you think?"

"The next thing will probably be that you will be given anti-Mormon literature."

They looked sheepish. Alfred stood and returned with several pamphlets. "We're already getting them. We read some of them before we were baptized but haven't felt good about reading them now that we're members. What should we do?"

"Well, there are two things you can do. You can read them with us and we can help you discern the truth from the lies, or you can just discard them and let your faith win."

They looked at each other. "We'd appreciate it if you'd take them away."

"I will if you prefer, but I don't like to even touch them. They seem to glow with evil."

Eleanor spoke up. "That's what I said, Alfie!"

Alfred stood and stepped into the kitchen, and we heard a garbage can lid slam shut. "That's where they're going from now on," he said happily as he returned.

The very next Sunday, Eleanor hurried over to me after church and said, "It happened! Someone hurt my feelings really bad in Relief Society." She seemed almost triumphant, even though her eyes were red.

"What happened?" I asked.

"It was in the Relief Society lesson. The teacher was talking about me and my weaknesses, and it embarrassed me to death."

"What did you do?" I asked.

"Well, I remembered what you had said, and so I went up and asked her if she was talking about me. The teacher was shocked, and she began to cry and apologized to me over and over. I cried with her, and we're sisters now. I know she loves me and would never intentionally hurt my feelings. But, if you hadn't warned me, I would have never come back to church!"

These three simple obstacles each occurred (and sometimes repeatedly) to both Alfred and Eleanor in the next few months. But, having been warned and having taken heed to the warning, they triumphed.

The last I heard from them was many years ago, but they were—and I believe they still are—faithfully moving forward with their spiritual lives.

The actual point of this story is that the evil ones are organized. They have well-designed programs and plans that they use and reuse. This simple process of getting newly baptized Latter-day Saints to falter has worked for hundreds of years now. They just use it over and over. Knowing this gives us the powerful ability to plan and to have inspired defenses.

It would be interesting (although probably spiritually destructive) to study the dark ways, to see the trends and the steps that are used over and over. I believe we would find that there are evil, cleverly modern "programs" for severing us from personal revelation and for breaking up temple marriages, destroying families, turning teenagers against parents, drug and alcohol abuse, pornography, cheating, lying, depression, infidelity, sexual impurity, homosexuality, and every other challenge to our spiritual journey.

They are planning our demise with evil intent and great malice, and we're watching television.

Brother John

An Eye Single

A few years ago I was asked to speak at a Single Adults fireside in my stake. I arrived with an outline and scriptures, prepared to address the topic their leaders had selected. As I stood and looked out into their faces, I felt a wave of anxious need and deep frustration coming from each one of them. I knew that I needed to talk about something other than what I had prepared.

I stood there for a long moment pondering what the Spirit was bringing into my soul and then asked them, "What is the most important goal that you have right here, right now?"

They all replied that they deeply desired to find a worthy eternal companion.

My heart went out to them. I said, "Frustration and anxiety come when we focus upon the wrong goal. When our lives are properly aligned with God's plan for us, we feel peace and safety. Temple marriage should not be your primary goal in life."

There was an audible gasp. I opened the scriptures and taught them that the greatest goal we should have is to make our eye single to the glory of God. I said that when we make our eye single to *anything* else, even something as worthy as eternal marriage or raising a righteous family, we have focused upon the wrong thing.

A sister near the front raised her hand. "A few months ago, my husband did inappropriate things with my kids, and he is now in prison. I had no idea it was going on; there were no signs I could detect until one of my children finally told me. My husband lied in court and said he was sure I knew what was going on, so the court decided I had failed to protect my children. They took my children away from me! I can't even visit them, and I haven't seen them for months!" Tears were streaming down her cheeks. "Shouldn't my primary goal be to get my children back?"

It was a hard story to hear, and I spoke kindly. "This surely seems like an impossible trial, something that is beyond your understanding and your ability to figure out." She nodded through tears. "But if you turn to Jesus Christ and make your eye single to Him, you will find that He loves your kids far more than you do. And *He* knows how to get them back."

She looked stunned, but her eyes showed less pain. I continued. "If you focus on your own needs and your own fears, you will not be attuned to the solutions Christ is trying to communicate to you. If you turn to Him, take the Holy Spirit to be your guide, and learn to hear His voice, you will begin to know what to do, step-by-step. You probably won't be given every answer all at once, but whatever is best for you and your children will sweetly take place. I promise you that the blessing you need will be manifested when you give your life to Christ and take His voice as your guide."

About this point, another sister stood and loudly insisted that eternal marriage *had* to be her greatest goal, and that nothing mattered more. Then she left the room, and everyone seemed relieved. The Spirit returned in greater abundance.

I told them that the liberating truth is this: When someone is married in the temple, that person's greatest accomplishment in this life is to learn obedience to Christ. When someone is single, that person's greatest accomplishment in this life is to learn obedience to Christ. When someone is rich or poor, young or old, beautiful or plain, dumb or dumber, that person's greatest accomplishment is always to learn obedience to Christ. I explained that a single person (or an unhappily married person) can just as easily become born again, sanctified, and filled with joy and light as a happily married person can. This gift comes to everyone who genuinely takes Christ's voice as the unfailing guide—no matter what their marital state may be.

A sweet peace had settled upon the room. I told them that feelings of neediness, pain, and frustration didn't have to remain in their lives if they would replace their missing puzzle pieces with devotion and obedience to Christ and to the words of revelation He is whispering to them every hour of every day. If they would do that, I explained, they would be led step-by-step to accomplishing everything that they had covenanted to do before they were born.

I challenged them, "Lay your desire to be married upon the altar, and walk away. Sacrifice your will, your needs, and your fondest dreams to the will of Christ."

A glimmer of hope came into the eyes of everyone there, for the Spirit was testifying to all of us that this was truth. I gratefully continued, "Here's what will happen. As a disciple of Christ, you will become a creature of light and joy. Happiness and peace will radiate from you. You will be empowered and guided through your trials. You will be healed of your aching. You will realize that you don't need a husband or a wife in this life to be whole and happy. You will feel content with your life in Christ and at peace about your eternity.

"When you arrive at the point where you no longer need or ache for marriage, but remain submissively open to it, the Lord will send someone to you who will be attracted to your inner beauty, your peace, and spiritual wholeness. This can happen either in this life or in the next—but you will be at peace, because you'll know that it *will* happen. Together you will be an equally yoked couple, for you will both possess similar characteristics that attracted you to each other.

"And the very thing you placed upon the altar will be returned to you a hundred fold."

Brother John

The Journey Home
Part VI: Six Months to Live

After we returned home to Alaska in April of 2009, John was basically an invalid. He spent the rest of the year recuperating from the trauma of Costa Rica but was blessed to continue his Alyeska work at home to support his family while taking on additional responsibilities in the stake.

By January of 2010, he had recovered a bit, and although yet very weak, he went to the oncologist to assess what had happened during the nine months of recuperation since his operation. The news was not good. The cancer had returned in force, and the doctor gave him six months to live. We were told that if John started chemo immediately, his life may be prolonged for an indeterminate amount of time, but that was our only choice if we wanted more than six months.

We were shocked by the news, and yet a continual sweet peace surrounded us. A great part of that peace came because a few months previously, John had decided that he needed to start a blog for his children and close friends to record his testimony of Christ and his life's experiences. Because he has a way of expressing the gospel of Jesus Christ in such a transparent and understandable way, and I suppose because he was a known LDS author, John's blog soon began to be read and appreciated by many others not in our family. In a flash of inspiration, it became clear to John that the Lord wanted him to expand his blog, and soon "UnBlog My Soul" was born. This work brought tremendous joy to him even as he was enduring the chemo, not only because he could freely share his testimony of Christ and the restored gospel, but also because he delighted in the powerful testimonies of those in what he called the "UnBlog Family."

Following a difficult three-month regimen of chemo, the doors literally flew open for us to move to Utah. We laughingly acknowledged that the Lord was kicking us out of Alaska! It was somewhat bittersweet because we still had family and precious grandchildren there, but we also could not deny that the Lord was finally granting John's dream of over twenty years—although we didn't know the full ramifications of what was in store for us. Eventually we came to realize it was necessary for John to be in Utah to associate with the rest of our family, to continue his blog, to meet the people he needed to meet, to give numerous firesides, to receive the support and affirmation of many new friends, and to write Visions of Glory. *This was John's last mission; this was the marvelous spiritual growth and opening of the heavens he had envisioned when his health first started declining in 2006.*

Would we have dreamed that it would take a life-threatening illness and, as Lemony Snicket bemoans, a series of seemingly unfortunate events to get us to where we needed to be? No; and yet we humbly acknowledged the obvious hand of the Lord in it all.

So we sold our business and just about everything we had and came to Utah. And we praised the Lord all the day long.

—*Terri*

Chapter Seven

Feasting on the Scriptures

The Banquet of Truth

Having just written the UnBlog on Peace, I asked myself, "What is the most important thing I, myself, have learned in my life?" What came to my mind was a little different than peace. Let me explain.

If I had a chance to write something in the heart of every Latter-day Saint that would automatically be believed and applied, it would be this: "Not only is the restored gospel true, but it works. It functions as in any dispensation past. It has inherent within it the very power of God, and by obedience to law and through the Atonement of Christ we can obtain every blessing, miracle, vision, manifestation, or visitation, for ourselves, that any generation of the past has obtained. Nothing is withheld. We have it all."

It is manifestly clear that we in the Church may possess unknowingly, but we *do* possess it.

If we read the scriptures and find an instance where someone saw angels, then we can seek and obtain that same gift. If we read of people walking on the water, raising the dead, dividing the waters, or speaking with the God of heaven, then these things are readily available to us. Why do I believe this? It is because I have studied, pondered, and tested these promises and found them to be true. I have dined at the banquet of truth and have drunk long and deeply from the river of grace. As the least of all saints, I have seen and heard remarkable things and have opened every door upon which I have knocked. I am not telling you what I think or what I believe; I am telling you what I have seen, touched, and known.

Having said the above, it is worth noting that these things do not happen according to the timetable of man. What we want and when we think we are ready to obtain it are not the driving forces. These things happen according to the timetable of God, which means that great patience is required, because when the qualifying laws are met but the timetable is premature, then we receive divinely spoken foreknowledge of promised blessings. We must wait upon the Lord to lay our hands upon those things, especially those that have specific fulfillment in the pre-millennial day. I'm speaking of the miracles of Zion, of moving mountains and rivers, or of calling down fire to defend the City of the Living God. In that day, we who have received those promises will participate without being surprised or amazed.

But until then we must wait and feast upon the bounteous scriptures we have been given, which fill our hearts and minds with these glorious possibilities and truths. The delicious blessings of which we read—visions, manifestations, and miracles of faith—are all part of the divine banquet available to us all—of which I am a happy witness.

Brother John

Who Wrote the Book of Mormon?

I have been reading the latter-day scriptures since I was an early teenager. I have probably read the Book of Mormon cover-to-cover two dozen times, and I have also studied it very thoroughly by subject. When I was a teenager, I determined it was true because I had a spiritual experience, which lit that flame in my soul. Every time I have read it thereafter, I consistently have had that flame enlarged by the Spirit of Truth.

At the same time, during my spiritual progression, I have learned continually greater and more magnificent truths about the gospel. I have found the promise to be true that those who seek will find, and that the great mysteries are indeed revealed to those who seek them. As a life-long seeker of truth, and as a student of all scriptures, I can see a long evolution of my doctrinal understanding. In other words, I understand the gospel much more now than I did in my teens or twenties.

At each phase and plateau of my understanding, those truths were enthroned in the Book of Mormon, alive with the Holy Spirit to testify of their grand power in my life at that time, to my then-current understanding, according to the light that I then enjoyed. This has always proven to be true.

Here's my point: Joseph Smith came forth with the Book of Mormon when he was twenty-five years old. His understanding of the gospel was basic, immature, unsophisticated, and lacking depth. His writings from those times reveal a searching yet unsophisticated doctrinal mind and a stunted use of language. For example, he learned about baptism while translating the Book of Mormon! This being the case, the Book of Mormon should logically be doctrinally primitive from page one, and evolve as Joseph's doctrinal knowledge evolved.

But it doesn't evolve. Chapter one of First Nephi contains the most advanced doctrine of the latter-days—so much so that most readers still don't view it as doctrine, but just as a wonderful happening. When Lehi saw God upon His throne in verse eight of chapter one, Joseph was writing about deep and spiritually profound doctrine that he himself did not understand or teach until later. The doctrine that man can qualify for a personal visitation of God, see visions, receive promises, ask for an endowment of divine providence, and still remain mortal, is one of the greatest truths ever taught to man and only made possible by temple ordinances that Joseph did not receive until almost a dozen years later.

That Joseph lacked the sophistication either as a writer or a theologian at age twenty-five to write the Book of Mormon is well established, so much so that his enemies have proposed other means and other people to explain the existence and profound effect of the Book of Mormon. But here is the eye of the needle for any proposed alternative theory about this inexplicable book: Whoever wrote it not only understood deep and profound doctrinal mysteries, but also somehow convinced God to testify to anyone who sincerely reads it that it is true! Only a God-sent, genuine, powerful prophet could ever write words so harmonious with God's work and glory that He personally would inspire millions of readers to "know" that those words are true.

So, if Joseph didn't write it, who did? That's easy: Nephi, Jacob, Enos, Jarom, Omni, Mormon, and a host of others. Each of these had the singular qualification of being a prophet of God who understood the profound doctrine that Joseph did not, doctrine that begins in verse eight of chapter one. Each prophet-writer had inspired license to pen truths of which God Himself is bound to testify, until the work of eternity is completed.

This is why the Book of Mormon is so profoundly befuddling to enemies of truth, and why it is so gloriously testified of by God. It is true on every level of investigation: True for a teenager who can barely understand the stylized English, true to the casual reader of inspired stories, true to the basic searcher for truths, true for the determined and inspired seeker, and true for those whose eyes and ears are already opened to the mysteries of God.

Brother John

Die Boek van Mormon

I was searching through my books in storage a few days ago and came across a first edition of the Book of Mormon in Afrikaans. I served a mission in South Africa from 1971 to 1973. I had interesting and challenging experiences. But this was one of the most riveting:

I attended the special conference in Johannesburg on May 14, 1972, when the new translation of the Book of Mormon into Afrikaans (Die Boek van Mormon) was presented. It was an electric moment. People wept. Some had waited all of their lifetimes to read the Book of Mormon in Afrikaans. Many people had learned English for the sole purpose of reading this scripture. The Spirit was strong among us as we rejoiced.

Remembering back more than forty years, I can still remember Professor Felix Mijnhardt as he spoke of his experience in translating that sacred book. We also had a special zone conference a few days prior where our mission president, Harlan Clark, recounted his involvement with and experience of the translation of the Book of Mormon. I had a good friend who was an assistant to President Clark who later shared with me his experiences of being in meetings with Professor Mijnhardt and Elder Clark several times. I can no longer remember who said what exactly, but I remember what I felt and how it affected my newly minted testimony as a young missionary. I will retell it as best as I can recall.

Professor Mijnhardt was invited to come to the stand and speak about his experience in translating the Book of Mormon. He recounted how he had been given a gift of languages from God from his youth. He said that he was fluent in over sixty languages. He was presently employed at Pretoria University as a language professor. He said he had been praying that the Lord would give him some task, some divinely important task, that would justify his having this gift of language from God.

He said that in about 1970, he had visited a group of Mormon leaders, including a Bishop Brummer, Mission President Harlan Clark, and others, who sought to commission him to translate the Book of Mormon from English into Afrikaans. He said that he knew of the Book of Mormon from his religious studies, and his initial reaction was that he did not want to be involved in translating it.

However, that evening as he prayed upon his knees, as was his habit, the Spirit of the Lord convicted him. The message was something on the order of, "You asked me for a great, divinely inspired task of translation, I sent it to you in the form of translating the Book of Mormon, and you declined." Professor Mijnhardt said he could not sleep through the night because he knew that translating the Book of Mormon would get him into trouble with his university, which was owned and operated by the Dutch Reformed Church. When morning came, he agreed to begin the translation immediately.

Standing at the pulpit, he described the experience. He said something like, "I never begin translating a book at the beginning. Writing style usually changes throughout a book and becomes more consistent toward the middle. Accordingly, I opened to a random place in the middle of the Book of Mormon and began translating."

He said, "I was startled by the obvious fact that the Book of Mormon was not authored in English. It became immediately apparent that what I was reading was a translation into English from some other language. The sentence structure was wrong for native English. The word choices were wrong, as were many phrases."

He asked, "How many times has an Englishman said or written, 'And it came to pass'?" We all laughed and knew he was right, of course.

He explained that when he realized this, he knew that he had to find either the original language or a median language and then proceed to translate it into Afrikaans. He listed a half-dozen languages he tried, all of which did not accommodate the strange sentence structure found in the Book of Mormon. He said he finally tried Egyptian, and to his complete surprise, he found that the Book of Mormon translated flawlessly into Egyptian—not modern, but ancient Egyptian. He found that some nouns were missing from Egyptian, so he used Hebrew nouns where Egyptian did not provide the word or phrase. He chose Hebrew because both languages existed in the same place anciently.

He said he had no idea at that time why the Book of Mormon was once written in Egyptian, but he said that without any doubt, the Book of Mormon had been authored in Egyptian or a language with very similar syntax. I heard him say this over and over. Then he said, "Imagine my utter astonishment when I turned to chapter one, verse one, and began my actual translation and came to verse two, where Nephi explains that he was writing in the language of the Egyptians, with the learning of the Jews!"

He said, "I knew by the second verse that this was no ordinary book, that it was not the writings of Joseph Smith, but that it was of ancient origin. I could have saved myself months of work if I had just begun at the beginning. Nobody but God—working through a prophet of God, in this case Nephi—would have included a statement of the language he was writing in. Consider how many documents written in English include the phrase, 'I am writing in English'! It is unthinkable and absolute proof of the inspired origin of this book."

He noted that he was one of the few people in the world with any knowledge of old Egyptian writing. He was certainly the only person who was also fluent in Afrikaans and English. He indicated that when a verse would not translate directly into English, he used Egyptian as a tool to arrive at a correct translation into Afrikaans.

Professor Mijnhardt spoke of many other things regarding the translation of this book and then said, "I do not know what Joseph Smith was before he translated this book, and I do not know what he was afterward, but while he translated this book, he was a prophet of God! I know he was a prophet! I testify to you that he was a prophet while he brought forth this book! He could have been nothing else! No person in 1827 could have done what he did. The science did not exist. The knowledge of ancient Egyptian did not exist. The knowledge of these ancient times and ancient peoples did not exist. The Book of Mormon is scripture. I hope you realize this.

"I have since been asked to translate the book you call the Doctrine and Covenants. I got part way through and set it down. It is not like the Book of Mormon. Anyone could translate it into Afrikaans. It is not scripture in the same sense that the Book of Mormon is scripture. I declare that the Book of Mormon is of ancient origin and is scripture of the same caliber as the Old Testament, or for that matter, the New Testament.

"I have taken this book of scripture, this Book of Mormon, and presented it to my Board of Regents and urged them to embrace it as scripture. They declined, of course. I took it to the head of our Dutch Reformed Church and demonstrated why the Book of Mormon is scripture and urged them to at least study it, even if they did not canonize it or even share it with the people of the church. I urged them to just think what having a new and profound book of scripture could mean to the church—to my church, the Dutch Reformed Church. I pointed out that they need not become Mormons, in the same way that they did not need to become Jews to embrace the Old Testament. They considered my presentation for a very few seconds and then rejected it. They next threatened me regarding my belief in the Book of Mormon, threatened my employment, and ejected me from their presence. I am deeply disappointed, but I am not deterred. I will keep promoting this book as scripture for the remainder of my life—simply because it *is* scripture, and I know it."

He paused and then added, "I am not a member of your church and do not expect to become one. I have been asked many times why I have not joined your church, and my answer is because God has not directed me to join you. If He had, I would be standing here as a fellow Mormon. Perhaps my mission in life is better served outside of your church. I haven't studied your doctrine or your history since Joseph Smith. The only thing I know about you is that you have authentic, ancient scripture in the Book of Mormon, and that all of the world should embrace the Book of Mormon as scripture. It simply can't be denied. I believe every religion could embrace the Book of Mormon without becoming a Mormon. You probably disagree with that, but it is my present belief, and my message to anyone who will listen."

I have pondered that experience for half of a century now. I do not know whether Professor Mijnhardt ever joined the Church. I know my memory of his exact words is wanting, but my memory of what I felt and what I knew and how potent it was to hear his testimony of Joseph Smith and the Book of Mormon is one of those things that I will never forget.

Brother John

Terri's Note: For anyone interested, the current location of the transcript for the May 14, 1972 Transvaal Stake meeting in Johannesburg is in the Church History Library, call number LR 9256 24, Folder 1.

Studying the Scriptures 501

I was asked a great question: How can I get more out of the scriptures?

Over many years, I have found that there are two ways to absorb the scriptures: 1) Reading them over and over as a story, and 2) Studying them by subject.

When I read the scriptures for the sequence of events (or the story line), I feel the Spirit and learn from the lives of the former faithful. However, I learn very little doctrinally. It is actually interesting to me that many Gospel Doctrine teachers tend to take this approach—to retell the story.

Yes, it is important to know when Lehi left Jerusalem and who went with him, but it is far more important to know the spiritual process that brought him into the Lord's presence than the details of how he left Jerusalem.

I began studying the scriptures by subject about twenty years ago, and it has opened my eyes to things I never even guessed were in the scriptures. It takes more time and more thought, and you don't get to tell your friends that you just "finished" the New Testament or the Book of Mormon for the umpteenth time. But if you really want to have the doctrine of the priesthood become alive and operative in your life, here is how I believe you can do it.

I prefer to begin in the Book of Mormon, but any book of scripture will yield its treasures to this method.

1. Read until you find a point of doctrine that grabs your attention. As an example, one of the first spiritual events in the Book of Mormon is Lehi seeing God upon His throne. We'll call this verse your "first scripture."

2. Write your "first scripture" reference on a blank page with enough of a description so that you can remember what it said.

3. Look up each of the footnote references on your "first scripture." Write each of those footnote references in a numbered list on the page for your "first scripture." When you go to the verse for each footnote reference, use a fine point red pen, and write the reference of your "first scripture" in the margin. This is invaluable because it creates a thread you can follow in both directions through your scriptures. When people are discussing that verse, or as you are teaching a lesson or making a comment, your scriptures will contain many threads that will take you to every place that particular doctrine is discussed. People will think you're a genius—which you will humbly deny of course.

4. This is important: Write down on another blank page the first reference you were sent to from your "first scripture." This is your "second scripture." Again, include a short description of what it says. Do the same for the next reference to which you were sent from your "first scripture." Each additional reference will be your "third scripture," "fourth scripture," and so on.

5. When—not if, but when—you have an inspired thought, write it down on the page for the scripture you were reading.

6. I like to underline each footnote as I read it, or I sometimes read the same one several times. I circle footnotes that lead me to beautiful or especially enlightening scriptures.

7. Now, go to the "second scripture" on your list, and after turning to that scripture, do the same as above and go to and read each referenced scripture. You will notice that many of the references take you to where you have already been. Just underline them in the footnote, and if you can remember what it said, don't read it again.

8. As you are working on this second scripture, you will be adding to the page for the second scripture a numbered list of the footnote references on that "second scripture."

9. You will eventually look up every footnote of every scripture on that subject. It doesn't take that long because it becomes circular after a while, or further footnotes are taking you back to scriptures you have already read.

10. When you find no new scriptures by this means you now need to use your commentaries and conference talks.

11. If you have GospeLink, you can click on the verse number, and it will bring up every commentary ever written on your "first scripture." Read the ones by authors you trust, such as General Authorities, Bruce R. McConkie, Joseph Fielding Smith, and others. You will find that they used most of the scriptures on your list. If they come up with an amazing quote or statement, or a new scripture you didn't find, add it to your "first scripture" document. Then do the same thing for your "second scripture," "third scripture," and so forth.

You can accomplish this same thing, though a little slower, by searching lds.org, GospeLink.com, and other places. The point is to search until no other scholar is telling you something new. Search until the information begins to be repetitive.

12. Now, using the information you have gathered, write an essay on what you learned. Move the quotes you've found to their logical place in your essay. This can be one paragraph or a hundred pages. Include in your essay the scripture references from your list. Write as if you were explaining it to a believing, but doctrinally unsophisticated person. Include your thoughts, feelings, and revealed insights.

Besides the blessing of scholarly learning, something greater happens as you do this. The Spirit of the Lord comes into your heart, and you learn much more than you read. Your heart is changed, and you feel power, knowledge, and peace at the same time.

Even though most of what we learn of the "mysteries" comes from the Holy Spirit, the greatest tool we possess in inviting the Holy Spirit and creating an environment wherein we can receive revelatory insight is to study the scriptures as described above.

By the time you have accomplished this exercise, you will know everything the scriptures can teach you on a particular subject. You will quite literally be a scriptural scholar on that topic, because this is precisely how scholars study. They pick a topic, read everything that exists on it, come to some conclusion, and then write an essay and pretend they're "scholarly."

After you have written your essay, find another intriguing doctrinal subject (often piggybacking off or related to the first subject you studied) and begin the process all over again. You only need to do this for doctrines that interest you, or about which you are not clear.

Don't be discouraged or think it will take too long or be too hard. You're going to do something with your time in the next week, month, or year. The difference is what you intend to have gained in that time. Doing nothing will yield nothing. Entertaining yourself will yield entertainment. Traveling will thrill your eyes and give you stories to tell. Cleaning the house will yield a clean house.

"Subjectively" studying the scriptures will yield revelatory insight, blessings of truth and light, and a staggering understanding of the Lord's plan for you personally.

This is the advanced course.

Brother John

Look and Live

When the children of Israel were afflicted in the wilderness with fiery (poisonous) serpents, the Lord instructed Moses to make a brass serpent and place it upon a pole. "And it came to pass, that if a serpent had bitten any man, when he beheld the serpent of brass, he lived" (Numbers 21:8–9).

But even after seeing their fellows saved by this simple act, there were some whose hearts were so hardened "that they would not look, therefore they perished. Now the reason they would not look is because they did not believe that it would heal them" (Alma 33:20).

Alma asks, "If ye could be healed by merely casting about your eyes . . . would ye not behold quickly?" (Alma 33:21). I can almost hear an "Oh, for crying out loud!" tone in his question. If all you had to do was look at something to save your life—why wouldn't you? The answer is that it was too simple. They didn't believe something so common and so simple could save them, so they refused to look— and it cost them their lives.

A few chapters later, Alma expands his teaching to include the Liahona, which was fashioned by the hand of God to guide Lehi through the wilderness and into the Promised Land. It was a physical object, like the brass serpent that Moses raised up, and if Lehi's family looked upon it, they would live. But for a larger part of their journey, they did not look, and they "tarried in the wilderness, or did not travel a direct course, and were afflicted with hunger and thirst" (Alma 37:42).

Why didn't they just look? Because it only worked when they believed God "could cause that those spindles should point the way they should go" (Alma 37:40). When they didn't believe that God "could" or "would" cause the Liahona to indicate His will, it didn't matter if they looked at it or not; all they saw were brass spindles, not the will of God.

It is easy to read about their stubborn unbelief and shake our heads, feeling sure that if *we* had been there, we would not have allowed unbelief to keep us from looking upon the serpent, or into the Liahona with believing eyes.

Before we get too smug, let us compare our own spiritual situation with that of Lehi and his people. After all, the Liahona was *not* a one-of-a-kind work of God. It may be the only time this work was executed in brass, but God has done this same thing throughout the long eternities. Lehi was given the Liahona because those in his company needed a physical, tangible witness of God's directing hand. Without it, they would not have arrived in the promised land.

You and I stand upon a taller ladder because of the faith and teaching of our parents and because we are not surrounded by barren wilderness but by millions of believing souls, by the greatest collection of scripture of all time, and by living prophets. So, we do not have, or apparently need, a physical Liahona. But this directing work of God did not begin with the Liahona, nor did it cease after it.

Then and now, as Alma asserts, the "word of Christ" is our Liahona. Many people in the Church assume this to mean solely the scriptures—and yes, scriptures are an integral part of God's directing work. But in addition to and verifying the truths found in scripture, Christ speaks to us *personally* every moment of every day. As with Lehi, these words of direction are empowered or disabled by our own belief that God truly is in the little pointers in our heart. If we doubt it, then the words cease. When we believe and take the words of Christ as our guide, then "just as surely as this director did bring our fathers, by following its course, to the promised land, shall the words of Christ, if we follow their course, carry us beyond this vale of sorrow into a far better land of promise" (Alma 37:45).

On the UnBlog, we have harped and hammered and belabored this principle unrelentingly. The reason is, most of us in this world are still not looking. After one knows that Jesus is the Christ, then hearing and obeying His voice is the pivot point of salvation. This is our Liahona, and most people only glance in times of need. We peer a little harder when we're in trouble. We try to believe when we are in pain and sorrow. But we don't really "look." We don't turn our spiritual eyes and ears upon the Holy Spirit—which are the "words" Christ speaks, and upon our personal Liahona spindles—and then never take our eyes away.

All persons I know who have chosen to look—and then never look away—have accomplished vast and eternal things in their lives. They walk with faith and joy daily toward God's ordained destination for them. They have a calling that gives them peace and direction. They know what to do each moment, largely without seeing the broad picture of where it is taking them. They are at peace because when each footfall is directed by the voice of God, then the only possible outcome is safety, miracles, joy, and exaltation.

The funny thing is that it is actually very easy to do—as easy for us as it was for Lehi to look upon his Liahona.

"Do not let us be slothful because of the easiness of the way; for so was it with our fathers; for so was it prepared for them, that if they would look they might live; even so it is with us. The way is prepared, and if we will look we may live forever" (Alma 37:46).

If your eyes are even distantly focused upon Zion, consider what "we may live forever" might mean in light of that approaching destination.

Brother John

Scripture Mastery Key

Terri's Note: The actual "Scripture Mastery Key for the Book of Mormon" is located in the Appendix, along with the "Scripture Mastery Key for the Doctrine and Covenants."

I want to share a powerful tool I've found for scripture mastery. It's simple to use and requires a tenth as much memory power as memorizing hundreds of scriptures.

I learned this on my mission almost forty years ago, and I still remember most of it. Here's how it works: Instead of memorizing hundreds of scriptures, you just memorize important chapter headings. For example, 2 Nephi 9 is about the Atonement of Christ. Once you memorize that information, every time you try to remember "that scripture about the Atonement," the odds are it is in 2 Nephi 9. You can flip to that chapter, look at your highlights, and find it in a heartbeat. It actually gives you scripture mastery with minimal effort.

I have prepared a document I call "Scriptorian's Key to the Book of Mormon." It has only ninety simplified chapter headings, which give you mastery of the whole book! They are short and easy to remember.

Here's what I suggest: Get up each morning, do your morning routine, sit down for two minutes and memorize one more chapter heading, and then review the previous four days. Then say your morning prayers and head off to your day. Add one and review four every day until you are finished.

In less than three months, you will be a Book of Mormon scriptorian. Imagine that!

Here's a potent additional aid to memorizing this list. Ask your spouse, roommate, or friend to help by memorizing the list with you. Then decide on some reward you both want. The person who can stump the other one the most times wins the reward. My missionary companion and I used to "gamble" for iced soft drinks. In Africa, that was a golden reward indeed, and we sparred relentlessly to stump the other so we could be the lone (gloating) guzzler at the end of the day. In not many weeks neither, of us could prevail because we both had the list down cold.

To challenge the other "player," you either state a chapter and the other has to repeat the synopsis or you paraphrase the synopsis, and the other has to correctly identify the chapter. Easy.

God bless,

Brother John

The Greatest Volume of Truth

I have a testimony of the Book of Mormon. I would like to tell you why.

There are actually two reasons I know that the Book of Mormon is the inspired document it claims to be. I'm going to start with the second-most important reason I know this.

Long ago, I began studying the scriptures subjectively. By that I mean by subject. I would happen upon a principle or subject I wanted more understanding about and would begin looking up every scripture I could find on it. Often I would use the references at the bottom of the page, sometimes the study guide. More often, I would use reference works like those penned by McConkie or Joseph Fielding Smith. As I found the references, I would record the previous and next reference by each scripture, thus making a trail forward and backward through my scriptures.

What I found was that the Book of Mormon is doctrinally consistent throughout. What that means to me is that it always teaches the same things about a doctrine such as faith. It doesn't teach faith in one way at the beginning and then another way toward the end. The reason this is important is mankind constantly evolves in his understanding. When you write a long document on any subject, your understanding is naturally going to be more evolved at the end than at the beginning. The way I personally deal with this is to just plan on rewriting the first few chapters many times. Joseph Smith translated the Book of Mormon one time and then immediately published it. Yet, there is no evolution of doctrine. This tells me that Joseph Smith simply didn't write it, he translated it, and the previous authors were prophets of God.

Another tool I found as a writer was Deseret Book's GospeLink program. With this software, I have been able to look up a scripture and then by clicking a button, read what every other LDS author, prophet, or thinker has had to say about that verse since the beginning of the Church. With a single click, anyone can determine that the doctrine of the Book of Mormon, and the way LDS leaders have interpreted it, has not drifted in the last 175 years.

Unaided by anything technological we have today, Joseph Smith translated this book in a little over ninety working days and promptly published it. It has had minor corrections for spelling and grammar, but the book has not been doctrinally edited—ever. It is in its original format just as Joseph spoke it and as his scribes recorded it. Joseph did this without reference material, without looking up passages from the scripture, without the benefit of more than a third-grade education, and without any prior understanding of world history, South American history, or even geography.

Joseph Smith wrote of nations, continental migrations, wars, methods of wars, cultural and economic complexities, animals that are now extinct, cultures that are now nonexistent, and facts of those cultures that were not proven to be accurate until one hundred years later. Yet, everything he said they did or said they were can be bolstered through modern discoveries.

But the greatest thing that Joseph Smith accomplished in translating the Book of Mormon wasn't the history of an extinguished civilization; it was the preservation of their beliefs and doctrine of Christ. When I first read the Book of Mormon, I was interested to find that everything I believed was also believed by those ancient people. But my understanding at that time was comparatively infantile.

Forty years later, my understanding of the doctrine of Christ has matured. Through consistent study, and through personal revelation over this long time, I have come to understand concepts that Joseph Smith couldn't possibly have imagined or believed when he first sat down to translate this book. Records of his life show that Joseph didn't understand simple things like baptism by immersion for the remission of sins! Yet, the lofty and mystery-shrouded doctrines, those things that can only be acquired by a lifetime of righteous seeking, are all present in the Book of Mormon. These are things that Joseph could not have of his own intellect and genius included in anything he wrote. But he could have *translated* the works and doctrine of much more mature authors—which is the claim he made.

Speaking personally, having written many books and published a few, I know that I could not write a Book of Mormon. With years of accumulated doctrinal understanding, all of the resources and history books, the Internet, and every modern source of unlimited information at my fingertips, even with inspired words and truth flooding my soul, it would take me several lifetimes to write even an approximation of the Book of Mormon. After writing and rewriting, I can promise that my attempt would be infinitely less, greatly flawed, and of far less eternal consequence than the Book of Mormon. No future generations will ever find one of my dusty books, or anyone else's, hidden under a rock and therefrom forge a religion authorized of God, attested to by angels and manifested by miracles—not even close.

No, the Book of Mormon stands alone, mighty and majestic, as an improbable compilation of inspired ancient authors whose words came through an unschooled and ignorant young man. Joseph Smith did not "write" the Book of Mormon but translated it from the writings of many great men whose lives spanned and included vastly more experience, wisdom, inspiration, and doctrinal purity than Joseph Smith possessed when he translated this book.

But, undergirding and overarching all of these intellectual "evidences" of why the Book of Mormon is scripture is this one thing: By the workings of the Holy Ghost, I have sought and obtained for myself the most high and holy witness that this book is quite possibly the most important book that will ever be written. It is the accumulated effect of God's guiding hand upon righteous and inspired men who lived out their lives, shed their blood, and gave their all to bring this amazing book through millennia of preparation into the hands of an unlettered school boy, to become the greatest volume of truth to ever come forth.

This is the first and most important reason I believe.

Brother John

Once More into the Breach

*O*nce more into the breach, dear friends, once more.

In peace there's nothing so becoming a man as modest stillness and humility. But, when the blast of war blows in your ears, then echo the courage of Christ. Stiffen the resolve, gird up the loins, despise the comforts of Babylon, and drink the bitter cup with unflinching boldness that God will raise you up, though the arrows of war embrace you. (With apologies to W. Shakespeare, from *Henry V*, act 3, scene i)

Which is just to say that today is chemo once more. I'll be back shortly.

Brother John

The Journey Home
Part VII: The Gauntlet

Do you recall Indiana Jones's amazing escape from the collapsing cave? Every step was critical, every corner awaited with dangers popping out of nowhere, and the odds of our good Dr. Jones succeeding were ridiculously small. Yet, he made it—with his hat.

The reason this comes to mind is because some days, writing this UnBlog seems like running the Indiana Jones gauntlet. There are so many things to disturb the flow of the Spirit, and they seem to need my attention all at the same time. When I don't UnBlog on a certain day it is usually because some arrow or stone (or rolling boulder) made it through the few defenses I command.

I have so far been resolute that I would not write unless the Spirit is present, which makes it an amazing gift that I have written much at all. These past few months have been times of illness, steep climbs, and glorious views. But I have nevertheless rejoiced mightily and shouted praises for what seems like an unending flow of joy in UnBlogging my soul.

Thank you for making that journey possible and precious—and for being patient with my inability to post every day.

I send you my love,

Brother John

Chapter Eight

True Power in the Priesthood

Power in the Priesthood

There are two levels or degrees of priesthood power that I would like to discuss with you. The first is obtaining and exercising power in the priesthood exactly as we have it today. The second pertains to the "fulness of the priesthood," which we have been promised, but which we do not presently exhibit.

Those who have obtained a "fulness of the priesthood" do not operate as mortals do. They have been given a degree of power that makes them "the greatest of all," and "all things are subject unto them in heaven and on the earth" (Doctrine & Covenants 50:26–27). We will discuss this "later and greater" priesthood as we detail the "oath and covenant of the priesthood" further on.

The Melchizedek Priesthood we presently hold gives us the authority to act in certain binding priesthood ordinances, and it gives us the right and the responsibility to use the priesthood to heal the sick, raise the dead, speak prophetically of the future, give inspired guidance, and to speak all the words that revelation puts in our mouths.

It seems that there are three things that must be present for every priesthood blessing to be instantly efficacious.

1) The Lord's will must be done. It is not possible for us to see a pronounced blessing come to pass if it is not the Lord's will. Whatever we say, whatever promises we give, must be the same Jesus Christ would have pronounced had He been present Himself. We are not able to bestow a blessing that is contrary to His divine plan. In my opinion, this is the greatest reason some blessings fail to deliver the full promises—because we have not delivered the Lord's will.

We acquire the ability to know His will through the walk of obedience in our lives long before the priesthood blessing. We learn to recognize His voice, and we acquire faith through long experience with obedience. By the time we place our hands upon someone's head, the pathways of revelation should have been opened years earlier.

2) When we bless by the priesthood, and we speak in that moment under inspiration, then the priesthood holder does not just believe, he does not only hope, he *knows* that his words are inspired of God, and his faith is perfect in that one thing. Speaking without such an inspired knowledge damages and inhibits the priesthood servant's faith and can limit the power of the blessing.

3) The recipient of the blessing must have faith to receive the blessing. Even when it was Jesus Christ whose voice commanded the miracles, He acknowledged that the faith of the blessed had healed them. In our day, the ability of the recipient to actually receive is significant in the outpouring of the blessing. We will talk a little more of this in coming days.

It is of great interest to me that the worthiness of the priesthood servant is less significant than these prior three factors. It is certainly true that an unworthy servant will have less access to the inspiration of empowered words, and less sensitivity to the guiding voice of Christ, but it is not always an obstacle. The pivot point of power is whether Christ's will is being performed, not the relative perfection of the priesthood holder. We all fall short, even the very best of us, but Christ never does, and when His will is being faithfully performed, the miracles occur.

Brother John

Lesson from a Pig Farmer

When I was thirteen, my little brother, Jimmy, drowned in an irrigation ditch and died. He was just two, barely out of diapers. It was a deep, deep tragedy for our entire family. As I write these words I feel my heart swelling with—I almost wrote pain, but I think the right word is *memories*—sad and wonderful memories.

It was a beautiful July morning, and I left early to milk the cows. It was summer vacation, and I had a lot of work to do that day. Timmy picked up a bucket and begged to go with me. "Pleath, Johnnie, let me milk the cowth," he begged. It wasn't safe for him to be around the cows, and I told him no a bunch of times before I left him in tears. It was hard for me to tell him no, because I loved that little guy with a fiercely passionate love. He never seemed to want to leave my teenage side, and there was a special bond between us that made my life worth living.

As I recall, we had four cows at that time. I milked them and put the milk in the cooler, which circulated brine water chilled to twenty-five degrees over the metal cans, cooling them rapidly. Our milking parlor was just a block from the house, but I drove the old truck to and from the parlor because the equipment and milk were heavy. As I drove home, I had a growing fear that something was wrong with Timmy. As I approached the concrete bridge that crossed the irrigation ditch to our home, I had a strong impression to look down into the ditch to my left. I dismissed this feeling because I was in a hurry to find Timmy. I don't know what I would have seen, but I know that I didn't do what I was supposed to do.

I jumped out of the truck, ran toward the house, and called to my mother, who was just coming out the front door to look for Timmy. He had been gone only a few minutes, but she, too, had a feeling that something was wrong. We ran around the house, into the fields, and down the road. Neighbors saw our increasing panic and joined in the search. I saw my mother head off down the ditch into the neighboring fields. She climbed through a barbwire fence and continued to follow the ditch, searching the muddy water frantically. I thought she was making a mistake.

By now, at least twenty minutes had passed. Then I heard Mom scream for help. I ran in her direction, and about one hundred yards down the ditch, I saw her jump into the water. The ditch was about six feet across and maybe four feet deep. The sides were steeply sloped and covered with slick moss. It was hard for an adult to get out of the ditch. The water moved slowly when it was dammed up for irrigation, as it was that day.

When I arrived, Mom had pulled Timmy out of the water and

was already performing CPR on him. I don't even know how she knew to do it; CPR was almost unknown at that time. Then my Dad arrived. I never did know who called him, but it was probably one of my siblings. It normally took about thirty minutes for Dad to drive home from his veterinary clinic; he must have driven insanely fast to get there so soon. He ran to my mother and helped with the CPR. I stood there with my brothers and sister in horrified silence, powerless to do anything, as time went into slow motion and every moment seemed to last an eternity.

Suddenly my mother looked up. This little sad scene was surrounded by maybe a dozen neighbors, half of whom were priesthood holders. Mom's lips were swollen and her face was white. I can't even describe the look on her face. It was part terror, part anger, and part grief. She cried out, "Someone give my baby a blessing!" She said it with deep urgency and then went back to her CPR with Dad.

Her words seemed to have the effect of slamming those brethren in the chest, because they collectively took a step backward. Ten seconds later, Mom looked up and was astonished to see that only one man had not stepped backward. He was a neighbor from several blocks down the road, a pig farmer who hadn't been to church in thirty-five years. He stood there in filthy overalls, twisting his hat in his hands.

She cried out, "Rulen, I know you hold the priesthood. Give my baby a blessing!" It was not a request. It was a shouted command.

"Ann, I ain't worthy," he replied softly.

She looked at him with eyes that could have stripped the paint off a tractor. "God will bless my baby. I just need you to say the words."

Rulen took a step forward and then very slowly knelt at my brother's head. I saw tears streaming down his face. He laid both hands on Timmy's damp head. As nearly as I can remember, he said, "God, I am a sinful man. Please don't hold my sins against this little baby. In the name of Jesus Christ, I command you to come back." He said this in a sort of sobbing whisper. He stood quickly and stepped back and then disappeared back into the crowd. I think he left and walked home almost immediately.

By this time it had been thirty to forty minutes since we had found Timmy. Permanent brain damage occurs at three minutes. My dad straightened up and with a look of grief told my mother it was time to stop. My mother screamed "No! You keep working on him. He's not dead!"

An ambulance finally arrived, and two white-coated young men ran up to my parents and just stood there. They didn't have anything in their hands at all. My dad demanded that they help, but they said they were taxi drivers and didn't know anything about medicine. It was evident they knew it was hopeless. It was obvious to everyone but my mother that Timmy was dead.

At that moment, Timmy took a breath. My mother screamed, "Bob, I think he's trying to breathe." My dad felt his neck. "He has a pulse!" he cried. "Quick, let's get him to the hospital."

I ran with them as they carried Timmy to the ambulance. The drivers didn't know how to turn on the oxygen tank in their overgrown station wagon/ambulance. They didn't even know what those green tanks were for. When my dad finally got it going, there were no face masks. The last thing I knew as the ambulance roared away was that my dad was cupping his hands over his son's face, trying to get oxygen to his lungs.

The next few days are a terrible blur. I don't remember anything except a hollow, impossible hope. Timmy was alive but in a coma. He was breathing normally. All of his bodily signs were normal. The doctors were incredulous and guardedly hopeful. This was a miracle no one could deny. Timmy should not be alive.

My mom and dad took shifts to stay with him twenty-four hours a day. We were allowed once to go see him. He looked perfectly normal. His skin was warm to the touch, and he was wearing his own pajamas. He just looked asleep. I felt hope. My sister cried, and then I couldn't help it—I cried.

It was late at night, and my mother was watching him when Timmy opened his eyes and said, "Mommy, I love you." My Dad arrived just after he closed his eyes again, and Mother was so relieved, so full of hope, that she decided to go home for the first time in a week. She went home, bathed, and went to bed, planning on returning to the hospital early in the morning. My Dad called her a few hours later. Timmy had died peacefully.

I remember sobbing until my eyes couldn't even blink. My tear ducts were exhausted. I remember a thousand sad faces as I stood near the casket and shook people's hands. I hated it. I remember a few things about the funeral and the burial. Mostly I remember Rulen Jorgensen. I remember his words, his tear-streaked face, his look of utter helplessness as he blessed my little brother. I remember his big, rough hands trembling on Timmy's tiny head.

Mostly I remember the miracle of when the pig farmer raised my brother from the dead.

Rulen straightened up his life and went back to church. I heard years later that he taught a Sunday School class, which one of my younger brothers attended. I don't think Rulen knew that my brother was related to Timmy, because once he told Timmy's story and wept. He wept for the wonder and power of being the instrument of God, and he wept as he said, "I am so ashamed that the only way God could reach me was through the tragic death of a little boy."

Timmy's death was Rulen's miracle, but it wasn't the only purpose for his passing. It was my miracle, and a lot of other people's too.

When I bear my testimony that I know there is power in the priesthood, I am speaking from painful experience. When I say I have seen someone raised from the dead by the priesthood, I'm not exaggerating. That day, Rulen taught me to believe—to believe all things, to hope all things, to have great faith that anything that is right is possible

Now when I lay my hands upon someone's head, I think of Rulen and know that God can use anyone to accomplish His will, even a pig farmer who hasn't been to church for most of his lifetime. When I hope for glorious things, for Zion and the miracles that will accompany and precede the building of that glorious city, I think of how many pig farmers there will be who don't step back when it's time to raise their arms to the square and exercise the power of God.

Brother John

Priesthood Blessings That Work

I *still remember the first few times I gave priest-*hood blessings. I was on my mission—it was terrifying. I had never done it before. I didn't know what to say. I didn't know what the person expected. And my faith wasn't sufficient to tell me that *my* priesthood could actually bring down a blessing upon the person involved. So, I did what I had seen everyone else do; I said comforting words, prayed for blessings I thought that person needed, and closed the blessing with feelings of inadequacy.

That was forty or so years ago. Since that time, the Lord has worked hard on me to instill several powerful principles into my priesthood soul. When I am asked now to give a priesthood blessing, and the Holy Spirit concurs that I should, instead of thinking, "What should I say?" my thoughts turn to three keys that correctly govern the giving of priesthood blessings. When these are right, you will find yourself completely confident in the words and outcome of any and all blessings.

1. Voice the will of the Lord.

The most important principle governing priesthood blessings is that we must voice the will of the Lord. We are not privileged to "order the Lord across the heavens" as Elder McConkie said once. We are there to voice the will of God and to pronounce blessings He would not otherwise send without this act of authority and faith.

I discussed the need for personal revelation in priesthood blessings in a previous UnBlog. It requires a lifelong process of learning to hear and recognize the voice of revelation. It cannot be acquired by crushing need in the thirty minutes prior to a priesthood blessing. It isn't something one learns the night before by gritting one's spiritual teeth. It is the result of a lifestyle of righteousness.

I once heard a talk by a Franciscan Monk who had converted to Mormonism. He had several doctorates in English, and his voice and language were like a symphony to hear. When the Holy Spirit began to paint with his brilliant language, it was far more than eloquent. At the end of the talk a young lady asked him how long it had taken him to prepare for his talk that night. Without hesitation he said, "Fifty-five years." It was the right answer.

Living a lifestyle of righteousness will also cleanse your inner vessel, giving you a more pure motive for the priesthood blessings you perform. Purity matters, since the "pure in heart shall see God," and the pure in heart are increasingly like Him. No longer is the concern "What should I say?" or "What do they hope to receive?" The questions are "What is the Lord's will?" and "What blessing does He have in store for them?" Since your soul is attuned to the fountain of all truth, that knowledge and those words will come.

2. Do not think beforehand what to say.

Don't analyze the situation at hand and try to think of the best outcome or the most hopeful promises. Don't let your love or fear or concern dictate the words of the blessings. The best way to do this is to separate your personal feelings far away from the moment. Turn off your emotions. Open your heart. Listen—and when there is a flow of truth, speak. Until then, say nothing.

Separating yourself from the emotion of the moment may not be easy, especially when you are deeply invested in the outcome. But when your emotions are heightened, the still small voice is very difficult to hear. The nearer you can make yourself into a blank sheet of paper, the easier the Lord can write upon it.

3. Have courage.

Be courageous! It takes courage to just let words tumble from your lips without editing them first. Courage isn't to act in the absence of fear; it is to do what is right in spite of fear. It is to say the truth (as given by the Holy Spirit) without editing it before speaking. It is to decide to not care what others may think but to courageously speak the words the Lord puts into your mouth.

4. It's still true.

Last, what was true ten minutes ago is still true. Have faith that the words and feelings that came to you in the moment of priesthood service remain true long after people's faces exhibited hopeful belief, after the glow of revelation fades. Bear testimony of the particular truths you just received for them. Tell them why you believe. Tell them that the Lord gave you the words. Tell them great blessings require great faith to claim. Tell them the blessings are theirs, and instruct them to go forth and claim them. If the Lord told you there were a million-dollar diamond in your living room, would you just glance around and then give up?

Tell them to go claim every blessing just given.

Brother John

I'll Say What You Want Me to Say

*I*t was 1978, and I was serving as elders quorum president in the first Wasilla Ward. That part of the vineyard was a fertile field heavily strewn with immovable rocks of opposition. We struggled mightily to find and minister to those in our growing flock. It was a time of rapid learning for me. I was too inexperienced to realize that what we were trying to do was almost impossible and too innocent to doubt we could do it. I just naively assumed everything would be as it should. Our ward boundaries extended three hundred miles east, two hundred miles north, and thirty miles south. Some of our *active* church members came to church once or twice a year by bush plane.

I was driving home from work sometime in the late spring when I distinctly heard the Holy Spirit instruct me to visit the Jones family (which of course is not their real name). They were active in the Church, full of life and happiness, and a pillar of strength to everyone who knew them. I drove to their home and knocked. Sister Jones answered the door, and I was astonished to find that her face was dark and angry. She greeted me curtly and said this was not a good time for a visit.

"Sister Jones," I replied, "I was just directed by the Spirit to come to your home. I think this is the best possible time for a visit."

She reluctantly stepped aside and led me to their living room. It was a large home with nice furnishings, a grand piano, and beautiful paintings. Brother Jones, a respected physician, was sitting on the sofa, his eyes red and puffy. He stood and shook my hand without saying a word. At this point, I was feeling that I was in way over my head. They had teenage kids, and I was in my middle twenties with a one-year-old. They were well-to-do, and I didn't have a trade or a profession yet. In addition to all of that, I didn't have any idea what was going on, and I was quite sure I wouldn't know how to help them if I did.

I was also sure the Lord had sent me.

We sat as Sister Jones explained, "We just sent the kids to the neighbors because we were discussing whether or not to get a divorce. We had just decided to go through with it when you knocked on our door."

I should have been shocked, dismayed, and frightened because I had zero experience dealing with domestic issues. All I could think was that they were older, smarter, richer, and better than I. Instead, however, the Spirit put words into my mouth. "Given the fact that the Lord just sent me to your home at this very moment, what do you think His opinion is about your getting a divorce?"

Brother Jones looked relieved. Sister Jones looked shocked. Her husband was wise enough to let her phrase the answer. After a long pause she said, "He is not pleased." Brother Jones just nodded and looked from his wife to me several times.

I continued earnestly. "Then the question isn't whether you *should* get a divorce, but if you have enough faith to obey the Lord, put aside whatever is alienating you, and go forward with your lives."

Let me add a sidenote here. I'm not anywhere near this bold in real life. Even if I had known what to say—which I truly didn't—the natural man in me would have stumbled around and been careful not to offend anyone, and probably would not have been able to deliver the message with enough force to accomplish the Lord's will. No, these words were coming from the Holy Spirit. I knew it so powerfully that I could practically feel light coming from my skin. I know this is an odd way to describe feeling that kind of power, but it is how I felt at that moment.

She stood and walked away toward the big window. "I don't think I am able to stay in this relationship."

I didn't know what to say, but the Lord put the next words in my mouth. "Then, your husband will receive all of the blessings of your temple covenants, including the eternal family blessings, and you will not."

She grew angry and stomped her foot. "I have been through hell to make this decision, and I don't think it is anyone's business but mine!"

I should have been terrified, but her words triggered a response from the Holy Spirit. I turned to her husband and said, "Can you bring me one of your kitchen chairs?"

He looked confused. I said, "I'm going to give you both a blessing. Is that acceptable to both of you?"

He nodded and left to get the chair. She nodded after a moment.

I placed my hands on her head. I felt very calm as the impressions came into my mind. It was a long time ago, but the message was simple. I commanded the spirit of anger and resentment to leave her. I told her that she was struggling not only with anger toward her husband but with anger toward the world. She had let that anger grow in her until the adversary had inflicted her with unseen enemies that now felt like her friends. When she was angry, they were happy and gave her a sense of righteous indignation, even pleasure. I told her that as long as she recognized the feeling of rising anger and realized it was coming from the adversary of her soul, she would be able reject it—and by doing this, keep those feelings away all the rest of her life.

I asked Brother Jones to sit, and as I recall, primarily told him to act in his role as the leader in his home, to quit walking away from his duties because of fear of his wife's anger, to always be kind and loving to his wife, and to be valiant in serving his family and the Lord.

I put on my jacket, shook their hands, and left them without further comment. That was thirty-three years ago, and they are still my friends, still married, and still pillars of strength in their ward. Sister Jones changed that day. For many years, I called her "Sunshine" because she was so cheery and pleasant to be around.

This is what I learned that day: You don't need to know any of the answers to serve with great effect. You don't need to be better educated, better informed, more experienced, or smarter than those you serve. You just need to have the humility to know your own nothingness; ears to hear; and the courage to go where He wants you to go, say what He wants you to say, and be what He wants you to be.

Brother John

Spectacular Failure

I promised you a tale of spectacular failure. What made it spectacular was that my failure, for reasons I don't understand, did not inhibit the Lord from pouring out the blessing I didn't have the courage to deliver.

This event occurred about 1995. I was sound asleep when the phone rang at about two o'clock in the morning. My first thought as I ran to the phone was that someone had died. It was my very good friend's wife on the phone. She was in tears and told me that her husband, my friend, was in the hospital. He was bleeding internally and was not expected to live through the night. She asked if I would please come and give him a blessing.

I told her I would be there as quickly as I could. I threw on my clothes and jumped into the car. While I drove, I prayed earnestly. Sometimes I know exactly what blessing to give, but most of the time I merely have peace without knowing beforehand what to say. In this rare case, I received both content and words. I was to bless him that he would be quickly healed, and that he would "spend the rest of the night in his own bed." It was exciting and a bit intimidating, but I knew it was his blessing to receive. All I had to do was say the words I had received.

I arrived at the emergency entrance of the hospital about an hour later. It was as busy as midday. People were scurrying around urgently. I had a hard time finding my friend; nobody seemed to know who or where he was.

I finally found him in a small curtained-off cubicle in the emergency ward. As I arrived, he looked as pale as the sheet he was lying on. He truly looked like he was dying. Nurses and doctors were urgently popping into his cubicle to do tests, draw blood, and consult. It seemed certain that there wouldn't be even thirty seconds of peace to give him a blessing. My poor friend looked so horrible, and his wife looked so scared, that I finally suggested we just give the blessing while people were coming and going.

I laid my hands on his head and had just barely begun when a doctor walked through the curtain talking loudly; seeing our heads bowed, he awkwardly excused himself to wait outside the curtain.

Then a nurse strode through, saw what I was doing, and stepped outside. I became rattled by the noise, the interruptions, the bustle, and by my friend's awful state. So instead of delivering the blessing I knew was his, I mealymouthed it. I spoke in general terms instead of specific promises. I spoke softly so as not to be heard easily, instead of with the surety I had felt earlier.

As soon as I finished, the nurses and doctors blasted back in. I quickly excused myself and left to go home.

The next day was Saturday, and I awoke early and called the hospital. They said my friend was no longer in the hospital, but they refused to give me any details. I truly feared he had died. I quickly called his home, and his wife answered. When I asked about him, she said brightly, "Oh, he was healed shortly after you gave him the blessing. We went home, and he spent the rest of the night in his own bed. He is perfectly fine now!"

I hung up the phone, feeling chastened and foolish. I had known the exact blessing my friend was to receive, but I hadn't found the courage to say the words. I have never forgotten that night or the price my fear could have cost my friend, if not for the grace of God. I praise the Lord that He saw fit to deliver the right blessing, in spite of my imperfect performance.

Brother John

The Mantle of Authority

*There is a spiritual phenomenon that is intrigu-*ing to watch and breathtaking to experience. It is when the mantle of a calling falls upon a newly called servant of God. It is one of the evidences of God's intimate involvement in the Church that bears His name. When someone is called by authority to an office, the Lord very rapidly upgrades and qualifies that person for the office. We call this rapid upgrading by God "receiving the mantle" of the office.

There is a real and powerful change that takes place due to the priesthood mantle. When the mantle settles upon someone, the spiritual gifts necessary for that office are received. No matter the calling or our prior spiritual growth, if we are humble, the Lord will graciously endow us with additional power, charity, and wisdom to bless the lives of His children through us. Some callings require the more profound complement of gifts and inspiration that that office deserves and requires.

I have seen men and women changed so dramatically that it is literally astonishing and glorious, like calling Lazarus forth from the tomb. I was also closely aware of one brother who was called who was not changed by the office. He remained the same as before and struggled in office. He was proud and self-promoting. He made many mistakes and offended many people. Less than a year after his calling, he confessed to certain crimes and ended up in prison for almost twenty years. The mantle will refuse to settle upon unworthy shoulders. Fortunately, this rarely happens.

I have seen bishops called who surprised me because I judged them to be a long ways from being prepared to be a bishop. Yet, by the next Sunday, the change had happened, the mantle had fallen, and they served long and well, with love and righteous inspiration. I have seen the same mantle fall upon Sunday School teachers, Primary choristers, Relief Society leaders, nursery coordinators, and every other calling.

I also watched it settle upon Thomas S. Monson. I always felt that Elder Monson was fairly jovial and carefree prior to President Hinckley's death. After Elder Monson was called and ordained as the prophet, there was a new greatness that settled upon him. He seemed older and wiser and a little more weighed down by his new office. By the next general conference, he was back to being strong and buoyant, but still sober and dignified. He spoke differently, wrote differently, and acted differently. This is the mantle, the upgrading that the Lord brings about to qualify those whom He calls.

Without it, God's church could not exist as it does today. Without this gift of mantle, few could serve in office without destroying the office and damaging the faith of those they serve. There are roughly twenty-eight thousand bishops, three thousand stake presidents, three hundred-forty mission presidents, fifty-five thousand missionaries, and fourteen million members. Just the fact that every person who serves is a lay servant without special training, ministerial degrees, or even crash course training is a vivid witness to the existence of this mantle and an equal witness that this is in fact Christ's church.

The mantle is like a super power the office holder must learn to use. It is a spiritual magnifying glass that takes every inspired act and amplifies it, making it sufficient for the office and for those it serves. It takes a simple prayer and opens the heavens. It takes a moment of silence and turns it into a vivid insight. It takes an awkward or challenging event and turns it into a teaching and saving moment. It takes a stumbling but willing servant and turns him or her into a man or woman of God, fully empowered to move the work onward.

When the release comes, it can be painful to feel the mantle lift. Where spirituality was so easy beneath the mantle, it now may return to a struggle as before the calling. Where once there were instant insight and sudden understanding, there may now be shade and shadow. When once the scriptures spoke to our souls in echoing thunder, now they may merely whisper their truths and force us to wield pick and shovel, just as before. Such is the case for every seeking mortal.

If you are presently in an office, wearing the mantle and feeling the spiritual power, I hope you see it clearly for what it is. This is the grace of Jesus Christ, amplifying you beyond your natural ability, beyond even your worthiness—and it will end. The only way to not stumble and fall to the ground after the mantle lifts is to do the things now, today, that you would have done before: study the scriptures diligently, seek in mighty prayer, repent, recognize your total dependence upon the Lord, fast with purpose, and most of all, not allow yourself to mistake this great gift as some evidence of personal greatness.

As Father said to Adam and Eve, "Dust thou art, and unto dust shalt thou return" (Genesis 3:19).

Brother John

The Holy Order

In March I posted a list of topics I intended to discuss on the UnBlog, and because of comments and questions (and chemo), I haven't gotten very far down the list. I would like to touch on one principle on that list that is of considerable relevance to the latter days—The Holy Order.

Throughout history have been a notable few who wrought mighty miracles by the priesthood of God: Moses dividing the Red Sea, Enoch moving mountains, Elijah and Elisha, and many others who possessed great power from God.

In the latter days of Zion, during the gathering and gleaning of the 144,000 throughout the world, this same "greater" priesthood power will again be manifest. Since, as we discussed earlier, *we* (meaning this dispensation) will become the 144,000 along with the returning citizens of Enoch's Zion, there must be a grand evolution from the functioning priesthood power we exhibit now into what we will wield in awe-inspired glory then.

The difference is merely this—that there is a "fulness of the priesthood" that we have been promised yet have not fully received. What we hold today is the priesthood of keys and presidency. We possess and righteously use all of the priesthood keys and temple ordinances. We possess the power by faith to heal the sick and administer to the faithful. But we do not presently possess a fulness of that same priesthood.

This is the way it should be. Nothing is amiss. This grand fulness of the priesthood and the Holy Order of those who possess it are not presently due upon the earth—but in my opinion shortly must be. When it is—when its time has come—then God will provide it through our living prophet.

These greater priesthood powers, this fulness of which we now speak, are always found possessed by those who have spoken to God face to face. In every case recorded in scripture, those who have companioned with deity returned with extraordinary gifts and powers.

Enoch was notable among these and was one of the greatest because of the gifts of translation he acquired for himself and his city. The scriptures refer to such people as belonging to the "order of Enoch which was after the order of the Only Begotten Son" (Doctrine & Covenants 76:57).

This Holy Order of the priesthood arises from the Melchizedek Priesthood commonly received by ordination in the latter-day Church. However, entering or obtaining this Holy Order includes a further endowment of the full power of godliness.

Those who become members of this Holy Order are called

"priests of the Most High." They are after the order of Melchizedek, who was translated (JST Genesis 14:25–40), which is after the order of Enoch, who was also translated, which is after the order of the Only Begotten Son, who possesses all powers of the priesthood, including those of translation, of course.

Joseph Smith's translation of Genesis 14 indicates how Melchizedek was ordained "after the order . . . of Enoch." Verse 34 indicates that Melchizedek followed Enoch's example, leading a Zion-like community that obtained a place in heaven. The Lord further explained that both Melchizedek and Enoch were "after the order of the Only Begotten Son" (Doctrine & Covenants 76:57). This relationship was reflected in the original name of the higher priesthood (see Doctrine & Covenants 107:3). (Richard O. Cowan, *Answers to Your Questions about the Doctrine and Covenants* [Salt Lake City: Deseret Book, 1996], 89.)

The promises and privileges we potentially enjoy in this dispensation are enormous, such that they have no peer in any previous dispensation. Our blessings are intended to be the most glorious ever offered to a people or a time.

> 9 Having made known unto us the mystery of his will, according to his good pleasure which he hath purposed in himself;
> 10 That in the dispensation of the fullness of times he might gather together in one all things in Christ, both which are in heaven, and which are on earth; even in him;
> 11 In whom also we have obtained an inheritance. (JST Ephesians 1:9–11)

Two of those glorious "things" that will be brought together from heaven and earth are Enoch's (former day) Zion from the heavens and Joseph's (latter day) Zion from the mortal earth. They will be combined in the dispensation wherein we live, and we have obtained an inheritance through Christ within those holy walls of Zion.

Then there will begin a glorious day of righteousness which all holy men saw in vision and longed to share but could not, because it was reserved for this last great dispensation.

> 11 Wherefore, hearken ye together and let me show unto you even my wisdom—the wisdom of him whom ye say is the God of Enoch, and his brethren,

12 Who were separated from the earth, and were received unto myself—a city reserved until a day of righteousness shall come—a day which was sought for by all holy men, and they found it not because of wickedness and abominations. (Doctrine & Covenants 45:11–12)

Enoch's people did not at that time establish the Zion that would remain on the earth, because it was reserved until the latter days, a time when wickedness and abominations would be swept away by the closing scenes of all time. In their day, the world wasn't ready. There were many generations left to come to the earth and much work to be done—including the birth and Atonement of Christ.

In order to build Zion, we are instructed to become the priests of the Most High, after the order of Enoch, which will then usher in this last great dispensation of peace. Consider this following quotation:

53 And who overcome by faith, and are sealed by the Holy Spirit of promise, which the Father sheds forth upon all those who are just and true.

54 They are they who are the church of the Firstborn.

55 They are they into whose hands the Father has given all things—

56 They are they who are priests and kings, who have received of his fulness, and of his glory;

57 And are priests of the Most High, after the order of Melchizedek, which was after the order of Enoch, which was after the order of the Only Begotten Son (Doctrine & Covenants 76:53–57)

There is power in these words we don't dare misread. When one becomes a member of an order, one assumes the attributes and abilities of all other members of that order. This is the very reason it is called an order, because all the members are alike in the attributes that define the order.

Thus, to be a member of the order of Enoch is to possess the priesthood of Enoch and the powers Enoch possessed, including the powers of translation and his unmatched command of the earth and her elements. To be after the order of Melchizedek is to possess all of Melchizedek's gifts, which included translation. To be after the order of the Only Begotten Son is to possess all the powers of heaven, which is what the Father covenants to bestow upon us as noted in verse 55.

Observe that those who are sealed by the Holy Spirit of promise are the Church of the Firstborn. Furthermore, when the referenced time comes for this verse to be fulfilled, then they have (not shall have at some future date, but *will* have) received all things.

How? How may we seek and acquire such a lofty blessing? The answer is simple: Seek the face of the Lord through the gospel plan and priesthood promises we currently possess, and while in Christ's presence, request it of Him personally.

Herein lies temple power: we are being taught and thereby invited into the presence of the Lord, there to request these blessings of priesthood, privilege, and Zion.

Brother John

Grace in Times of Need

My Dear UnBlog Family,

I received the results of my latest CT scan yesterday: "No visible cancer." In my case, this is unexpected and rare. My doctor is cautiously amazed and somewhat mystified. I will have to keep doing chemo, but at a reduced dose, with more of a life in between. This truly is grace in times of need.

I thought you would like to rejoice with me!

Brother John

The Journey Home
Part VIII: Beloved Friends and Family

For over two years after we came to Utah, Johnnie and I felt like kids playing in a shiny new playground, feeling childlike joy in fresh discovery, laughing together in the warm sunlight, and delighting in the sand between our toes. We counted every moment a gift from God. Our days alternated between chemotherapy, grandchildren tearing through the house, charming moonlight strolls by the lake, firesides with astonishing people, more of the dreaded chemo—and always, always the UnBlog.

In 2011, John (through a series of miraculous circumstances) met a compelling man who is known as "Spencer." That day changed John's life because he not only found a new friend, but he also discovered another facet of his mission on this side of the veil. The two eventually audio-recorded Spencer's near-death experiences, and John wrote them into Visions of Glory. I can tell you that Spencer, like John, is a good and sincere man, and after personally coming to know him and feeling the spirit that he brings, I believe that Spencer truly experienced what is recorded in that book. I am so grateful that in the last months of his life, John was finally able to meet this beloved friend who blessed our lives tremendously.

It seemed to me that the culmination of my husband's mortal journey was the "UnBlog Family Reunion," which was initially requested by the UnBloggers themselves. Through reading John's blogs, responding with their own commentary, and reading the commentary of others, those "UnBloggers" had truly become a family. Some of them expressed a desire to John that they would like to meet together in a type of reunion, although they lived all over the world. And so on September 1, 2012, just three months before John's passing, many hundreds of "UnBloggers" met together for one glorious afternoon and evening. Being with them was a joy I know John will never forget, in this life or in eternity.

But the very next day, John's health seemed to decline. His life's work seemed to be finished, and through the Spirit he knew and accepted that fact with graciousness and surrender, all the while continuing to believe every promise he had personally been given by the Lord. John's mantra had always been, "Be faithful, be fearless, be patient." And he was. But the next few months would teach him what it truly means to endure to the end.

—Terri

Chapter Nine

Perfected in Christ

Perfect in Christ

Like you, I have labored my whole life to try to understand what actually constitutes being righteous and then to do all of those things all of the time. I have since come to understand that this approach does not work.

I have discovered that for me there are just too many "things"—acts, commandments, assignments, jobs, and callings—to do all of them all of the time. Discipline simply is a smaller horse than mortal weakness, and when you hitch them back-to-back, discipline will always be dragged backward until it simply must give up and start over. This is a matter of divine design. No amount of good works or faithful acts can make one righteous.

Before someone chokes to death on that statement, let me quickly add that there is a path that includes works, which does not lose the tug-of-war to human weakness, does not exhaust us, and is sweet and joyful.

It is also very challenging, but it almost instantly makes anyone who crosses that line *righteous*.

The line we must cross is this: Christ considers those who hear and obey His voice to be righteous, and those who can't or won't hear His voice to be wicked.

Consider Alma 5:37–39:

> 37 O ye workers of iniquity; ye that are puffed up in the vain things of the world, ye that have professed to have known the ways of righteousness nevertheless have gone astray, as sheep having no shepherd, notwithstanding a shepherd hath called after you and is still calling after you, but ye will not hearken unto his voice!
>
> 38 Behold, I say unto you, that the good shepherd doth call you;

yea, and in his own name he doth call you, which is the name of Christ; *and if ye will not hearken unto the voice of the good shepherd, to the name by which ye are called, behold, ye are not the sheep of the good shepherd.*

39 And now if ye are not the sheep of the good shepherd, of what fold are ye? Behold, I say unto you, that the devil is your shepherd, and ye are of his fold; and now, who can deny this? Behold, I say unto you, whosoever denieth this is a liar and a child of the devil.

I mentioned that there is a way to instantly become righteous; here is how it works. Since those who hearken to Christ's voice become His sheep, and are of His fold (which is another of our phrases meaning "righteous"), then to commit, to covenant, and to dedicate oneself to always hear and always obey, is to become righteous in that instant. Our Shepherd may lead us through a process of repentance and purification, but even during that walk we are considered righteous, and a righteous walk will in time yield "righteous-ness."

Best of all is that since Christ's voice is living, it is also kind, loving, and understanding. It leads us to obedience that is within the scope of our abilities. We need never be overwhelmed because not only are we led by Christ but He also strengthens and uplifts us, making us more and more like Him. In time, His voice leads us where *we* want to go, because His will, His desires, and His joys have become ours. In other words, we have become "one" with Him.

We will never, in this lifetime, become perfect in our own right. But when we employ all of our heart, mind, and strength in obeying His voice, and trusting in His empowerment, then is His grace sufficient for us (Moroni 10:33). In other words, He will atone for those things wherein we err and give us with His strength to overcome all along the way.

In this state of grace, then, we become righteous "in Christ." We have "come unto Christ and [been] perfected in Him" (Moroni 10:32). Under the umbrella of His Atonement, we will have qualified—not earned, but qualified—as one who is at last "perfect in Christ."

32 Yea, come unto Christ, and be perfected in him, and deny yourselves of all ungodliness; and if ye shall deny yourselves of all ungodliness,

and love God with all your might, mind and strength, then is his grace sufficient for you, that by his grace ye may be perfect in Christ; and if by the grace of God ye are perfect in Christ, ye can in nowise deny the power of God. (Moroni 10:32)

As Moroni explains, we are never perfect in and of ourselves, but only perfect in Christ. We cannot *perfect* ourselves either; only Christ can perfect us. Our part is to love God so completely that we choose to listen and obey His voice—in other words, deny ourselves of all ungodliness. When we do, His grace becomes sufficient, and we are changed and made perfect in Christ. Then after receiving this gift of grace and its accompanying perfections, we must never deny and forever acknowledge that it was *His* power that perfected us, and it was *His* power that made us "righteous."

For some, this concept may challenge your present understanding. But if you will determine today to be unwaveringly obedient to the voice of the Spirit, you will discover for yourself that this process of being perfected in Christ is the joyful way to perfection—and the only way that really works.

Brother John

A Goddess in Embryo

I would like to tell you about a friend of mine. I will call her Lynne. I first met Lynne about twenty-five years ago while teaching adult Institute classes in Alaska.

We met in the high council room and sat around the big table. It was a lovely setting; each student had a place for books and scriptures, and I had a wide whiteboard behind me. We were studying the Book of Mormon, part one. It was nearly Christmastime and a time of partaking of the processes of spiritual growth with special people. We soared and rejoiced as we searched the scriptures together. The Holy Spirit was often strong in our classes.

About the fourth Sunday evening we met, a young woman walked into the room and sat away from the table, in a corner of the room. Her hair was unkempt, her clothing was heavy and worn. I walked around the room and introduced myself. She smelled of wood smoke and burned meat. She said her name was Lynne. She smiled shyly through yellowed and missing teeth and sat abruptly, looking away.

During the next few months, Lynne said absolutely nothing. She declined to participate, she would not comment, she would not read scriptural passages, and she would not look up. She often arrived late and left early to avoid the need to interact. But she always came, and she always followed along in her manual, making copious notes on a spiral-bound notebook. The only time I heard sounds come from her lips was when I stumbled on a scripture reference. I would say something like, "I don't know the verse, but there is a verse in Moroni that says—" and she would whisper the exact reference I was looking for. She knew them all, and she was never mistaken.

I found out as the class progressed that Lynne had a checkered past. She had been on a mission and then lost her membership in the Church. She married a guy who abused her kids. He ended up in prison, and she ended up penniless. Her two boys were in perpetual legal trouble, and one of them spent time in prison as well.

It was near the end of the semester when we were discussing how the scriptures had blessed our lives. I knew Lynne loved the scriptures, and I hoped she would have a few words to say. I asked every member of the class in turn to say just one or two sentences of testimony. I saw Lynne look up at me in fear. I smiled at her and nodded reassurance.

I forgot about Lynne and was listening to the sweet testimonies. Suddenly, it was Lynne's turn. She was not sitting at the table, but on a back row of chairs, her head bowed. I looked at Lynne, who was struggling to find words to say, and to my great astonishment, I saw a vision.

Instantly, I found myself standing in a beautiful sunken garden. There were four white stone pathways rising up a few marble steps out of the small formal garden I was in. Exquisite flowers and sculpted bushes filled the space with beauty and sweet perfume. The pathways led away from the center of the garden, where I was standing. The light was more yellow or golden than normal, and the flowers were more pinks, mauves, and pastels than the bright colors one normally associates with flowers. Each flower seemed to be singing in its soul, rejoicing and radiating love and faith. I found myself completely enthralled by the experience.

I sensed someone and looked up. A short distance away, a beautiful woman was walking toward me. She looked to me like a goddess in a long, white, gossamer dress. She literally glowed with righteousness and was so stunningly beautiful that I could scarcely look at her. I felt like a bashful little boy, out of place and at a loss for words. She radiated love and joy. She walked down the steps and toward me with such grace and confidence that I did not know how to address her, or even if I was worthy to talk to her.

She stopped and smiled broadly, as if she knew a secret. I was astonished to feel that she loved me. She waited a moment and then asked, "You don't recognize me, do you?"

"I'm so sorry, but I really don't," was my reply.

She smiled so happily that I felt my soul overflowing with joy. She took both of my hands in hers and said, "I'm Lynne, from your Institute class."

The vision closed up, and I found myself looking at the mortal version of this glorious, celestial being. No time had elapsed, and our mortal Lynne was still struggling. Finally, she just shook her head in shame and leaned back into her chair. I nodded at the next class member, and the discussion progressed around the room.

Now, this was astonishing enough, and the message was clear enough, but it is not the end of the story. I went home and wrote about this in my journal, but I never spoke to any other person about it. This sudden vision of a lowly and self-abused human's true worth has deeply affected me and has shown up in my novels a time or two, but the event is real, and I saw what I saw.

Nearly ten years later, I was serving in a bishopric and was walking through the stake center late one Sunday afternoon. By sheer chance, I happened upon Lynne in the hallway. She was pacing back and forth. She still looked worn and tattered. Her hair and clothing were still the same, and she still smelled of wood smoke. The only thing I could see different was that she was older, and she was very angry.

I greeted her. "How are you, Lynne?"

She shook my hand one pump and yanked her hand back. "I'm

here to get my name taken off the records of the church," she said. It was practically the first time I had ever heard her speak a complete sentence, and it was not the one I had expected.

"Why is that?" I asked.

She explained how someone had deeply offended her and embarrassed her so badly that now she couldn't even come to church anymore, because everyone looked at her differently now. She had the signed letter in her hand, ready to give to the stake president. Her appointment was in a few minutes.

The same vision I had seen many years ago came forcefully to mind; the memory of it was as fresh and astonishing as when I had first seen it. I asked her to give me a few minutes. She looked at her watch and nodded.

I told her of that day, sitting there hoping she would say something in class, and then suddenly seeing her in vision, so full of light and righteousness, glowing so gloriously that I deemed her to be a goddess. I told her about how I knew that of all the people on earth, she, herself, did not understand her own worth, her own glorious soul, and how deeply she is beloved of God. Why else would God show me that vision, I asked her, other than for His love of her, so that at this critical moment I could tell her who she really is?

Lynne wept. I wept. She pulled the letter from her coat pocket, ripped it up, and dropped it in a trash can. She shook my hand warmly, forced her chin up where it belongs, and walked from the church.

I have seen Lynne many times since over the years, and her hair and clothing are still worn and tattered. But she holds her chin up, and her face glows as she smiles and speaks, because she finally is beginning to know who she is.

It was a loving and tender mercy that filled my heart and senses with her true worth. I have often wondered at Father's love for Lynne, at the goddess she inwardly is, and I am ever grateful for the privilege it was to be there for her at that critical moment.

From what I saw of her then, I still think she is underestimating her worth a great deal. I think we all are. If we all could only see ourselves as Christ does, if we could only realize what Christ can and will make of us, we would never hang our heads again.

Brother John

Purity that Parts the Veil

*I*n my thinking there are two aspects to purity. The first and most understandable is an absence of sin. Little needs to be said about sinlessness, except to note that it is through the grace of Christ and through obedience to the voice of the Holy Spirit that we become as sin free as mortals may.

The second type of purity is more difficult to grasp and, therefore, to achieve. In my opinion, this type of purity may best be described as an unfettered soul, or a heart that is unpolluted by lies and false ideas.

This purity is more than an absence of sin. It is an inspired pattern of believing that is unpolluted by the mental refuse mortality dumps into our souls.

Throughout life, much of what we are taught by the world is lies. We are taught we're not popular because we're fat-skinny-tall-short-white-black-different, or we're unlovable, or we're a bad boy, or that we "have" a temper just like Dad—and we believe these things, because smart people told us so. Some "big person" tells us we're naughty, and we believe it and act it out for the rest of our lives. We experience something very unpleasant in our childhood (like fried liver or not knowing what to say when bearing testimony for the first time) and avoid a repeat experience for the rest of mortality—even though that thing is wholesome and even valuable. We come to fiercely believe what we have experienced and use avoidance, anger, resentment, hate, and even irrational behavior to avoid things that we believe are true.

It's amazing how many decisions most adults are still acting upon that happened prior to their second birthdays.

"I must make people happy, or they will not like me."

"Eat all your food, or children will go hungry in India."

"Mothers yell at their kids."

"Fathers almost never come home."

"Church is boring."

"I get the most attention when I am sick—naughty—funny—cute—complimentary—disobedient" or any of a thousand other behaviors.

Other lies encompass relationships, body issues, philosophies of men, educational fallacies, corrupt politics, false doctrines, false religion, false tradition, and every aspect of our mortal experience and what we believe our world to be.

These lies can fester in our being for years and years until, in time, we come to accept and embrace them as truth. These incorrect beliefs seem simple and innocent, but they are lies that originate from the evil one, and we can't approach the veil with lies in our heart.

If the pure in heart shall see God, then the *impure* in heart shall never see God.

In the beginning, our minds are like a beautiful white wall beside a busy road. Mud and dirt get splashed on our wall by careless drivers, especially during rain storms and adversity. Although mud is slung, we only become impure when it sticks. Remember that we aren't only becoming impure by sin but also through the unavoidable processes of this mortal existence. To embrace the dirt as being a part of our structure is to not understand our true identity as spirit beings or our true potential. To be able to view these smudges as pollution that is foreign to our most intrinsic goodness is to strip them of their power and to coat our souls with spiritual Teflon.

Eliminating these lies is an inspired step toward that purity of heart, which, when achieved, allows us to see God. So how do we acquire such an ethereal form of purity? How do we jettison the baggage of mortality of which we may not even be aware?

The answer is that such highly refined purity is a function of humility and of a willingness to let the Lord sequentially purge us of these impurities. Through the workings of the Holy Spirit, He teaches us the real truth about ourselves and everything and everyone else. This process often involves experiences that bring the baggage to the surface, where we may unwittingly use it to hurt ourselves or others. The Holy Spirit then quietly corrects or chastises. If we chose to humbly comply, He starts purifying our inner self, and a tiny circle of pure white appears on our mud-spattered wall.

Over and over, the Holy Spirit communicates truth in small things: speak kindly, say you're sorry, ask for forgiveness, walk away, abandon your pride, put it back, pick it up, and on and on. As we choose to obey, the Spirit rejoices and purifies us from the inside out. If we have a difficult time in acting upon what we are inspired to do, we plead with the Lord for His grace and assistance, which He always gives to the sincere seeker. Thus, the impurities that have nothing to do with sin are triumphantly conquered.

The wise man looks beyond the obvious and sees a larger process at work than just driving the speed limit when prompted to do so. The Holy Spirit is asking us to lay aside our pride, to submit to law, or to learn any of dozens of lessons that stand between us and purity. If they weren't important to our salvation, the Holy Spirit would be silent on them.

Things like love, kindness, forgiveness, charity, mercy, service, and a correct understanding of who and what we are matter deeply to our salvation. Therefore, the Holy Spirit speaks, and the Holy Spirit empowers. To abandon the arrogance of "This is who I am— deal with it" and to let the forces of divinity reshape us is to yield to the Holy Spirit and put off the natural man, replacing him with that purity, which ultimately parts the veil.

Brother John

Consecration Made Easy

There is a simple elegance about the way the Lord's program works. It is not complex, though it may be complex in the blessings it bestows. But the actual process is very simple. That process is—start where you are, hearken to the voice of the Holy Spirit in the things of your everyday life, and when the next "line" or "precept" appears before you, embrace it through obedience.

We all have a comfort zone of things we are willing to do. Let's consider Brother Joe Mythical, who goes to church and pays a full tithing. He does about half of his home teaching. He calls family prayers twice a week or so after his wife urges him, and he feels guilty about not doing Family Home Evening but is uncomfortable trying to do it. He'll give a priesthood blessing if someone really needs it and asks many times, but he has to desperately pray and mentally prepare for a while to get ready, and then he doesn't really know what to say. He doesn't study the scriptures but does read the Ensign occasionally. He is the second counselor in the elders quorum but doesn't really understand his duties. He goes to the temple a few times a year when he feels a need, or as a date with his wife, but he doesn't understand it. He prays almost the same prayer each night before going to bed. He wants spiritual blessings, but he does not see them happening around him, and he wonders what is wrong.

What Brother Joe doesn't know is that his life has several thousand "lines" of spiritual enticement dangling before him. All day long, the Holy Spirit is urging him to upgrade his spiritual performance in every aspect of his life. Every decision he makes, every time he "forgets" family prayers or overlooks home teaching once again or prays without real feeling, the Holy Spirit is reminding and urging him to choose a better course. If Brother Joe hearkens to even one prompting, his life will begin to change. All it takes is one "hearkening" to begin. He will then feel the Spirit more loudly in other parts of his life, and other spiritual "lines" will become more apparent and joyful.

If he chose to hearken to all of the promptings he receives, in a very short time he would be receiving answers to his prayers; feeling joy in service; and experiencing revelations, bursts of spiritual truth and understanding, power in the priesthood, guidance in family and personal matters, and greater love for his family. And every other aspect of his life would rocket spiritually higher. However, right now Brother Joe isn't ready to hearken to *every* prompting, because this seems like a grim sacrifice that he is not yet willing to make.

Every act of obedience seems to require a sacrifice large or small. Staying on your knees an additional couple of minutes is sacrificing your tired body's will to your spirit's unending desire to return to God. Each act of obedience is sacrificing our mortal will to the will of God.

What one learns over time, however, is that *nothing we do is actually a sacrifice.* We can never make God a debtor, because every act of obedience is immediately repaid with a blessing far greater than whatever it cost us in sacrifice to qualify to get it (Mosiah 2:24). There is a divine accounting about these things that always keeps us in the Lord's debt. When a spiritual pilgrim discovers this—when we truly gain a testimony that every apparent sacrifice actually blesses our lives, opens the windows of heaven, and qualifies us for greater inspiration and greater blessings—then it no longer feels like drudgery, a challenge, or a sacrifice to obey. It becomes a joy to hear the Holy Spirit urge us to some additional obedience, because it is seen by the believing heart as an additional dispensation of blessings for which we pay very little.

Having learned by inspired experience, by walking the path of obedience and observing the divine arithmetic of obedience, there comes a powerful assurance of the love of God and of His guiding and blessing hand in your life. This is when the erstwhile pilgrim, now the spiritual warrior for Christ, looks around and asks the Lord what His will is for him or her today: "To whom shall I go? Where would you have me serve? How can I serve and honor Thee today? What would You have me do?" The simple answers enter like flashes of joy. "Call family prayers. Do your home teaching," We receive them just as before, but this time we are under divine commission. Christ grants us a brighter knowledge of how to pray, how to succor, how to bless and uplift and testify of Christ's love.

From there, the voice of revelation proceeding from the lips of Christ leads us to all other "lines" and "precepts" that make us priests and priestesses in His service. We are endowed with power, and in the Light of Christ we see through the dim glass of mortality more clearly.

This is "consecration made easy": you begin where you are right now and choose to obey. This is a divinely ordained progression that will bring you from any plateau upon which you presently stand to these greater blessings you seek but can't even comprehend. It will all roll out before you like a heavenly red carpet upon which you may walk with feet quickened by joy and perfect faith.

> Then shall thy confidence wax strong in the presence of God; and the doctrine of the priesthood shall distil upon thy soul as the dews from heaven. The Holy Ghost shall be thy constant companion, and thy scepter an unchanging scepter of righteousness and truth; and thy dominion shall be an everlasting dominion, and without compulsory means it shall flow unto thee forever and ever. (Doctrine & Covenants 121:45–46)

The best part is that it does not take a long time. These changes can be made in Alma the Younger style if we can make as determined a choice as did Alma. Most often, it is a journey made longer by ignorance of how to remain on the path, kind of like riding a bicycle in traffic with no understanding of the handlebars or brakes. There will be some spectacular failures. But when we finally understand the "easiness of the way" (Alma 37:46) and turn our whole souls to Christ, the resulting blessings and spiritual power will flood into our lives faster than we can receive them.

Brother John

Doing Less, Being More

I would like to speak to the brethren for a moment. Being a male, and being endowed with the full range of the weaknesses of guy-ness, I want to issue a call to reach further than we are.

Brethren, for many years, I took a lot of license because I was so busy with my profession, with the Church, and with family, that I excused myself from the heavy lifting of creating profound righteousness in my own life and soul. I just figured there is only so much a mortal can do, and I focused upon those things I could lay my hands upon, touch, and turn with a wrench. I don't want you to misunderstand—I was very active in the Church, working in every way for family and home, and doing a lot of cooking, cleaning, and washing dishes to be a good husband.

It took a tragedy in my life to realize that I was avoiding the most important thing of all. When the tragedy came, I was not prepared to call down constant revelation for the solution, to get immediate answers to my prayers, and to work miracles in my world. I was handicapped spiritually. I had been so busy *doing* righteous things, that I had failed to *become* righteous.

It was during this and subsequent crises that I began to spend hours on my knees (precious hours I usually needed for sleep) in deep, mighty, pleading prayer. It was at that time that I began to fast whenever prompted (usually during demanding times at work, when I knew it could only harm my job performance). It was then that I realized I had been "doing" the gospel, and "doing" my family, and "doing" my marriage without much inspiration or feeling. I was using the same determination to "do a good job" that I had learned in the hayfields and corn rows of my youth, to "do a good job" at my adult life.

Eventually, I gave it up. I realized I could no longer "do" everything and be everything for everyone. I laid down that yoke of perfect "doing" with a broken heart, realizing that I had failed. Then over a period of years, I learned to take upon myself Christ's yoke through obeying His voice, and I learned to serve Him instead of myself or anyone else.

And guess what? He told me to get up each morning and go to work, just as before. But this time I went in His name, with His guidance, and it was a joy instead of drudgery. Jesus Christ sent me on my Church assignments, but they were now guided by revelation and power, and I felt the full joy of Christ as I served Him—where I had been serving the Church, or my fellowman, or something else before.

I was a better husband, a better daddy, and a better man. More than that, I was a disciple of Christ. I had learned to quit "doing" my life and just to walk in Christ's divine grace. All of these other things—things which I had laid down, things wherein I had failed to fully "do" everything I knew I should—Christ did with my hands, and they were all done in a way that blessed everyone as He would have done.

Shortly after that, Christ asked me to write a book about that journey. I obeyed, with a great sense of inadequacy. But it was His work, and the book is still in print eighteen years later.

I don't remotely claim to have been perfect in anything—only obedient, or as obedient as my ongoing imperfections allow—but it has mercifully been enough to make my life a joy. In the things I used to "do," His voice now leads the way to His glory, not mine.

I find I like it that way.

Brethren, my hope is only this, that we can stop "doing" so much, and "become," in Christ, men of God whose word can, if called upon, move a mountain or raise the dead, because I suspect the time is approaching when these things will need to happen, long before we will see them coming and have time to prepare.

If you lack a place to start, here are a few ideas:

Stop believing you can "do" it all—because sooner or later, you will find you can't.

Listen carefully for the Holy Spirit to lead you, and walk with courage in that light.

Fast every time you are prompted, no matter how hard or inconvenient it may seem.

Pray a minimum of twenty minutes a day, and longer when prompted. Learn to pray while the Holy Spirit is guiding you. This is the gateway to miracles, profound revelation, and promised blessings.

Open the scriptures again and study them, search them, read them by subject, mark them, write in your journal about them, and pray over every concept. Don't read them sequentially from beginning to end, but let the Holy Spirit show you each day where to read.

In all your doing, allow Christ to "make" you more.

Brother John

Be Ye Therefore Perfect

I would like to speak to the sisters as I recently addressed the brethren in "Doing Less, Being More."

Sisters, I think many of you suffer from the same malady as men, but to some order of magnitude greater. You expect more of yourselves, you love more and serve more and demand more of yourselves—and because of this virtue, you get much more tightly ensnared in "doing" your lives, and "doing" your families, and everything else that your kind hearts tell you must be done in order for you to be perfect.

God commanded, "*Be* ye therefore perfect," not "*Do* ye therefore perfect."

Jesus Christ obtained His perfection at long last by obedience to His Father's voice. He did only those things that the Father showed Him to do. Everything else He simply didn't do. Thus, He "became" perfect—though He did not "do" everything perfectly, according to some telestial standard. Why do I say that? Because I'm sure there were times when He could have healed someone who wanted it and desperately needed it but who wasn't prepared for it. So He passed them by, not "doing" the healing because He was "being" perfect, which required obedience to a law higher than immediate healing. Thus, He was perfect in all His "being" and "doing," because He always did as the Father directed.

Jesus Christ set the standard for perfection by obedience to His Father and now asks us, as His spiritually begotten sons and daughters, to hear His voice and likewise become perfect in Him by going where He sends us, and being all He asks us to be. In this obedience, He will apply the empowering grace of the Atonement, which will cause us to "be" perfect—not because we get everything done, but because we are perfectly obedient, as was Christ.

Somewhere in that female mixture of life there may also be a slight resentment or feeling of inferiority, or a suspicion that others may secretly deem you inferior—partly because of how history has treated women, and partly because the Church is patriarchal in its leadership.

First of all, sisters, know and trust that God will richly, profoundly, and perfectly compensate you (as well as the brethren) for every injustice you or your predecessors have ever had to endure. God is not capable of respecting one person, sex, or race above the other, and He values His precious daughters equally as much as He values His precious sons. This is not a platitude; it is a fact of divine law. In eternity, God has reserved every blessing for you that He has reserved for His sons. It may not appear so to the myopic telestial eye, but if you inquire of the Lord, you will be given to know that this is absolutely the case. Believe it, trust in it.

Not knowing or understanding that truth, some sisters stumble upon feelings that they have been (or are being) mistreated, and they militate against the obviously male-dominated world. Some lose their testimonies and resent the present order of the Church, or what they perceive it to be. Some engage in power struggles at home and radiate resentment when they feel less than in command or that their opinion is not appropriately valued. Some withhold their godly grace, nurturing love, or physical love when they feel such is not deserved.

Likewise, some men fight against taxes, some against gun control, some against government in general, some against a rival sports team, some against an unfair employer, or an unfair marriage. Some men are abrupt, mean, and abusive at home and elsewhere to prove some lie about how "real men" really are, or that they have a right to control or belittle at will, or to prove that masculinity is superior to femininity.

The truth above all other truths is that these mini-wars we are waging are sucking the virtue out of our lives. We were sent here to prove that we would "do all things whatsoever the Lord their God command them," not necessarily to see if we would rise to the cause of gun control or equal rights. All these earthly battles will pass away in the fiery blast that cleanses the earth, and then the supposed kings, queens, and captains of these tiny empires will wish the mountains could fall upon them to hide them from their shame of long disobedience.

Clearly, God does call some people to fight these outward battles, to stand up in politics, and defend what is right. He occasionally inspires some to champion unlikely causes. He sends inspired women into battles wherever gentle and godly hands can heal. He sends inspired generals into critical battles and empowers men and women whose only weapon is a pen to start nations, record scripture, and defeat evil.

But mostly, He calls us to take our place at the head of the table and call family prayers. Mostly He calls us to lay kindly hands upon unkind people and speak loving words to someone presently unlovable, to dispense compassionate service, and to be a loving and forgiving spouse whose "weapons of war" were long ago buried deep in the ground, lest we impale our immortal souls upon them.

Sisters, I urge you, do not withhold the power of your grace. This divine, nurturing grace—which, like Christ, you give to someone because it is needed but not deserved—is the balm of Gilead to your husbands, to your children, to the Church, and to the world. We need your grace. We need your forgiveness. We need your strength. We need you.

These acts of Christlike obedience and grace and resultant "being" are what truly define us now in mortality and in the day of judgment. God bless us all of us, men and women, to see the real battles that stand between us and salvation. And God bless us to trust Christ to empower us to win them.

Brother John

The Comfortable Deception

Judging by the sheer number of comments on the UnBlog "Be Not Deceived," I am going to declare "Avoiding Deception" as the greatest concern of the UnBlog family we have uncovered so far.

The problem with a deception is that it's so deceiving, if you know what I mean. Another way to say this is that the very nature of a deception is that it's believable, logical, and plausible, and when you buy into it, you become comfortable that you are not being deceived—hence the power of deception.

If you study a rat in a maze, from your lofty perspective, it is easy to see when the rat is deceived, because no matter how hard it tries, it doesn't know where each passage leads and keeps running from dead end to dead end, rarely getting to the end of the maze to get its treat.

Like the rat, the way we can tell if we are deceived is if we keep running from dead end to dead end but never really realize the great blessings (or treats) of the gospel—which are living with faith, hope, charity, miracles, angelic visitations, power in the priesthood, revelation, prophecy, and true joy in our lives, along with not feeling defeated, lost, or overwhelmed by the gospel or its requirements, and having a bright hope that any spiritual goal is attainable.

I believe the key to finding the end of the maze is to prayerfully and with mighty intent ask God *how* to get to where you think you should be. If you are seeking to be born again or to experience your Calling and Election or to have a better relationship with your teenager or whatever, just ask with real intent how to get there, and then yield the direction of your life into Christ's hands. Let Him shepherd you to where you desire to be. Don't worry about the details; just let go and let God. And then be willing to flawlessly obey His voice at all costs.

What I suspect will happen is that your life will be changed. You will experience some event or spiritual epiphany that redirects your thinking, devotions, wants, and desires. When you determine that this enlightenment aligns with the scriptures and the living prophet, choose to yield to this new direction. After a while—perhaps a long while—you will find yourself at your desired destination. It will just amazingly appear before you as you walk the sweet path that Christ leads you down.

I think most of the time we place far too much emphasis on "I can do this! I am determined to seek and find! I am going to work and work until I overcome this! I'm going to knock really hard and watch it open!"

It sounds great, but the problem with every one of these declarations is the "I" in the statement. Really, "I" can't do anything, because "I" am a fallen man, and "I" am not capable of any great spiritual accomplishment. Unregenerated in Christ, and in this fallen mortal state, "I" truly am nothing. The only thing "I" can do is to yield my life into the hands of the loving Christ, and then "We"—meaning my Savior and I—"can do this! We are going to seek and find! We are going to knock and behold it opening up before us!" And then, together you do.

My humble point is that we need to quit running like rats from here to there, trying to conquer the maze using our shortsighted rationale and limited abilities, and just ask Christ to take us to the treat. We do the walking . . . Christ shows us the way. But this means we are not tricked by that comfortable deception that includes the word "I."

"I" have failed many times. "We" never have.

Brother John

Holy and without Spot

Mention to someone "I'm surprised you're not translated yet," and they take the compliment to mean they're almost perfect! I even jokingly use it that way sometimes. But the truth is a little different. The requirements to qualify for any gospel blessing don't include perfection. It's always about obedience.

Here's how it works. We come to understand some principle or requirement of the gospel. Let's assume it's something hard for you, like giving up smoking or pornography. Conquering these things doesn't require perfection or perfect discipline or perfect control of our lives. It requires obedience.

When we obey some principle of truth, we in that way "deny [ourselves] of . . . ungodliness" (Moroni 10:32). When we do, "then is his grace sufficient for you." The practical application of this is that when we love God enough to obey Him, no matter the cost to ourselves, then the grace of Christ changes us so that over time we no longer desire the sin.

We obey, though still riddled with doubt, weakness, and mortal addiction. We submit because it is right and because we love God—and then He changes us. The addiction loses its pull. The sin loses its fantasy. With repeated and ongoing obedience, the pain or weakness lifts from our heads, and then we miraculously become "perfect in Christ."

As Moroni tells us, we cannot become "perfect" because of our acts, our works, or our strength. All we have done is to "deny ourselves." This is an act of discipline that we can do by our will, but we cannot change our inner man by an act of will. One can stop speaking curses and still have them echoing in the mind. One can stop looking at porn but still be overwhelmed with desire. We can't change the desire or our natures. Mortal man can only control the act. So, we accept our limitation, bow our heads, and "deny ourselves."

The motivation we deploy in choosing to deny ourselves is all-important. Just denying ourselves because the sin is destroying our life isn't a pure motive. The only motive that really works is when we do it because we "love God with all [our] might, mind, and strength." The divine word then goes on to say, "Then is his grace sufficient for you, that by his grace ye may be perfect in Christ" (Moroni 10:32).

I consider that *wanting* to quit any sin—being willing to deny ourselves—is an easier mind-set to acquire than wanting to do it because *we love God* with all our might, mind, and strength. As an example, it's easier to want to quit smoking because it's a nasty habit than wanting to quit because of our love of God, which love propels us to change.

I also believe that getting our motives pure is the hardest part of repentance. This is where the hours upon the knees, fasting, and weeping come into powerful play. Not only can we pray for forgiveness but also for a *desire* to repent. Just as powerfully, we can also pray for a *desire* to have a *desire* to repent. In other words, a very powerful prayer in claiming the grace of God to change us is to pray for our motives to become pure, so that we are doing it because we now love God with all our might, mind, and strength.

It might be easier to see this process in a series of steps.

Step One: Obtain a pure motive. We do this through fasting and prayer and by doing things that bring the Holy Spirit into our lives. This may be the hardest step of all, but it is eternally essential. Pray for the desire to have a desire to want to love God—or however many iterations you lag behind. Such prayers do work. And then pray that you will feel that love of God in your bosom.

Step Two: When your motive is pure, then deny yourself of that ungodliness. Don't worry about everything else. The point is not to be perfect; it is to be obedient. Just do the one thing right. For this to work, it must be a lifelong commitment, not another attempt or temporary act of will. Empowered by the "pure love of God," a lifelong commitment is not only possible, but it is the only correct manifestation of pure love. Remember, Christ is going to change you—but only after you choose to forever deny yourself, no matter how hard it may seem to you from the bottom side looking up.

If you feel that physically denying yourself is impossible, plead with God to assist you in that very deed, as well as in the desire. With God, nothing is impossible, and this empowerment is all within the scope of Christ's grace to the humble and willing seeker.

Step Three: Feel the grace of Christ changing you—over time—so that you not only no longer desire this thing anymore but it literally becomes repugnant to you. Now you are becoming, and will be, "perfect in Christ" in that one thing. As well, your very nature is being changed, and you will find that other sins soon fall, like one domino falls upon another. Other flaws will surely linger, but they too will yield to this process.

Step Four: Having experienced the power of Christ's atonement and grace and the glorious retooling of your soul in this one thing—now stand upon this new mountaintop you own and make a lifelong commitment to "deny yourself of *all* ungodliness." If you must, do it one flaw at a time. But the desire soon comes to give away all your sins, and it becomes no longer necessary to peel the onion.

Step Five: Then, "by his grace ye may be perfect in Christ." Again, it is Christ who does the heavy lifting. He shed precious blood to be able to "save" you, body and soul, heart and hand. When the desire for all sin leaves you, it won't be because you did it by some Zen of great discipline. It will be because you became "perfect in Christ." It is a far easier way! And it is the only way that actually works and can deliver exaltation.

Step Six: No person who experiences this grand upgrading of the mortal soul can deny that it was by the power of Christ that one is changed. We were powerless before, lost and imprisoned by our weakness, and now we are free! We must never forgot whose blood paid for our freedom. We must never take credit to ourselves or deny Christ's power of deliverance. "If ye by the grace of God are perfect in Christ, and deny not his power, then are ye sanctified in Christ by the grace of God . . . unto the remission of your sins, that ye become holy and without spot" (Moroni 10:33).

We are talking about the journey of a lifetime here, not some-thing to do in the next two weeks. Don't fear the greatness of what you are doing. You are a son or daughter of God, and not only *can* you and Christ do this together, but eventually *you will have to* before you return home to God.

Becoming perfected in Christ is the way—the only way.

Brother John

The Doer of All Our Deeds

This is the razor's edge of salvation: that point when mortals turn over their lives to Christ. This is the point when the Atonement becomes personally powerful, when the enabling power of the Atonement is received, and we are mightily changed, when faith blossoms sufficiently to move moun-tains, when we suddenly realize the promised joys of the gospel, and our eyes are opened to infinite vistas of eternal possibility.

Elder F. Enzio Busche described it this way:

This is the place where we suddenly see the heavens open as we feel the full impact of the love of our Heavenly Father, which fills us with indescribable joy. With this fulfillment of love in our hearts, we will never be happy anymore just by being ourselves or living our own lives. We will not be satisfied until we have surrendered our lives into the arms of the loving Christ, and until He has become the doer of all our deeds and He has become the speaker of all our words. ("Truth is the Issue," *Ensign*, November 1993, 25)

This should be the whole focal point of our effort and our surrender—to come unto Christ and, by yielding our will to His, to become one with Him.

Brother John

Light All through the Night

*Y*esterday, we were sitting in a small restaurant. I was in that funk zone where you feel nothing at all when my sweetheart started telling me about her recent spiritual journey. Her seeking has been to understand the meaning and purpose of my health situation. She had come to a simple conclusion, which startled me and snapped me out of the zero zone.

She recalled all of the improbable forces that had brought us here to Utah, and of all the miracles we have continued to receive like rose petals falling from the sky. She concluded by saying that no matter where it has taken us, no matter how many mistakes we have made, the path we are on is the right one—even if it ends in our leaving mortality what appears to be too soon.

As she spoke, as I listened, I felt the flow of the Spirit and a confirmation that she was exactly right. When you experience a gold-plated miracle that dramatically changes your life (although not the aspect you initially wanted to have changed), then you know you are in God's hands, in His sight, and under His care. You know you are in the straight way, or these miracles would be absent from your life. And that one pressing thing (in this case, my health) for which you are most earnestly seeking is also in His tender care. Fear is not appropriate, nor is it necessary. All is well, all is well.

Many years ago in a stake priesthood meeting in Idaho, I heard Bruce R. McConkie ask this question. "How can you tell if you are living a life that is acceptable to God? How can you tell if you have been forgiven of a past sin for which you've repented?" His answer was, "If you feel the presence of the Holy Spirit in your life, if you are receiving personal revelation, and if you receive answers to your prayers, then you are in the straight and narrow way and your sins are forgiven, because the Holy Spirit does not dwell in unholy people."

This is what my eternal companion was saying for both of us. We are in the straight way, and all is well, because we do walk in the light of the Spirit. Having this truth re-illuminated was a tender mercy to me, as I continue to watch my health deteriorate and my life slipping fast away. It was especially sweet to hear it from the lips of the person I trust most, and who has been better able of late to perceive the light all through the gathering night.

Brother John

The Journey Home
Part IX: Excuses, Excuses

I'm sorry to stay in "UnBlog-Lite" mode so long. Usually I'm feeling better by now, but the chemo has been harder to shake this time.

I keep coming back to this sense of joy in my heart because of my blessings. I look forward with rejoicing to the future because I am excited to discover its treasures the Lord has hidden along my path. I'm thrilled to think of what lies on both sides of the mortal veil, with so much yet to do on this side, and eternities of wonders on the other.

I spent several fascinating hours talking with Spencer (not his real name), preparing for the new book I'm writing about his near-death experiences. I'm still not sure how close we are to the end and really have no desire for it to end. What he was shown and has told me is so explicit and revealing that I'm wondering at this point how much I dare publish. I'm looking forward to beginning the actual writing of the manuscript to see where the Spirit lets us go. Even if I were allowed to publish only a small fraction of what he has told me, it would be electrifying information. In the narrative so far, he has just started to tell me of the journey of some of the companies of Saints from Salt Lake City to Missouri. The incredible events that seem to be in our near future would almost be unbelievable if it wasn't for the fact that the Spirit burns brightly as I write it down.

Without any exaggeration at all, it is the most detailed and explicit vision of which I am aware that any mortal has seen of these times, or at least been allowed to speak about. Most of these types of visionary experiences come with an "unspeakable" clause. In the case of Spencer, he was held to that standard for over thirty years until just recently.

Thanks for your patience. I promise we'll get back to meatier matters soon.

Brother John

Chapter Ten

Ushering In the Millennium

Hope for Our Times

*I*t is hard to look at the pace at which our world is power-diving toward prophetic destiny and not feel frightened. Twice in the last week I received comments from separate readers about a vision they had seen during the night regarding a destructive earthquake in Salt Lake City. In each case, the dreams were remarkably similar.

As I watch the Constitution being violated and our way of life being sucked into economic ruin and war, I wonder how far the fabric of democracy can be stretched before it rips. When I see the rise of terrorism and the face of the anti-Christ growing ever more visible, it is not difficult to see the end times approaching rapidly.

So, where is our hope and our peace?

First, the bad news: This telestial world must end, and we will be present when it does.

Now, the good news: We rejoice in the demise of this veil of tears. Its purpose is accomplished, its life is spent, and its time past. I share everyone's trepidation about being here when the earth goes through its wash-and-spin cycle to become clean. But I rejoice in the fact that its days are numbered. Even if we personally must die, the next step is to watch from safety until it is over, come back with Christ in the glorious Second Coming, and then enjoy a thousand years of millennial peace.

Those of us who endure these times will raise our children without sin and without satanic interference throughout the Millennium. Who wouldn't be willing to give their own lives so that their grandchildren could grow up in such a world?

But there is even better news. The Lord has prepared a place of security within the yet-to-be-built latter-day Zion. There we will watch in safety as the world self-destructs. We will be commissioned by Jesus Christ Himself to go out with the citizens of Enoch's Zion into the chaos around us and save with tremendous power—raise people from the dead, heal them, teach them, and bring them back to Zion. These will be the greatest days mankind has ever seen, not because of their destructive reality, but because of the unapologetic display of godly power we will unleash to save the just and the innocent. It will make superhero movies look silly.

And—there's more! By following the course laid out in the scripture and in the principles we have been UnBlogging, we can and will be invited to be a part of that great army of 144,000 warriors of light. *We*, not some future generation, but *we* will populate the city of Zion, and *we* will call down fire from heaven and miracles from above. *We* will command the elements and defend with great power.

Herein lies hope for our times—that we have the ability, the power, and the privilege to prepare ourselves to build Zion, receive Christ at His coming, and end this telestial world once and for all. Christ will not return until we build Zion. This is our greatest challenge and our greatest potential. These words seem to echo from eternity: We delay no longer, the call is heard, and the silence is broken.

We have begun.

Brother John

Building a Mansion

*M*uch more than a place or a city or a society, Zion is a state of being. To be a part of a perfected Zion society in any dispensation, we have to become a Zion individual. It is roughly like saying, to live in the air, one must become a bird. To enter the rarefied environment of the latter-day Zion when it has reached its full potential requires a specific and powerful change to re-create a body and soul into the Zion format.

As we continue to explore Zion, it will become apparent that to be a participant in Zion is to become pure, to be endowed with the fullest priesthood power, to rise above the mortal sphere, to be endowed with power that transcends life and death, to have author-ity in heaven and on earth, and to quite literally dwell with God.

Having said all that, I am convinced that the previous paragraph is a textbook example of knowing things by faith without believing them. As we read such statements, each assertion "feels" true, so little thought is given to translating them from truisms into personal beliefs.

Consider for a moment one of the statements just above. "To be a participant in Zion is to rise above the mortal sphere." What an amazing statement! Our initial reaction is to believe the words, because the Holy Ghost attests to the soul that they are true. They were true of Zion societies past and will be true again. But there is raw power in those words that apply to us today. To rise above the mortal sphere is not to leave mortality but as a mortal to no longer be subject to the trials of mortality, to live beyond pain, hunger, even death. Such privileges have belonged to past generations of Zion individuals and will belong to this dispensation of those who seek and obtain Zion.

We are speaking of the powers of godliness, power that transcends life and death, power over personal injury, immunity to disease and sickness, and of literally having power over our own death.

Such a Zion lifestyle exceeds our present paradigm so powerfully as to make it inconceivable—not in the perception of Zion *someday* being like this for someone, but in the perception of Zion being like this in our day, for you and me. We can't conceptually place ourselves in that Zion. In other words, we don't believe what our faith actually tells us. Thus, we have ceased to strive for the very thing that would bring us our greatest triumph in mortality and our greatest joy.

What is even more exciting is that everything we do, believe, and strive for in this gospel is bringing us toward Zion, even if we didn't realize it. But we cannot rise above the limits of our own belief. We cannot accomplish things of which we can't conceive, and we cannot build Zion when we have no concept that it remains yet to be.

We stand with the tools and boards and nails in our hands with the intent of building a cottage, whereas if we studied the blueprints, we would realize we're actually building a mansion.

Brother John

The Pure Love of Christ

On this Easter morn, I worship my Savior and bow my head in deep humility for His sacrifice and triumph on my behalf. I would like to share with you an account of an experience of years ago wherein I learned somewhat of the power of His love, which is the defining quality of all those who will inherit Zion.

When I was fourteen years old, I had gone to Sun Valley, Idaho, to work for the summer. It was my first extended time away from home. It was a challenging and eye-opening experience. While I was there, I attended church regularly and was intrigued to find that without my parents sitting beside me representing what I "should" be feeling and thinking and doing, I actually felt the Spirit freely and felt my testimony growing tremendously.

One Sunday, one of the sacrament meeting talks was on charity, the pure love of Christ. I remember being very earnest in wanting to experience charity and praying diligently throughout the meeting and into the evening that I could have the gift of charity. Nothing identifiable happened that day.

Nearly thirty-five years later, I was preparing to leave for work, pulling on gloves and hat, when I felt something go through my body like an electric shock. It was during a time in my life when I had been fasting often, praying diligently, and exerting all of my discipleship to grow and obtain. What I felt was a type of spiritual thrill, a kind of high-voltage spiritual influx unlike anything I had experienced before or since. It left me feeling spiritually alive, but nothing else I could name at that moment. I pondered it for a moment and then left out the door.

It was a dim Alaska winter morning with deep snow, frosted windows, and bitter cold. I started my pickup and scraped the windows. By the time I was ready to drive, I was chilled and uncomfortable. I turned onto the main road and was startled to see people driving toward me who I was very sure needed me to do something. I didn't know what, but I knew they needed me. I watched each car with deep concern, tears pooling in my eyes. I came to a stop sign, and the vehicle opposite me was an old Subaru wagon with frosted windows. The defroster was apparently not working because the occupant was scraping at the glass with his fingernails. I felt overwhelmed and deeply concerned, and I started to open the door to run across the street and exchange cars. I had a good pickup, and I had the means of repairing that Subaru. But the Spirit restrained me and said I could not.

I didn't understand; it was painful to drive on. As I watched the Subaru lurch and chug away, I felt as if I had left a naked child in the street to die. I drove on past the parking lot of a large grocery store and realized that not everyone would be able to purchase what they needed. I started to turn in. I was going to stand in the door and ask everyone whether they had been able to buy everything they needed. I planned on going to the bank and withdrawing money for them. It was such a relief, such a joy, to think that I could do that; but the Spirit again forbade me, and I very reluctantly turned back onto the main road.

Something similar to this happened with every vehicle I saw at every intersection. It was the most painful thing I have ever experienced. I had to stop, I just had to—but the Spirit would not allow it. I finally arrived at work and began helping a customer, to whom I began promising things for free and offering to not charge for anything. One of my employees saw this, gave me a funny look, took over, and pushed me aside. I forced myself to go into the office and close the door, and I wept. The idea of letting my employee actually charge this person money was distasteful to me. I felt physically ill.

Still, at the same time, I knew something had changed in me. I realized these feelings of deep, overpowering love and concern were not originating with me. I sat there for hours praying, trying to understand. The burden was increasing. The weight of the concern was crushing. I was going to die under the weight of these feelings if I didn't get up right then and find a way to rescue someone. I stood and walked in circles. There were so many needs, so much pain, and I had so little resources to help them—and I didn't even know where they were or what they needed.

Finally, I bowed my head and very softly asked that these feelings would be lifted. In that instant, they were gone, and I was myself. Nothing of those feelings remained, only the memory. It was astonishing to me then, and is to me now. I simply no longer felt the weight of love and concern of moments before. I sat again and asked for an explanation. This experience had left me weak, exhausted, and emotionally devastated, as if I had watched loved ones suffer and had done nothing. It had lasted only a few hours. I knew that if it had continued, I would have found a way to give away everything I had for them, including my life if necessary; and the world would have judged me insane and locked me away.

Then the Spirit reminded me, actually showed me an image of myself sitting there with my head bowed, pleading for charity when I was fourteen years old, in Sun Valley, Idaho. It had taken me thirty-five years to prepare for my answer, and when it came, I found it crushing.

It was then that I realized why my Savior would have been willing to die for me—for us. With such an exquisite feeling of love, with this pure form of charity such as only a God can experience, He would have agreed to *anything* that would deliver the people of His affection from their sins. Some part of Him didn't want to; when the time came, a part of His mortal being shrank and resisted. But the eternal part of Him, the part that was defined by charity, the part that was our Savior, rejoiced and willingly laid Himself upon the altar.

As for me, it has taken a long time before I've been ready again for another endowment of charity such as this. I have loved such as mortals do and have prayed for the type of charity that brings compassion and a deep willingness to sacrifice for others. But lately, as I grow in the knowledge of Zion and look toward the millennial day, I find myself longing for a greater bestowal of the Savior's charity in my life, no matter the cost. It is only when we are prepared and ready to be filled with His all-encompassing love that we will ever hope to qualify for Zion and live comfortably with Christ and our brethren in that blessed setting. As I have acquired new eyes, I am beginning to understand why the pure love of Christ is not only a requirement of Zion, but the fulfillment of the deepest desires of a Zion heart.

Until that day arrives, I think back on this experience of glimpsing the pure love of Christ for a few hours, and my eyes fill with tears, and I wonder and worship at His feet.

Brother John

Our Everlasting Privilege

*We stand in approximately the same position rela-*tive to the Second Coming, and the cleansings that must precede it, as Enoch stood prior to the cleansing of the wicked earth by the flood. At the beginning of Enoch's ministry, no city of righteousness glowed in the evening darkness. He boldly preached to the spiritually unwashed and impure. There were certainly other believers than Enoch upon the earth, and many who understood at least a part of God's dealings with man. Enoch undoubtedly went to these first, and many believed and joined him. Those who believed were taught and received the ordinances of salvation and exaltation. As individuals, they grew until they were worthy of the divine presence, and thereafter, because of their collective purity, they were instructed to build a city upon whose gilded streets Deity walked and talked on a familiar basis.

Just as Enoch had to build his Zion to save the righteous from the universal destruction of the flood, we must build up Zion in our day to save the righteous from the universal cleansing by fire that will accompany Christ's glorious return. Since He will not return until after we build Zion, can it be that the Lord isn't delaying His return unto the end of the world—but that *we* are?

Moses spoke of the New Jerusalem this way:

> 62 And righteousness will I send down out of heaven; and truth will I send forth out of the earth, to bear testimony of mine Only Begotten; his resurrection from the dead; yea, and also the resurrection of all men; and righteousness and truth will I cause to sweep the earth as with a flood, to gather out mine elect from the four quarters of the earth, unto a place which I shall prepare, an Holy City, that my people may gird up their loins, and be looking forth for the time of my coming; for there shall be my tabernacle, and it shall be called Zion, a New Jerusalem. (Moses 7:62)

Observe the sequence of events:

- Righteousness and truth will sweep the earth as with a flood.
- The elect will be gathered from the four quarters of the earth.
- A Holy City, the New Jerusalem, will be built.

- The elect may gird up their loins (take courage) in Zion.
- The Second Coming will occur.

The implication of this is that we, the stewards of the latter-days, cannot be intelligently looking for the Second Coming until we have built Zion. Zion is the highest blessing of this dispensation, and because it is the greatest, building it is the greatest challenge we will ever face.

The prophet Joseph Smith taught: "Zion and Jerusalem must both be built up before the coming of Christ" (The Historians Corner, *BYU Studies*, vol. 19 [1978–1979], Number 3, Spring 1979, 393; italics added).

Elder Orson Pratt echoed the Prophet's teachings on this matter when he taught:

> The Christians of all denominations expect that he will appear in the clouds of heaven with power and great glory. The Latter-day Saints expect this in common with all other Christians. But before he appears in his glory he is going to build up Zion, that is, Zion must again be built up on the earth: and *if there is not a Zion built up on the earth before he comes, or in other words, if there never is to be another Zion built up on the earth, then he never will come.* (JD, 14:348; italics added)

If we don't build Zion, Christ will never come? Can it be true?

I don't believe Elder Pratt is proposing that Christ won't come at all, since prophecy indicates that Zion *will* be built, and that He *will* return in glory. What is being emphasized by this dramatic statement is the timing of Christ's return in relation to the building of Zion. Elder Pratt is teaching us that since Christ will come to Zion when He returns, then He can't, or better stated, He won't fulfill that promise until Zion exists.

We know from the scripture and from statements we will quote following that the date of the Second Coming of Christ is fixed. The date is known only to the Father (Matthew 24:36). When we speak of "delaying" the Second Coming, we mean only that in His foreknowledge of all things, the Father has fixed that date after the establishment of Zion. And since our own agency and faithfulness govern when we will get around to building Zion, we have an obvious influence upon that date, in effect, delaying it.

From all this it appears that by delaying the establishment of Zion, we have also delayed the Second Coming of the Lord. If this is true, it is startling. The idea that we, through our spiritual sleepiness, could delay the return of the Lord, and thus the day of peace so long sought by the righteous of every generation, is almost horrific.

Elder McConkie said it this way:

> *Though the day of the Second Coming is fixed, the day for the redemption of Zion depends upon us.* After we as a people live the law of the celestial kingdom; after we gain the needed experience and learn our duties; after we become by faith and obedience as were our fellow saints in the days of Enoch; after we are worthy to be translated, if the purposes of the Lord should call for such a course in this day—then Zion will be redeemed, and not before. (*NWAF*, p. 615; italics added)

Claiming the cause of Zion as our own and sacrificing to remake our own lives into Zion worthiness are the mission and purpose of our dispensation. The prophet alone can issue the call to build a city—but the command has gone forth for us to personally claim the blessings of Zion worthiness for ourselves and our posterity.

We have such a remarkable opportunity! Imagine—it is not only our duty, but our everlasting privilege, to walk up to the veil and claim our place in Zion! We have been commanded, and the way is open before us to end this telestial world of blood and horror, and invite Jesus Christ to return to rule the peaceful millennial world that our grandchildren and their posterity will enjoy.

Brother John

Telestial to Terrestrial

One truth I consistently forget is that the latter-day tribulations are much, much more than a descent into chaos and war. I have a tendency to look at those approaching times and think about food storage, economic chaos, foreign invasion, no utilities, and bands of hungry people. What I should be thinking about is that the earth is being changed into a millennial state, and we are being changed with it.

The earth is presently in a telestial state. We are all familiar with the trials and heartache of the telestial state. During the Millennium, Zion and eventually everyone and everything upon the earth will be terrestrial. In that glorious state, our bodies will not be subject to pain, hunger, disease, or aging. All of nature will produce without coercion to bless the sons and daughters of Adam. There will be no government but Jesus Christ, and peace will rule for a thousand years. This is the millennial-terrestrial state.

All change is painful. There is a birthing process of change that cannot be avoided. The greatest change will be ruled by the fact that nothing telestial can remain on the earth by the time the millennial-terrestrial day has begun. This includes people, buildings, traditions, infrastructure, religion, literature, landscape, and everything else. If it is not terrestrial, or if it is not capable of making the change into terrestrial—it must be destroyed. Or, perhaps better stated, it will not survive the change and will no longer exist. Even a telestial mind-set or idea must perish. This means that wherever the idea persists, it must be altered or the holder of the idea cannot enter the terrestrial day.

We know that the earth will "abide the day" of this transition and will become the new home of Zion, and the terrestrial state will cover her face. We are also informed that the earth will become the new celestial kingdom after the Millennium (Doctrine & Covenants 88:17–19, 25–26).

This means that everything telestial must be wiped off of her face. No trace or evidence of it can remain. Even the hills that were thrown up in the telestial day must be leveled, and the valleys that fell must be raised. Everything man has built that does not exactly conform to the terrestrial inspiration must be wiped away. Every philosophy, religion, principle, government, or thinking that is not equal to the terrestrial standard must be consumed by fire.

Our only hope of "abiding the day" is not in our food storage and other physical hedges against the tide of change, although they are important. But in all our necessary preparations, let us never forget that our true hope lies in our ability to use the gospel and priesthood ordinances to change by Christ's grace into the terrestrial state, prior to the earth doing it.

If you can lay hold upon this concept, it will literally save your life and ease your transition into the millennial day (Doctrine & Covenants 88:82–85). If we are already terrestrial, having laid aside everything telestial of our own free will, by our inspired discipleship, allowing Christ to make the changes in our hearts, minds, and homes, then when the birthing process of the Millennium begins, we will not be subject to the necessary cleansing of the earth as "she" changes. We will still feel the ground shake and watch the trauma of so much cleansing around us, but we will not fear, and we will not be moved but will stand in holy places. Those places will be made holy by our presence—because we, ourselves, are holy. The Holy Spirit will guide us (Doctrine & Covenants 45:56–59), and we will be a source of strength and peace to those around us as the changes occur.

If we are capable of making this change, but just choose not to, then in my opinion, the tribulations will be a great shaking and awakening of our souls. Those who awaken after the shaking begins will experience the fear and horror of those times, but in the end they will join the terrestrial evolution and come to Zion. This is not to say that all of them will physically survive. Some will be in the clouds of heaven coming with Christ, not physically upon the earth in Zion. There will be a large mortality rate among this group who decides to change after the testimony of earthquakes, floods, and fires begins (Doctrine & Covenants 88:89–91). But, happy day, happy day, all is well.

Those who cannot change, whose hearts are set so much upon the things of the world that they cannot evolve into the purity of the terrestrial world, will ultimately not evolve and must be wiped off before the earth can achieve its millennial glory.

This is the reason for the tribulations—not to punish us, not to wreak vengeance—it is to cleanse the earth so that Christ can come and make His abode in Zion. If we are to remain on the earth, then we must change in sync with the earth, so that when "she" is glorified, we will be glorified with her and be welcome in the millennial day.

As Christ prayed, we need to pray joyfully with Him: "Thy kingdom come, Thy will be done on earth."

Brother John

The Least among Us

Last Sunday, I sat two rows behind a darling little girl about six years old. She had beautiful, sandy brown hair tied up in a pink bow. She was sitting by her grandmother, who was clearly enjoying her granddaughter's love and affection. They quietly exchanged smiles and soft books and snacks as the service progressed. At one moment, the little one lifted her left arm to place it on her Grandma's shoulder and neck. Her arm ended at her elbow with one tiny deformed finger on the stub of her arm.

To my left, another young lady sat. She was all of four or five. She was dressed in a soft blue dress with ruffles, and her dark brown hair was adorned with a white bow. Her face was twisted up slightly on the right side. She sat quietly watching an interpreter sitting in the aisle facing her, signing to her what the speakers were saying. I could tell from the few signs compared to the many words that the little one was getting a very watered-down version of the meeting.

The young man, Jamison, who brought us the sacrament was accompanied by another young man who kept a constant hand on his shoulder, guiding him from place to place. Jamison is twenty-six but looks sixteen. He is a priest but has the mental capacity of about a six-year-old. His face is pinched, and his body is hunched and wasted. He passes the sacrament with a beaming smile so big that it lights up the whole chapel.

Another young lady of indeterminate age comes to church in a complicated wheelchair that supports her every appendage. She is deaf, blind, and profoundly retarded. She sits through sacrament meeting squealing and sometimes screaming.

The man in front of me is seventy-something, a former mission president. He's tall and handsome, with a full head of white hair. He has Alzheimer's and knows it. He tries to communicate but forgets what he was going to say before he begins. His face shows frustration and embarrassment. He stands up when the deacons stand to pass the sacrament because he thinks the meeting is over. His mother gently pulls him back down. She's in her nineties. Her mind is as sharp as a tack, but her body is frail. She's living with him and his angel wife because she can no longer take care of herself. The mission president's wife is a registered nurse. She works full time and then comes home to care for her beloved husband and mother-in-law every day. She looks completely exhausted, but she brings them all faithfully to church every week.

My heart aches every time I meet with these people. My eyes fill with tears because I want to heal them. I want to take that short little arm and hold it, stroke it, and pray over it until it resumes its normal shape. I want to hold Jamison until he is physically and mentally twenty-six. I want to pour out the love of God upon all of these, who are indeed the "least among us."

But, the Spirit restrains me because this is a day of quiet miracles, when the telestial world rules over our lives with prolonged suffering and approaching death. So, I pray for Zion. I pray for the day that I enter into that sacred terrestrial world where all little girls' arms reach all the way around their grandmothers, where all Jamisons run and jump and bless the sacrament in a clear and inspired voice.

And so I write and write and write with all of my heart, to continually hold these things before my eyes, and to prepare the world to be worthy of that day—that day when the telestial world ends, and miracles become our daily fare.

I do not believe it is far off. I hope it is not far off. And, when it comes, I'm going to run to all of the Jamisons I know, and all of the little ones who are not whole, and heal them.

Brother John

And Have Not Been Deceived

As we turn our eyes on the times around us and view the churning events that seem to tell us the promised days of Zion are approaching, the possibility of being deceived grows ever greater.

Let me say as strongly as I possibly can that The Church of Jesus Christ of Latter-day Saints is operating as Jesus Christ directs it. Only a few times in history has it happened that we, the people, actually laid hold upon the full blessings being offered by the living prophet and established Zion in that dispensation. Every other time we gave it a shot, we failed, and the Lord withdrew the privilege for a time.

The problem has never been a failure of the living prophet. It has always been a failure of the would-be saints to climb the holy mount to the face of God—which is the final step in establishing Zion. We become so caught up in the details of survival, society, and seeking prosperity that we forget, or we never see, the foundations of our Zion being built all around us.

> And at that day, when I shall come in my glory, shall the parable be fulfilled which I spake concerning the ten virgins. For they that are wise and have received the truth, and have taken the Holy Spirit for their guide, and have not been deceived—verily I say unto you, they shall not be hewn down and cast into the fire, but shall abide the day. (Doctrine & Covenants 45:56–57)

As we read in the verse above, there are three steps we must take to not be cast down into the fire and abide the day.

1) We must receive the truth. It is tempting to say that the truth is found within the Church, but saying so sets you up for embracing a deception. The truth is found within the gospel, which is righteously and correctly being administered by the Church. But the Church cannot save us. The Church programs can't save us. The temple can't save us. Only Jesus Christ and the gospel that circumscribes His every truth and power and grace in our lives can save us. We come unto Christ and are perfected in Him (Moroni 10:31–32). We do this in large part by ordinances and by giving our loyalty and love to the latter-day Church. But it is *Christ* that saves us. This truth gives us the safety of searching all truth, laying hold of all good things without regard to what we see others doing, and not stumbling because of real or perceived flaws in the Church.

2) We must take the Holy Spirit to be our guide. Why? Because the Church publishes manuals and scripture, but the "gospel" only publishes truth via the Holy Spirit. The only way to partake of the purest truths is by being guided there by the Holy Spirit, which is always in direct alignment with the truths taught by the Church. This purest truth is the voice of Christ, and it is what brings us to Christ in order that we might be "perfected in Him."

3) We must not be deceived. The truth is there are one billion or more ways to be deceived, and only one way—through the gospel

blessings and the voice of Christ—that we may not be deceived. There is one straight and narrow path to show us the way through these times, and a billion other ways to get lost.

There seem to be two types of people whose deceptions take them away from the restored gospel. There are those who never caught the spiritual power of what they have and for some reason become disenchanted with the restored gospel and step away. They don't like something they think is amiss in the Church, or they were offended, or they were proselytized away by anti-minded imps.

The second group consists of people who view the gospel as a great blessing, and who have begun to experience great things in their personal quest. The scriptures become clearer, the Holy Spirit feeds their souls, and they leap into blessings they read about in the scriptures but have never heard a living person claim. Occasionally, they begin to look back at the Church and wonder why they don't see more people rising spiritually or why certain subjects are not more clearly taught in official church meetings. They soon begin to wonder what's wrong. If these wonderful people have not fully taken the Holy Spirit to be their guide, they sometimes step away also. They often do so sadly, and at other times with a smug attitude that they have evolved beyond the Church. Such is surely a most dangerous and satanically inspired deception.

Deception nearly always entices and encourages us to sever our connection with the true and living Church. Pure truth always entices us to align our lives with the living Church and to remain "faithful and true in all things."

When the latter-day scenes are enacted, our living prophet and this latter-day Church will be the focal point of all that occurs. The latter-day Zion will be a blossoming of this Church, not a replacement. There is no scenario wherein Jesus Christ leads someone outside of His fold.

The comforting truth is that we who stay within the latter-day fold and lay hold upon all that the gospel offers are they who have not been deceived.

Brother John

The Times of Easy Preparation

You may be interested to know that I have completed the interview phase with Spencer for the new book. At this point we've recorded forty-six hours of interviews and narrative. My analysis of it is that it is the most intriguing story I have ever heard in my life.

Beginning today, I am going to be spending most of my time writing his book. If my energy and health hold out, it should take me a few months to write it and then almost a year of editing and rewriting. The publisher usually takes six to twelve months to get it on the market from there. I am honestly excited for this project to go forward!

As I have interviewed Spencer, it has become increasingly more apparent to me that the times of easy preparation are coming to an end. By this I mean the times when you can just walk into a store and buy anything, when everyone has resources, and spirituality feels good but is not a matter of survival, not the difference between life and death.

We may have years to get our houses in order, as our prophets have long counseled, or it may be weeks. I don't claim to know, but I do believe that the option to "wait and see" is over. The next step is forced preparation. This is like running out to buy a fire extinguisher while your house is burning down. The lessons of these times will be taught by the testimony of earthquakes, floods, and plagues. Most of us will survive, but the lessons will force us to our knees as we fast for days, weep for departed loved ones, and try to make spiritual preparations that should have been done a decade ago.

Soon the times of easy preparation will be over, and the times of rescue will begin. This is when you will sit in the ashes of your former lives, praying and praying that an angel of any form will come to rescue you, bring you hope, and point the way to Zion. This is a very real stage. Eventually 144,000 "angels" will be dispatched to gather what remains of the people, who by trial of fire will then be fit to enter Zion. It will not be a moment of rejoicing, because the cost will have been life-shattering, but it will be a time of great relief and of singing the songs of redeeming love.

My hope for us all is that *we* will be the angels doing the gathering, as we walk the streets of gold with Christ.

Brother John

Looking Back on the UnBlog

I have had about two years now to think about what the mission of the UnBlog is and to refine it, to watch it grow and evolve. It has been an enlightening journey. When I began the UnBlog, I was very ill and felt inspired to write down the spiritual experiences and events of my life so that my children and grandchildren could read them and know that they too can reach into the heavens and pull down great blessings upon their heads. It was in a moment of inspiration that the Lord instructed me to post those things on an Internet blog and to call it "UnBlog My Soul."

About a year later, I distinctly came to the end of that which I was supposed to record from my own life, and I thought there was nothing more to write. I considered ending the UnBlog because it seemed to have served its initial purpose.

But the Spirit whispered that there was much more ahead. By this time, I was halfway through chemotherapy and feeling extremely mortal. I didn't think I had much time left on earth, and I decided to continue the blog by writing a few points of doctrine that, if understood correctly, can assist anyone in obtaining the profound promised blessings of the gospel, including miracles, visions, angelic visitations, and even qualifying to be in the presence of the Lord. Over about the next year, I think we accomplished most of that. The UnBlog archives now have over 450 articles on various gospel subjects, most of them with this one goal of illustrating how to seek and obtain the vast and glorious gifts of heaven while yet in mortality.

Somewhat like Nephi, I glory in plainness, not only in saying *what* is possible, but in defining *how* to achieve it. For most seekers, the first thing we glimpse is the great blessings way beyond where we presently perceive we are. Just seeing a destination but no possible path to get there is torture. So, I always write about the path, the *how* of reaching for these great things. As I contemplate the end of my journey to the veil, it has been my hope that someone else's journey could be illuminated by something said here, either by myself or by one of you.

Additionally, the UnBlog has taken on the unexpected role of witnessing to a very important fact, which is that each seeking soul is not alone in the spiritual quest. I have spoken to many, many people who said something equivalent to "Until I found the UnBlog, I thought I was the only person on the planet who was seeking these glorious blessings from God." It may be true that all of us have felt the "great alone" at some point. I certainly did.

Last, I think one of the missions of the UnBlog has been to say over and over that The Church of Jesus Christ of Latter-day Saints is not broken. It is not somehow true-but-not-functioning, or a kindergarten class one must enroll in and then graduate from to go beyond. The voice of the UnBlog is that this Church is profoundly true, that it is operating as Jesus Christ directs it, and that it will be the organization through which He finally authorizes and orchestrates the building of the latter-day Zion. Stepping outside of the fellowship of the Church is stepping outside of the very pathway leading to the blessings you think you will find beyond.

Looking forward, I cannot see the UnBlog future with any more clarity than the day I wrote the first entry nearly two years ago. But I see that God's hand is upon us all, and I humbly rejoice to be a part of it.

Brother John

The Journey Home
Part X: Into the Valley

After the UnBlog Reunion, John's personal mortal "Journey to the Veil" took a decidedly downward course, and within just a short time, he could not eat anything at all or keep much water down. Even smells in the house made him nauseated, so I stopped cooking, and the family would eat outside or elsewhere. But there was a special sweetness that permeated our home and an opportunity to daily express love that perhaps would never have happened otherwise.

One by one, the children all came home to see their Dad and spend precious time with him. One daughter quit her job to be by his side until the end; I could not have physically cared for John without her there to help me. John's brothers and sisters sacrificed to travel from England and Texas to see him; his dear mother visited regularly, and our many friends from the ward and from his UnBlog were a constant support. Our home teacher (who happened to be our stake president) would regularly show up on our doorstep, not insisting to see him, but just to offer deep consolation that only someone so profoundly spiritual could have afforded. The humble priests faithfully came to give John the sacrament, even when he couldn't swallow, and they brought the priesthood's strengthening power with them. Our ward family wrapped their arms around us in such a show of Christlike compassion and service that I hardly knew how to express our thanks before another wave of service and love was offered!

And then there were the hospice angels: the doctors and nurses who cared for John, who mitigated his pain, who made the experience a healing one for him and our family. I have never experienced such compassion as they brought to our door, no matter how inconvenient it surely must have been for them in the wee hours of the morning.

I learned something important: The end of life can be as beautiful as the beginning of life. Ever since I gave birth to my first baby, I have always loved attending births and giving birth myself, because the veil is so thin and the angels are always, always present as that new spirit arrives. But I discovered that this thinning of the veil and attendance by *angels is also the case with the end of life! This realization has filled me with wonder and awe as I have comprehended more fully the infinite kindness of the Lord, even as we venture wide-eyed into the valley of the shadow of death.*

—*Terri*

Chapter Eleven

The Christ-Empowered Life

The Christ-Empowered Life

We Latter-day Saints seem to be able to understand our responsibility to demonstrate and support our faith with daily effort and work. It is much harder for us to embrace the truth that we fallen mortals are not capable of changing ourselves, through works, into Christlike souls. No amount of effort, no amount of good works, no amount of service or temple attendance or tithing or teaching Sunday School, important as they are, can affect the transition. We are kind of like puppies who think that by working very, very hard, we can grow up into horses.

The law that "the natural man is an enemy to God" has stood since the moment Adam and Eve transgressed the law and were driven from the Garden of Eden. The effect of the Fall cannot be overcome by man, no matter how determined his effort.

But provision is made for all the wee puppies, through the Atonement of Christ, that if we hearken to His voice, and obey Him, and submit to His will, He will change us into the ponies we yearn to become. As we submit, we are disciplining ourselves to obey any path, process, or purification the Lord sees fit, which process may take us through many other experiences than obvious evolution toward ponyhood.

This is the domain of faith wherein, by submitting to His will, we allow ourselves to be led into pathways whose destination we can't possibly predict. We allow ourselves to be disciplined, humbled, changed, and stripped of pride. We submit to whatever schooling or lessons or pathways of pain we must—and we let obedience, not self-will and determination, chart our course.

Elder Bednar explained it this way:

I suspect that you and I are much more familiar with the nature of the redeeming power of the Atonement than we are with the enabling power of the Atonement. It is one thing to know that Jesus Christ came to earth to *die* for us. That is fundamental and foundational to the doctrine of Christ. But we also need to appreciate that the Lord desires, through His Atonement and by the power of the Holy Ghost, to *live* in us—not only to direct us but also to empower us. I think most of us know that when we do things wrong, when we need help to overcome the effects of sin in our lives, the Savior has paid the price and made it possible for us to be made clean through His redeeming power.

Most of us clearly understand that the Atonement is for sinners. I am not so sure, however, that we know and understand that the Atonement is also for saints—for good men and women who are obedient and worthy and conscientious and who are striving to become better and serve more faithfully. *I frankly do not think many of us "get it" concerning this enabling and strengthening aspect of the Atonement, and I wonder if we mistakenly believe we must make the journey from good to better and become a saint all by ourselves through sheer grit, willpower, and discipline, and with our obviously limited capacities.* ("In the Strength of the Lord," BYU devotional address at BYU–Idaho, October 23, 2001; emphasis added)

In the next several blogs, we will study what I call "The Christ-Empowered Life." You may find that this small refinement in your gospel paradigm, when properly understood, may be exciting and ultimately empowering. I have come to believe it is a grand key that has the power to bring the Saints of this generation to the Zion stature.

Brother John

The Miracle of Grace

Who among us has not confronted our personal weaknesses and found them stronger? Who has not sinned and repented, sinned and repented of the same flaw too many times to count? Who has not quit smoking, or something worse, only to start again, stop again, and restart? While it seems like an indictment against one's character, strength of will, or personal discipline, it is more a statement of the human condition.

As fallen man, as those subjected to the effects of getting tossed out of the Garden of Eden, we are by nature flawed, inclined to satisfy the needs of the flesh at all costs, passionate about pleasing our senses, and excited to dominate and control others. It is our birthright—not a worthy birthright—but it is something we acquired just by being born.

Since our Creator allowed—or "designed" might be a better word—for evil to enter the world and to afflict us all, He also provided a way for us to overcome the effects of the Fall at His expense. He is the engineer, the architect, and the general contractor of mortality. Of necessity, He ordained a place for evil in this world, to test us—and He engineered, designed, and constructed a means for us to overcome, paid for entirely by the shedding of His blood. This is how a perfect God could create an imperfect world and still remain perfect, just, and merciful.

The scriptures inform us that the natural man, the mortal man, is an enemy to God, and has been from the Fall of Adam (Mosiah 3:19). Why? Because God built it that way. The mortal body is the real testing ground. The war against evil is not being waged somewhere in Salt Lake City; it's being waged inside your body. On this battlefield, your spirit wears the white hat, and the flesh wears the black hat. The Spirit of God speaks to our spirit and attempts to guide us through the spiritual minefields. The spirit of evil attempts to influence our flesh and lead us to do the exact opposite (2 Nephi 2:29). For this reason, the natural man, the person captivated by his body, is an enemy to God.

The means our merciful Savior has provided for us to conquer in this stronger-than-everyone war is to yield to the enticings of the Holy Spirit and thereby put off the natural man, and thus become a saint through the Atonement of Christ (Mosiah 3:19).

The astonishing thing about this is that *we* don't put off the natural man. We aren't even capable of doing so by our own strength. Our job is to yield to Christ, and He puts off our natural man.

If we try to get into the boxing ring alone with the forces of evil, we will be beaten and beaten until we just can't do anything more than whimper for rescue. When we at last find our face against the canvas, with no strength to arise, then Jesus Christ steps into the ring, and because we are at last humble and obedient and willing to yield to His voice, He changes us. He empowers us against the dominion of the flesh. He takes away those weaknesses we were powerless to overcome by ourselves. He fills us with peace and joy, and we stand, repaired and reborn and fearless, because *He* conquered our demons. *He* put off our natural man.

And then by His grace, as a gift we qualified for but couldn't possibly earn, He empowers us to become as a child, "submissive, meek, humble, patient, full of love, willing to submit to all things which the Lord seeth fit to inflict upon him, even as a child doth submit to his father" (Mosiah 3:19).

This change is so powerful that we no longer have a desire to do evil but to do good continually (Mosiah 5:2).

This is the magic of the Atonement. This is the miracle of grace: beyond anything we could possibly offer except our self-will and token of obedience, *He* changes us. *He* lifts us. *He* empowers us. *He* pays the price for the sins that drove us into the ground in the first place.

Brother John

From Rags to Riches

I had such a wonderful time in Boise! It was the first time I have given two firesides in one day. But the Holy Spirit found us there, and doing two firesides didn't physically deplete me as expected. It merely doubled my blessings.

During both firesides, we spoke of the enabling power of the Atonement and how it changes us. As we were driving home, I remembered a family that I found and baptized as a missionary in Bulawayo, Rhodesia, Africa. I wrote about this family over a year ago, but would like to revisit that true story for you here.

We were tracting a neighborhood with little homes made of rough, red brick that had been painted white a very long time ago. Everything we could see suggested these people were in a social vice made of poverty and economic decay.

Every home was about twenty feet square, with a sun-bleached, red tile roof. Each was separated from the broken cobblestone road by about ten feet of red, hard-packed earth. There were no sidewalks, no street lights, and no house numbers, just rows of tiny homes baking in the heat and humidity of the African summer. It looked more like Arizona than tropical Africa.

There were very few cars, a few motorcycles, and lots of bicycles parked in driveways. It was late in the afternoon when we knocked on another sagging door, and a young mother came to the door. She was so skinny I wondered whether she was ill. Her dress was too large for her emaciated frame and very dirty. It also was so thin and tattered that it was apparent to us that she only wore the dress, with nothing beneath it. She had a black eye, bruised cheek, and an array of recent and older bruises on her arms.

A tiny girl clung to her leg. She was bony-thin and very small and seemed to be about two years old. I found out later that she was six and that starvation had stunted her growth. She was missing her two front teeth. Her hair was thin and missing in patches where she, or someone else, had pulled it from her head. I found out later her daddy had punched her teeth out in a drunken rage a few nights before, because the little waif wouldn't stop crying because of unrelenting hunger.

My companion introduced us, but instead of telling her we had a gospel message, as we usually did, he said, "We want to tell you about a program that can make your family happier." He was speaking about family home evening.

The woman replied, "Well, if there is any family in the world who needs help being happy, it is this one." She invited us inside. Their living room was so small that sitting on the ragged sofa our knees nearly touched hers, as she sat on the chair opposite us. The adjacent kitchen was so tiny that they had to move the sofa to have room to sit around the table. There were two bedrooms the size of closets. We explained how a family home evening could help her family and gave her a pamphlet explaining it. She invited us back to help them have their first FHE a few days later.

We returned and met her husband, Alfred. Her name was Eleanor, and their little daughter's name was Ellie. They watched us with an amused expression as we sang, prayed, and gave a lesson. Ellie sat on my lap the whole time and twisted my tie. About every ten minutes, I asked her to twist it the other direction. I didn't know the medical term then, but I am sure she was autistic, because Eleanor said the little child had never spoken.

We gave them a Joseph Smith pamphlet and left, thinking we had wasted our time.

It was nearly a month later when we were walking past their house late at night. It was dark, and we should have left the area an hour earlier. We were about to hurry on when both I and my companion said, "We need to check back on Eleanor." We didn't really want to because their home, their lives, and their outlook were so bleak; just being in their home was depressing and spiritually depleting. They had literally laughed at us during our attempted FHE, and it just didn't seem likely they would be interested in anything we could offer them.

But we were obedient to the prompting and knocked on their rickety screen door. She arrived quickly and shouted back into the house, "Alfie, the Mormons are back!" She almost dragged us into the tiny front room. He came in from a bedroom holding the pamphlet we had given them.

He looked at us with a confused expression. "We've read this pamphlet a dozen times and underlined some of it," he said, turning it so we could see the careful red underlining. "What I can't understand is why this isn't in the newspaper and on the TV. I mean, I had no idea God had called another prophet. This is important! Joseph Smith lived in 1820!" Alfred paused to check his facts from the pamphlet, then nodded. "So, that means he's probably dead, right? Why is it that we're just now hearing about it?"

He was visibly upset.

I said, "Joseph Smith isn't alive any more, but there is a current living prophet."

They hammered us with questions and wrote down Joseph Fielding Smith's name carefully on the pamphlet. They wanted his address (which we didn't have, of course) so they could write to him. They also wanted to know what else Joseph Smith had done before he died.

We told them about the Book of Mormon, and they were almost in tears. We handed it to them and they immediately began reading it out loud to one another. They asked us how to pronounce words and what some things meant, but they were enthralled. Their voices were reverent and excited. When we finally interrupted their reading, they asked how much the book cost, because they literally had no money. They asked if they might borrow it for just one evening, promising they would be ever so careful with it. When we said it was free, tears came to their eyes. They said the only other book they owned was a family Bible.

We returned a few days later, and they had read many chapters in the Book of Mormon. They had hundreds of questions, but never a criticism or word of doubt. They knew it was true and wanted to understand everything it said.

They had been given some anti-Mormon literature by Eleanor's mother. They had studied and underlined the anti-pamphlet too. He shook it at us. I was expecting some point of doctrinal disagreement.

Instead, he demanded, "Is it true Mormons don't smoke cigarettes?"

We said yes.

"And you don't drink liquor?" he gasped.

We said yes, expecting he was building up to ordering us from their home.

"I told you!" Eleanor cried out, shaking her finger at him.

"You were right, weren't you?" he said with his head down. Finally, he stood up and reached in his pants pocket and withdrew a pack of cigarettes. "Well, you better take these, then. I don't think I can throw them in the garbage. I've smoked since I was four years old," he said. "But, it's already been twenty-four hours since I decided to quit. If I'm going to be a Mormon, I'm going to be one all the way."

My companion and I were moved nearly to tears. We assured him that God would assist him with his righteous desires. He demanded, "What other fun things can't I do?"

We told him about tea and coffee. He took a big breath and nodded. "I can do that too. What else?"

We told him about tithing, and he turned white. We tried to tell him how paying tithing would actually increase his family's welfare. He interrupted us. "This isn't about money. It's about obedience, isn't it? And, if we're in, we're in one hundred percent."

Remember this all happened in the first thirty minutes of our second visit, the first one being our amateur attempt at "performing" a family home evening.

Alfred was not done. He said, "By the way. Do you have a church building, and are the meetings on Saturday or Sunday?"

We were in missionary Nirvana. I still remember the thrill, as if angels were singing and blowing trumpets. I couldn't even understand how people who were so low and hopeless could be so faith-filled and golden. It was, and still is, amazing to me.

They attended church for the first time a few days later. The church in South Africa had paid for and constructed a beautiful A-frame chapel there. It was large and spectacular compared to any other building in Bulawayo. The building had a grand piano and full-size organ in the chapel. It may have been the only grand piano in Bulawayo.

When Alfred and Eleanor and Ellie walked into the foyer, the little branch in Bulawayo almost jumped out of the pews to welcome them. They hovered and fussed and complimented and loved them. The branch president hugged Alfred and said he had been waiting all of his life to meet him. Alfred looked skeptical and then touched. He nodded.

Our investigators were dirty and ragged and still smelled of tobacco. But they knew in that instant that they had come home. That first week they attended church, they held each other's hands and laughed with wonder and hope. It was the first time I had seen Eleanor without a black eye.

Sister Eleanor told me later that they would have joined our church just to feel the love and fellowship. To her, the love was just a wonderful bonus to the fact that it was also true.

They were baptized four weeks from our shared family home evening. As the weeks came and went, the light in their faces increased into a beautiful glow. Their transformation was more apparent each time we visited them. Their rebirth and the accompanying changes were literal miracles I shall never forget. The first time we returned, their faces were washed and their clothing clean. The second time, little Ellie had a clean and less-tattered dress and little white shoes. Alfred had cut his hair and shortened his beard. Both he and Eleanor's faces were shining.

After they were baptized, he got a raise at work, because he was the only member of the crew who came to work sober. Besides the raise, they had all the money he no longer spent on booze and cigarettes. He told me that they were now "rich," and he proclaimed it was all because of paying tithing and living the Word of Wisdom.

They bought a small "American-made" (they were proud to say) refrigerator. It was very old, probably built in 1920, and had the big ceramic coil on top of the unit. When it started up, the whole building seemed to shake. They set it up in the living room because the kitchen was too small. They proudly served us iced water made in their very own refrigerator.

A few weeks later, Alfred bought a little Morris Mini car, which is little more than a motorcycle on four wheels. It scared me to ride in it. They could afford better food and better clothing. Little Ellie began to grow taller and to grow in her front teeth. She began to laugh for the first time in her life but saved her first words for the moment this little family stood with me on the train platform as I was preparing to leave Rhodesia. We shook hands, Eleanor cried, Alfred fought back tears, and little Ellie ran up and hugged my leg.

I lifted her up to my face and she said, "Eldah Pont, I don't want you to go on the twain!"

The train whistle blew, I kissed Ellie on the cheek and set her down. I turned and stepped onto the train, and it chugged slowly away.

It was the first time in my life that I had seen the power of the Atonement uplift, cleanse, and upgrade someone. Their change was dramatically powerful. Christ truly does work His greatest work among the poor and humble of the world. The transition I saw from that first chance meeting to the day they saw me off at the little train station was to me as great a miracle as Moses dividing the Red Sea. They were not the same people. They were born again, spiritually and physically. They were dressed well according to the world in which they lived. They were happy and full of hope.

Where once had been retched despair, now there was bright hope. They had been bitterly unhappy, bruised in body and spirit, and now they knew joy. Where once had been frigid doubt, now there was fruit-bearing faith. Thoughts of suicide had given place for hope and dreams for the future. Their faces and their souls were shiny clean, and I had been privileged to watch it happen.

This enabling and upgrading power of the Atonement is the very same upon which we call to purify ourselves and purge from our souls those things that man cannot change. This is why the scriptures teach us that when we "becometh a saint through the Atonement of Christ the Lord" that we "becometh as a child, submissive, meek, humble, patient, full of love, willing to submit to all things which the Lord seeth fit to inflict upon him, even as a child doth submit to his father" (Mosiah 3:19).

This is not because we change ourselves, but because Christ changes us. And we are born again, and again, and again.

Brother John

Saved by the Law?

Alma and his people were instructed by the Lord to keep the Law of Moses even though they knew that the law could not save them. "Now they did not suppose that salvation came by the law of Moses; but the law of Moses did serve to strengthen their faith in Christ; and thus they did retain a hope through faith, unto eternal salvation, relying upon the spirit of prophecy, which spake of those things to come" (Alma 25:16).

Abinadi taught, "If ye teach the law of Moses, also teach that it is a shadow of those things which are to come—Teach them that redemption cometh through Christ the Lord, who is the very Eternal Father. Amen" (Mosiah 16:14–15).

King Benjamin taught, "The law of Moses availeth nothing except it were through the atonement of his blood" (Mosiah 3:15).

For years I have wondered why the Lord would command them to keep a dead law. Why not just reveal to them the greater gospel law? But consider Moroni's summary of their entire history: "And there were many whose faith was so exceedingly strong, even before Christ came, who could not be kept from within the veil, but truly saw with their eyes the things which they had beheld with an eye of faith, and they were glad" (Ether 12:19).

In other words, the power of the Law of Moses was sufficient so that those who did not rely upon the law to save them, but who turned to Christ and relied upon the "spirit of prophecy," were able to develop faith that was so strong, even before Christ came, that they parted the veil and obtained marvelous and saving blessings during their lifetime.

The question this might bring up is: How could the Law of Moses, being "dead" (2 Nephi 25:26–27), bring them to these grand blessings—the very same blessings we seek today?

The answer is that all law is dead. Which of the "laws" we recognize today can save us? None of them can. If there were saving power in baptism alone, as an example, then you could baptize people against their will, or while they possessed an evil soul, and the waters themselves would "save" them. This of course is not the case.

The virtue of all "law" is the extent to which it brings us to Christ, where true saving occurs. Baptism, performed by authority, becomes saving after we repent, take upon ourselves the name of Christ, keep His commandments, are born again, and become the sons and daughters of Christ. The reason we partake of the sacrament each week, year after year, is to continually rededicate ourselves to our covenants with Christ and thus renew our baptismal covenants.

The old practitioners of Judaism believed that unrelenting performance of their rituals and sacrifices would save them. They thought that wearing certain robes and observing certain festivals and feasts would save them—no matter the blackness of their hearts or the depth of their unbelief. The same deception could be described as believing that "doing" the Church program can save one. The thinking that years of meeting attendance, temple service, and tithing alone will "earn" one a mansion in the celestial kingdom is not much different from thinking that faithful observance of festivals, feasts, and sacrifices will save you.

We call certain ordinances "saving ordinances" because they are indispensable to our salvation. But the ordinance itself does not save us. When an ordinance is performed by priesthood authority, that ordinance establishes a binding contract with God. We promise to do certain things, as noted above regarding baptism; in response, God promises to bestow certain blessings. This contract cannot be broken unless we fail to keep the promises we made. The same is true of all ordinances, in and out of temples. When we finally meet the promised requirements, then the Holy Ghost, acting as the Holy Spirit of Promise (a weighty subject for another UnBlog) judges us worthy and prepared, and the blessings promised by the ordinance are bestowed by God, not by the ordinance.

Imagine how crushing an eternal blow it would be to step up to the judgment bar thinking we had "done" everything required of us—attended every feast, offered every sacrifice, paid every tithe—only to find out that all of those performances did not have the power to save us. It is a scary image to think of spending our whole lives chin-deep in truth without knowing how to totally immerse ourselves but instead trusting tradition, rituals, and observance to save us. Tradition, rituals, ordinances, and observances are essential to our progression, but they alone do not have saving power.

How much better is it to understand the truth we are submerged in, to know how law and ordinances work, to know in whom we trust for salvation, to knowingly and diligently choose to come unto Christ and be perfected in *Him*? Then, long before we step forward at the judgment bar, we will know with absolute revealed knowledge that we have been true and faithful in all things and that every promised blessing is ours.

Brother John

Just Drink the Medicine

*I*n a previous UnBlog, I talked about spiritual growth from the bottom up, from the perspective of one struggling upward through the mists of darkness and flames of refinement. I would like to mention the challenges of those who are somewhere upon the ladder looking down. Since adversity swirls around us like a London fog, none are immune to the equal and opposite clause of opposition.

When seekers begin to experience the profound blessings of the gospel—the ministry of angels, the miracles of priesthood, and grand spurts of growth that can accompany such times—some seekers upon this part of the ladder occasionally buy into the lie from evil voices that there is something wrong with everyone else, or even the Church. The dark thinking is: if others knew what I know, they would all be growing as I'm growing; or if the Church was doing its job, we would all be growing as I am.

I want to squash this benighted bug once again. Everyone, from Adam to Enoch, from Joseph Smith to each one of us who were ever blessed to view mortality from any spiritual altitude, might have naturally taken a glimpse at fellow mortals and wondered why they were not soaring too. But to maintain any thought process that wonders what is wrong with everyone else, or with the Church that supports them, is inspired of evil.

If one lifted off the ground in an airplane, it would be unbelievably arrogant to think ill of the people still in the airport and wonder what is wrong with them because they are not flying yet, or to look down upon the airport as defective because not everyone is in the air. The very purpose of the airport is to prepare people to fly, just as it did you. The fact that you are a few feet off the ground is glorious evidence that the airport is doing its job, and when you land again, you will again be at the airport, waiting to get on your next plane.

If you are born first in a family and are in high school when your youngest sibling is born, it would be foolish to look at the newborn babe and wonder what's wrong with it because it is acting like a baby still or doubt your mother's parenting because the child is still in diapers. This is the divine order of all mortal things and mortal processes—even in the Church, we are all in diapers until we individually learn to soar.

I am now and will always be a warrior in defense of the Latter-day Church. Not only is it "true," but it works. It brings to our lives the very blessings we are seeking.

If you soar for a moment, the Church and the fact that Jesus Christ endows it with His power and His grace and His priesthood are the reason you are soaring. There is no other reason.

I often liken the Church, and the grace of Jesus Christ to which it gives us access, to a bottle of medicine that if taken will cure any disease you have. It will make you whole of any ailment or injury. Yet, when someone sees it, they wonder why the stopper is cork instead of a modern childproof cap, or they wonder why the label is hand-lettered and a little crooked—and they criticize and decline to drink the medicine that would have healed them of their spiritual maladies.

My argument is—just drink the medicine! The label on the bottle or the color or taste of the medicine is irrelevant—just drink the medicine! The weaknesses of mortals who administer the bottle are irrelevant—just drink the medicine! The chips on the bottle do not damage the power of the cure—just drink the medicine!

It will heal you and give you wings to fly.

Brother John

Grace for Grace

There is an intriguing formula given in Doctrine & Covenants 93 whereby Christ received a "fulness of the glory of the Father," for He "received not of the fulness at first."

The fulness of the Father was when Christ received "all power, both in heaven and on earth, and the glory of the Father was with him, for he dwelt in him." In other words, by receiving a fulness, Christ became perfect and acquired the full power of the Godhead. He became "one" with the Father.

Christ took upon Himself the work and mission of the Atonement, and the process of sanctifying Himself in oneness with the Father, so that "we," those whom the Father gave Him to save (John 17:24), would likewise have the ability, through the Atonement of Christ, to come unto the Father and become sanctified even as Christ was sanctified.

Consider the rest of John 17:

> Neither pray I for these alone, but for them also which shall believe on me through their word; That they all may be one; as thou, Father, art in me, and I in thee, that they also may be one in us; that the world may believe that thou has sent me. And the glory which thou gavest me I have given them; that they may be one, even as we are one: I in them, and thou in me, that they may be made perfect in one, and that the world may know that thou hast sent me, and hast loved them, and that thou hast loved me. (John 17: 20–23)

John, whom we call "the Baptist," explains that Christ received "grace for grace." We know that this grace was a gift from the Father because Christ "received" it. He didn't earn it but qualified for it by who He was and by acts of grace among His fellowman.

It works like this: Christ attuned Himself to the voice of the Father so that He truly did nothing except what the Father commanded Him (John 8:28–29). When the Father sent Christ to teach, heal, or bless, Christ obeyed the Father and thereby dispensed grace to fellow mortals—for which the Father then gave Christ an increased gift of the Father's grace. Thus, Christ received a little more of the "fulness" of the Father and became a little more "one" with the Father by each act of grace. In other words, He received grace for grace—the Father's grace in response to Christ's grace given to men.

The process is exactly the same for you and me. When we are born, we arrive in mortality with a certain set of abilities, gifts, and talents. These things constitute our mortal tool chest. Some people are physically strong and able to push a handcart across the plains. Some are born with great love or the gift of teaching, prophecy, faith to heal, or even music and science. The list of human gifts is vast, even though each of us has only a few. These are our mortal gifts that we are able to grant to others as grace. When Christ, through the Holy Spirit, asks us to serve someone by using one of our gifts, then we are giving grace to that person.

So, when we dispense our small grace to another mortal as prompted by Christ's voice—we bake cookies for someone, support someone in personal struggles, or help someone mow a lawn—then Christ dispenses His grace to us: His eternal grace in exchange for our mortal grace. The difference is that our gifts are cookies, and His are steps to the gift of exaltation.

The second step of this grand process is that we grow from "grace to grace." Just as Jesus Christ "received not of the fulness at first, but continued from grace to grace, until he received a fulness" (Doctrine & Covenants 93:13), we are powerless to obtain a fulness on our own. There is no other process of good works, service, ordinances, or church service that will bring us to a fulness. The only pathway to "a fulness" is to obtain continual grace from Christ, so that we grow from "grace to grace."

It is true that service, good works, and ordinances are vital to the process, but they must be done in obedience to the voice of Christ in order to activate this divine law of "grace for grace." Good things done for lesser motives on our part, out of duty or habit or even as selfish accomplishments, are not grace and do not trigger the divine mainspring of atoning and enabling grace.

Christ grew from one gift of the Father's grace to another, until He obtained a fulness, and so can we.

And thus we receive grace for grace, and grow from grace to grace, until we obtain a fulness. The key is always the same: Hear His voice and obey.

Brother John

Elder Brother

*I*t is not uncommon in the Church to hear Jesus Christ referred to as our "Elder Brother." I believe it is generally meant as a term of endearment, a statement of His care and involvement in our lives. It is actually true that Christ is our elder brother in terms of His being the firstborn of Heavenly Father's household. We are His premortal siblings.

A search of the scriptures does not contain the words "elder brother" in reference to Christ. The holy word contains terms such as "Mighty God," "Eternal Judge," "Everlasting Father," "Holy One of Israel," "Holy Messiah," and "Lord God Omnipotent."

As I have grown as a result of Jesus's grace and intervention in my life, my adoration has grown. I see more clearly not just how much He loves me, but how mighty and glorious and perfect He is. Every time I feel Him near, I feel His love encapsulating me in magnificent perfection and mighty power. As my adoration of Jesus Christ has grown, my language has changed from familiarity to worship and reverence. I no longer refer to Christ as my "Elder Brother" because that so magnificently understates my relationship with Him. He is my God, my salvation, and the lover and exalter of my soul. He has ransomed my soul from destruction by His grace with very little help from my personal worth. I depend upon Him for every part of my life and my hope of exaltation.

One of the unfortunate effects of referring to our Savior as our Elder Brother is that it causes non-Mormons to doubt we are

Christians. Without understanding our powerful, underlying reverence for His Godhood, Savior-hood, and glory, such language seems to demote Christ from Mighty God to "my buddy, Jesus." It is my personal impression that we must grow beyond the spiritually myopic to elevate our lives, by His grace, to His divine stature, rather than pulling Him to our level in order to better relate.

We are the offspring of God, our Heavenly Father, and we rejoice therein. However, that relationship is not exalting. Every person ever born, from Cain to Christ, is our eternal sibling. We know of nothing we did to gain that privilege, and we will reap no extraordinary benefit above any other mortal from being the offspring of Heavenly Father.

By divine design of the Father, the relationship that redeems and saves us is our relationship with Christ. This greater relationship is achieved when we become Christ's sons and daughters through His Atonement. When we refer to one another in the Church as "brother and sister," we are not referring to being children of Heavenly Father but to having been born again as children of Christ. It is a sweet and powerful reminder that everything we hope for comes from Christ. It is also a glorious compliment to refer to another as Christ's spiritual offspring, our spiritual brother or sister in Christ.

It may be noted that President Joseph F. Smith did use the term "Elder Brother" while the Church was somewhat isolated in Utah; but as we now work to build bridges with other Christians in the twenty-first century, refraining from using the term may help to clarify our belief in the absolute divinity of the Savior. Elder M. Russell Ballard explains it this way:

> We occasionally hear some members refer to Jesus as our Elder Brother, which is a true concept based on our understanding of the premortal life with our Father in Heaven. But like many points of gospel doctrine, that simple truth doesn't go far enough in terms of describing the Savior's role in our present lives and His great position as a member of the Godhead. Thus, some non-LDS Christians are uncomfortable with what they perceive as a secondary role for Christ in our theology. They feel that we view Jesus as a spiritual peer. They believe that we view Christ as an implementor for God, if you will, but that we don't view Him as God to us and to all mankind, which, of course, is counter to biblical testimony about Christ's divinity.
>
> Let me help us understand, with clarity and testimony, our

belief about Jesus Christ. We declare He is the King of Kings, Lord of Lords, the Creator, the Savior, the Captain of our Salvation, the Bright and Morning Star. He has taught us that He is in all things, above all things, through all things and round about all things, that He is Alpha and Omega, the Lord of the Universe, the first and the last relative to our salvation, and that His name is above every name and is in fact the only name under heaven by which we can be saved.

So let us be very clear on this point: it is true that Jesus was our Elder Brother in the premortal life, but we believe that in this life it is crucial that we become "born again" as His sons and daughters in the gospel covenant. (M. Russell Ballard, "Building Bridges of Understanding," address delivered to the Logan Institute of Religion, February 17, 1998)

I testify to all who will hear that Jesus Christ is my spiritual Father, my Lord, and my Savior!

Brother John

After All We Can Do

There is a certain mind-set among us that is hostile to our spiritual growth, which is that we must by our own discipline work out our own salvation. The thought is that if we are really, really good, "after all we can do," somewhere at the end of our lives, Jesus Christ will finally get involved and make up for what we were not able to do during our lifetime, and in the end we will be "saved by grace."

The flaw in this thinking is that it places upon us mere mortals a burden we cannot hope to carry—that of keeping every commandment, doing every good thing, raising perfect families, overcoming every weakness, paying our tithing, and a million other laws and rules, by obedience and discipline—waiting for the day that it is enough, and Jesus Christ finally gets involved, forgives those things we couldn't do, and fills in the blanks.

Unfortunately, this sets us up for a lifetime of struggle that isn't going to take us where we are anticipating.

The truth of how this works is that we are given choices in our life. We know right and wrong because of the Light of Christ, which we each receive throughout our lives—a gift of grace wrought through the Atonement of Christ. It is by grace that we even know what is good and bad, or to know what we should do. Thus it is by grace that we receive faith, truth, insight, inspiration, direction, guidance, truth, and power from the beginning to the end of our lives.

Then, when we make a right choice such as saying we're sorry or going to church or forgiving someone who doesn't seem to deserve it, Christ dispenses more grace, and we are changed. As we trust fully in Him, He enables and empowers us to keep the very commandments that He has given us. Then, as we choose to obey His voice and accept His empowerment, we become more like Him and are compensated (by orders of magnitude) much more than our token obediences could possibly warrant. We receive "grace for grace"—His mightier grace for our little grace—until we finally become perfected in Christ.

Thus, we live by grace every moment of every day.

When we come to the end of our lives, having walked in the Savior's grace, having partaken of His upgrading and empowering Atonement, we will know that we have been "saved by grace"—not in that moment alone, but throughout the walk of our entire lives. And it indeed will be "after all we can do," because the reward is far above and beyond all we ever could have done to merit such a gift by our own works, important as they are as tokens of our love and obedience.

When with tear-streaked faces and overwhelming gratitude we finally get a clear realization that the Lord's grace has permeated every moment of our lives, then every knee will bow and every tongue will confess that Jesus is the Christ. In that great day of judgment, we will at last comprehend with awe and reverence that He created us, He gave us life, He sustained our lives, He taught us right from wrong, He empowered us to choose the right, and then He forgave us when we stumbled—because He loved us, and we loved Him in return.

We will worship Him then and forever, because we will finally know that we walked our entire life in His grace, and "after all we can do," we were saved by it.

Brother John

Sacred and True

*S*ome of the comments following the UnBlog "Journey to Calling and Election" conveyed poignantly to me that you are seeking, hoping, and striving to believe that these great things do still happen in our day. By way of bearing testimony that they do, I would like to share just a part of a personal experience I have alluded to in a few firesides. I do so only with the humble desire that it might add to your belief, hope, and willingness to continue to seek after these great things until you obtain them. The path is not easy, but it is true, and many are finding it.

Many years ago I had an experience in prayer, which began as deeply searching and needing. This was a time in my life that had been truly excruciating in its trials. I had been mightily struggling and yearning for many years to flawlessly obey the voice of the Spirit to the best of my ability and to totally submit to the will of Christ, no matter the cost. This particular evening was a moment of exquisite despair; I recognized with anguish my utter nothingness before God and man. I cried out to the Father in full consecration of the last pitiful gifts I had to offer, knowing I would never be enough, knowing that I had failed in my life.

After about an hour of spiritual struggle, I felt a pure flow of knowledge that answered my need and ended my searching. It was like being plugged into a computer with the ability to download insight, wisdom, truth, and enlightenment in an instant. I felt so grateful for this powerful and timely answer to my prayers that I remained on my knees to thank God. I didn't want to leave. I felt welcome, at peace, and at home.

I prayed on into the night, sending my gratitude as high as my spiritual voice would launch it. As the Spirit filled me with greater and greater light, it formed the words I uttered. My words stopped being mine; they became more powerful than language, more beautiful than poetry, more profound than English can be. It was speech and song, worship and wonder that far eclipsed mortal language. I found myself rejoicing as I had never rejoiced before and was so enveloped with love that it consumed me. I felt on fire; my skin was burning, and I had the sensation of floating.

In the midst of this experience, the Spirit whispered to me that I should get into bed. "Look, you're cold and shivering. Get into bed." I realized for the first time that I was icy cold. I climbed into bed, and the experience continued. The primary feeling within me was of being infinitely and tenderly loved by God, of being profoundly welcome in His presence. My mind was filled with light. I opened my eyes to the darkness of night but saw light everywhere. I was given questions to ask and immediately received the answers. These were not questions I would have thought of but questions I should have known to ask. Every answer expanded my mind with more than just words; I "saw" the answers, felt them, assimilated them into my soul, and marveled over them. This continued for about an hour.

After this magnificent question-and-answer period had concluded, I suddenly felt a great presence of power. The previous feelings of great wisdom and truth, of vast love and acceptance, were still present. But this additional presence was power greater than if I had been laid upon a million-volt power line. It was power so vast that I was fully aware that if I had not come through the earlier process of prayer and worship, enlightenment and protection, this infinite power would have reduced me to atoms. This unspeakable power permeated my being, but I felt no fear. I was humbled to the dust and felt tiny in comparison, like a child who had been unexpectedly ushered in to see the King. I knew beyond a doubt that I was welcome but felt vastly unprepared to be there.

I then heard a voice that sounded to me like the voice of eternity. It was as if a planet had acquired lips and was speaking. The Voice combined every sound that humans can hear into one mighty vibration, like the rushing of a mighty wind or the sound of creation moving mountains and oceans into place or setting planets spinning on their paths.

This voice said two sentences, both of which startled me to the core. I could hardly imagine what I had just heard. I wasn't even sure that I had heard it correctly. My mortal mind wanted to doubt. After I heard these things, I saw two small visions, which I cannot share. Then, the experience stopped abruptly. I was left to myself to ponder what I had seen and heard. I lay there for quite a few minutes, pondering what I had seen, unsure that I could ever remember the whole of it—when it suddenly began again. I saw and heard exactly the same thing a second time.

During the second iteration of this experience, I grew very tired. It was by then early morning, and my body was exhausted. I sensed myself going to sleep, even though I willed myself to be awake. Then I felt something reach out and touch me, like someone stroking a child to soothe him. Sleep fled from me. I was suddenly fully awake until the experience concluded exactly as the first time.

Again I lay there pondering what had happened, reviewing it in my mind, rejoicing over and over. All doubt was gone. I simply *knew* all that I had seen and experienced. I was trying to understand what I had done to trigger this experience and why I would be worthy of such a thing when the familiar voice of the Holy Spirit said, "Get up and write it down."

I immediately went downstairs to my computer and turned it on. I had gotten up so quickly upon hearing the instruction to write it down that I had forgotten to pick up my glasses. I had to put my face right into the screen to start my word processor and open my journal. I sat there and knew in all of my heart that I could never remember every word. Each of the prior two experiences had taken about an hour. But the Holy Spirit said, "Just write."

I placed my fingers on the keys and typed, "I just had one of the most amazing experiences of my life . . ." when the same experience opened up a third time. The entire experience again happened as I wrote. I typed with wild haste, ignoring spelling, punctuation, and capitalization. I just wrote as furiously as I could, trying to convey what I was experiencing. When I was finished, I knew I had captured only a small portion of it, but what I had written was true, and to me it was astonishing. I saved the file and turned off the computer. The clock beside my desk said it was 5:00 a.m. I dressed and left for work, having spent the entire night in vision.

Throughout the day, I was invigorated and awake. I pondered all day long what had happened during that long, sleepless night. When I finally got into bed that next evening, I was no more tired than any usual night. I prayed for a long time, hoping to again have a vast experience, but it did not come. I closed my prayers, climbed into bed, and soon fell asleep.

Since that experience, I have wanted to share both what happened and why, but the Lord has laid a blanket of silence over those things for many years. In that intervening time, I have written extensively about *how* it happened. It happened because I was taught how to hear and then to obey the voice of the Holy Spirit, which is the voice of Christ. That is the only "how" there is. I have written volumes on this subject, adding up to millions of words describing this process. The only reason I know it is because God very gently led me through that process until I experienced blessings I didn't even know I was seeking. I had to look back to see that they were the very things the gospel, the priesthood, and the temple had promised me. They were. It was a startling insight.

It has only been recently that Father has allowed me to describe "what." What happens is that the heavens do open, and miracles do occur, to even the least of saints. What happens is that the promises of the latter days are fulfilled to the letter. We *can* approach the veil and accomplish everything we hope for.

I don't even know why I can say these things now. Perhaps it is because my life is nearing its conclusion, and I would not feel I could report my life as having been fully accomplished if I left mortality with these things in my head. Perhaps there is a sense of safety in knowing that once my life ends, nobody can take away what I said while yet alive. They can doubt, but they can't erase the fact that it was said.

When the Spirit suggested "UnBlog My Soul" as the name for this blog, I thought it was ironic. The idea and purpose of writing this blog came to me in a flash of insight. I was to publish all of these precious things in my soul so that death could not erase them. I wanted them to not be lost to my wife, to my children, to my brothers and sisters, or to anyone who could be blessed by them. To me, "UnBlog," unclog, unload, and unburden all mean the same thing: that my life not end before my soul has been emptied of these precious things.

I praise the Lord for this opportunity and humbly give Him all the glory. There seems to yet be more to UnBlog than I had ever envisioned, which means the Lord apparently isn't quite ready to draw the curtain on my life.

Until that day arrives,

Brother John

Chapter Twelve

Hurrah for Israel!

Hurrah for Israel!

Today's UnBlog constitutes the five hundredth posting. I find it hard to fathom—kind of like how a grandparent looks back upon the lives of his children with fond memories and thinks, "It went by so quickly!"

Pondering these marvelous days and the various subjects we have considered together, it occurs to me that I have had one overriding motive that kept me UnBlogging. It is also the most important thing I know about the gospel.

Not only is it true, but it works.

It works in our dispensation the same as it worked in Adam's or Noah's, Enoch's, Abraham's, Moses's, or Christ's. It has been taught in different ways, with different laws and different traditions, and with different degrees of success and failure. But the one thing that has not changed is that those who did—and do—dedicate their lives to Christ, regardless of what anyone around them believes or understands, did—and do—find the curtains of heaven opening and the glories of God brightening upon them.

This is my testimony and the reason why I keep writing and keep testifying: because it works! Of this I am a witness. It isn't easy, and it isn't quick. It is in fact the most demanding pathway one can choose through mortality. But, as we all must walk a thorny road anyway here in this world, taking the higher road is much, much preferred. It is the only path that brings joy in mortality, and the only one that overcomes this mortal condition and brings us back into the presence of God, who is our home. Every other pathway is a study in eternal physics—bouncing off obstacles, rebounding from unseen blows, bearing the weight of unexpected tragedy, burning with doubt and fear, crushed by the unknown and unknowable without Christ, weeping without hope, and waiting to die with looming terror.

So, standing upon this small hill, glorying in my Jesus, I testify to all who will hear. The gospel is true. It does work. The promises are profound, and they are ours to reach out and claim, just as they have always been.

Hurrah for Israel!

Brother John

Epilogue

Until We Meet Again

Until We Meet Again

Dear *UnBlog Family,*
This is Brother John. I have a few minutes to drop you a note, so I thought I would share with you a few things that have happened.

I am very sick and spent last weekend in the hospital trying to survive. The doctors tell me that I have between two and four weeks left, but they could be wrong, of course. Accordingly, I have been giving father's blessings to my children, having brief meetings with friends, and having many wonderful experiences among the harsh ones. I have also been learning how to type and spell while on pain killers. Believe me, it takes different pathways in the brain.

I have found that these days the house is filled with the Spirit and with angels. I have had a few startling dreams that I wish I could share but will probably never have the energy to write. I'm not sure I trust my present state of dreams right now, and they would be suspect for sure a dozen years from now.

I may write a little more as my health allows. As my dear friend takes over the UnBlog, you will notice some differences over time, but I do believe the same sweet spirit and spiritual "family" we enjoy here will grow even greater.

It is truly an amazing experience to die. I have discovered how much love and goodness there is in this area of medicine. I truly have had loving arms around me. It amazes me how kind and Christlike the hospice nurses and doctors are. They are astonishing. In the depth of these awful moments, I believe I have experienced Zion because of them. My wife wept too. Not just for the relief, but because these loving angels were *here*, and because they knew what to do and did it with love.

For now, my pain is controlled. Father has bestowed many blessings, and I really am looking forward to what lies ahead. I will try to keep you in the loop. There seems to be a spiritual process to dying, of which I am of course completely ignorant. If I am able, it will be fun to capture a few of those steps along the way.

God bless you all, until we meet again.

Brother John
November 6, 2012

The Journey Home
Part XI: A New Journey Begins

December 10, 2012

It had been the perfect Sunday. We had all our Utah children and grandchildren over, and John's mother and sister also came by. I served Sunday dinner as usual, but this time we went downstairs to avoid any smells that might waft into John's room upstairs. The grandchildren were laughing and playing rambunctiously, and I wondered whether this was bothering John, so I went into the bedroom to check on him. He was lying there just listening. He simply said, "It's so wonderful to hear the sounds of life."

But after they left, John's night was a hard one. He hardly slept at all. I decided that he wasn't getting enough pain medication and called hospice early the next morning to get more. In response, the hospice doctor came to our home to personally visit John, which astonished me! This doctor was incredibly personable, gracious, and congenial. After the doctor ministered to us and left our home, John seemed to diminish more every minute. My dearest friend and sister, Faith, was there with me (she felt impressed to come down from her home in Layton that day), and we each prayed over John at his bedside. The prayers were profound and inspired, filled with vision, light, and promise for his new future.

John's favorite Tabernacle Choir CD, "Peace Like a River," beautifully set the tone for the prayers and for the angels who attended his passing, which happened within a few minutes of those prayers. He passed away just after our two daughters living at home had returned and were with him.

John's passing was only a few weeks after the publication of Visions of Glory. Under difficult circumstances, John completed his last major assignment in mortality—the writing and publishing of Visions of Glory, which has become an inspiration to tens of thousands of Latter-day Saints.

And so John's mortal journey to the veil was completed, as all of ours will be one day. I know that he has now joyfully begun a new and even more fulfilling journey, unfettered by human frailty and pain, and this knowledge is supremely comforting to me. Yet as I have contemplated these things, I can't help but think how John Pontius had made another journey to the veil—a spiritual one—many years before. He had sought for the greater blessings promised to the extraordinarily faithful, and he had paid the price necessary to receive them. He had come to understand the simple but profound truths that surround these vast blessings, and the Spirit graciously gave him utterance to teach those truths.

I believe, as John did, that this is the true "Journey to the Veil"—the spiritual journey. The fulness of this journey can be made either in this life or in the life to come, but how much better to make it here as a mortal on earth, when we can then bless our posterity and others around us with the additional bestowal of light, service, godly attributes, and unique blessings that attend such a grand path.

God bless each of us as we continue on our own journeys, and as we spiritually prepare as individuals and as a people to build the pre-millennial Zion.

—Terri

APPENDIX

The Path of the Ancients

Most of my life, I have viewed the gospel taught in the scriptures and the gospel we are living in the latter-days as somehow being different. It used to seem as if the ancient faithful had a greater gift, more miracles, more prophets and prophecies, and more access to the Lord. I just didn't see the grand events of scripture (like Elijah's fiery chariot or Moses's dividing of the Red Sea) happening today. I wondered why the Lord was so willing to talk to Nephi and his people when I had yet to recognize a single peep from the heavens.

It wasn't until the Spirit taught me what the whole gospel plan looks like that I could understand how those of ancient glory had arrived at the blessings and miracles that defined their lives in scriptural history.

The value of the graph below is that it demystifies the miraculous process of walking the path the ancients used to obtain their great blessings. The ancient righteous were not born to spiritual greatness; they fought for it, sought for it, and paid the price for it. Having obtained, they recorded their lives and their experiences probably without ever suspecting that their words and their journey would become a part of actual scripture.

Observing their path makes it easy for us to realize that their path was the same as ours. There is only one way to obtain these blessings, and it has been the same for every man and woman throughout history. These glorious things must be accomplished sequentially, one by one, line upon line, until we have traveled as far as our obedience qualifies us. It generally is not possible to skip a step or to seek for a higher blessing when there are lesser accomplishments between us and the ones we think we want.

In the graph below, the principles and ordinances we can attain are listed along the bottom, from left to right in approximate order of sequence. You will recognize your own life in this list. These are the things you have done since childhood up to this day. If you are a seeker of righteousness, you are somewhere on this path.

The spiritual blessings resulting from participating in and applying those principles and ordinances are listed (vertically) along the top. These are the spiritual things we most desire in mortality! The spiritual blessings from "Spoken Directions" through "Prophecy" do not necessarily come in the order listed, nor do they necessarily come at the point indicated. However, generally, the frequency and magnitude of these spiritual blessings increase as one grows in light and truth.

You will note that the beginning point on the farthest left starts with a slight degree of spiritual ascent (the top curved line), which progresses upward with each succeeding step taken. This is the degree of sanctification we have obtained as we progress, or the degree of truth, light, and Spirit that we possess. You will notice that most of our life's journey is spent with slowly increasing spiritual power. We usually travel a long ways before our spiritual strength begins to progress steeply upward, which for most seems to begin somewhere around having one's Calling and Election made sure, and rises quickly and exponentially from there.

The vertical dashed line between "Visions" and "Doctrine Distilled Upon Soul" is approximately the limit of what most Latter-day Saints believe is possible for them to personally obtain. It is, in a real way, our veil of unbelief—wherever it exists for us. The things beyond (farther right in the graph) are the "greater things"—the mysteries that are absolutely available to all of us in this life, but which many people cannot see because they just don't believe it is possible (or perhaps even permitted) to participate in those blessings themselves.

Referencing the graph, we may surmise that if in our lives we are receiving revelations and seeing visions, then we have been born again, received temple covenants, have begun the process of consecration, and are approaching having our Calling and Election made sure. Using this graph, it is easy to evaluate your own progress—and thus plot a course to greater things.

May we all find the faith to rend our personal veils of unbelief!

Brother John

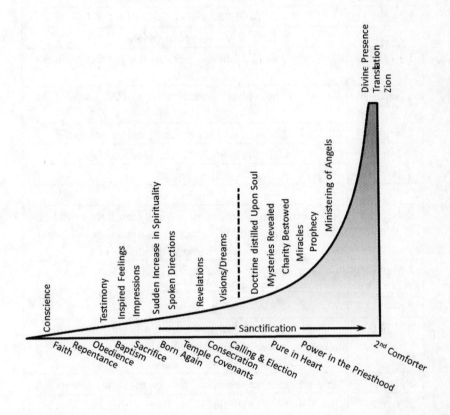

Scripture Mastery Key: The Book of Mormon

1 Nephi 1	Lehi called as a prophet, sees God on His throne.
1 Nephi 2	Nephi speaks face to face with the Lord.
1 Nephi 3	The Lord will empower us to do the things He commands.
1 Nephi 8	Lehi's vision of Tree of Life.
1 Nephi 10	He that diligently seeks shall find.
1 Nephi 11	Nephi's vision of Tree of Life.
1 Nephi 12	Vision of America.
1 Nephi 13	Church of devil. Plain and precious things taken from the Bible.
1 Nephi 14	Two churches only. Great and Abominable Church of the devil.
1 Nephi 19	Prophecy of Christ's suffering and atonement.
2 Nephi 2	Opposition in all things. Good and Evil.
2 Nephi 3	Three Josephs.
2 Nephi 4	Psalm of Nephi.
2 Nephi 9	Resurrection and Atonement. Save all men if they will hearken unto his voice. When they are learned they think they are wise. To be carnally-minded is death.
2 Nephi 10	Jews crucify their God. America land of liberty. Reconcile yourselves to the will of God, not the will of flesh.
2 Nephi 13	Wo unto the daughters of Zion.
2 Nephi 25	Nephi interprets Isaiah. We labor diligently to write to believe in Christ. Saved by grace. We talk of Christ, we rejoice in Christ . . .
2 Nephi 26	Priestcrafts. Many churches. Devil leads with a flaxen cord.
2 Nephi 27	Book of Mormon. Sealed book. Three witnesses. Marvelous work and wonder.
2 Nephi 28	False churches. Satan rages in hearts of men.
2 Nephi 29	We need no more Bible. Judged out of books.
2 Nephi 31	Take upon you name of Christ. Baptism of fire. Speak with tongue of angels. Straight and narrow path. Rely upon words of Christ. Only true doctrine. None other way.
2 Nephi 32	Angels speak by Holy Ghost. Continues from 2 Nephi 31. Holy Ghost will show you all things what ye should do. This is the doctrine of Christ.

Mosiah 2	King Benjamin's Address. Unprofitable servants. List to obey the evil spirit. Open rebellion against God.
Mosiah 3	Prophecy of Jesus Christ. Salvation only through the name of Christ. The natural man is an enemy to God.
Mosiah 4	Know your own nothingness and the greatness of God.
Mosiah 5	Being born again. Ye shall be called the children of Christ. Hear and know the voice by which ye are called.
Mosiah 7	Ammon finds Lehi-Nephi.
Mosiah 8	24 gold plates.
Mosiah 11	Abinadi prophesies.
Mosiah 12–16	Abinadi's trial.
Mosiah 17	Alma believes.
Mosiah 18	Waters of Mormon.
Mosiah 26	I covenant with thee (Alma) that thou shalt have eternal life. (Alma's C&E)
Mosiah 27	Vision of Alma the Younger. Marvel not that all mankind . . . must be born again.
Mosiah 28	Sons of Mosiah preach to the Lamanites.
Alma 3	Rewards every man according to his works. Receive wages of him whom he listeth to obey.
Alma 5	Rebirth of the spirit. Have ye been spiritually born of God? Ye are as sheep having no shepherd.
Alma 8	Alma and Amulek preach.
Alma 10	Unrighteous lawyers and judges destroy the people.
Alma 12	It is given unto many to know the mysteries until they know them in full.
Alma 13	Premortal calling of high priests. Called according to the foreknowledge of God, on account of their faith. Exceedingly great many who . . . entered into the rest of the Lord.
Alma 17–26	Account of the Sons of Mosiah.
Alma 29	O that I were an angel.
Alma 32	Faith. Plant the seed of faith (in Christ) in your hearts. Faith is not to have a perfect knowledge. God imparts his word by angels. Arouse your faculties even to an experiment upon my words.

Alma 33	Seed of faith defined: Believe in the Son of God, that he will redeem, resurrect, and judge you.
Alma 34	Atonement. There should be a great and last sacrifice. Cry unto Him in your fields. Do not contend against the Holy Ghost.
Alma 37	The Liahona is a type of spiritual things.
Alma 40	Resurrection.
Alma 41	Plan of Restoration (good to good—evil to evil).
Alma 42	Redemption and Atonement. Adam and Eve. Justice and Mercy.
Alma 45	Alma translated.
Alma 46	Moroni raises the Title of Liberty.
Helaman 3	Sanctification comes by yielding your heart to God.
Helaman 4	Zarahemla captured by the Lamanites.
Helaman 5	Nephi and Lehi preach to the Lamanites. Ye must build upon the rock of the Savior. Nephi and Lehi circled about by fire.
Helaman 6	Lamanites more righteous than Nephites. Gadianton Robbers take over the Nephite government.
Helaman 7	Nephi upon the garden tower.
Helaman 10	Nephi receives the sealing power.
Helaman 13	Samuel the Lamanite prophesies Nephite destruction.
Helaman 14	Samuel the Lamanite prophesies of Christ's birth.
Helaman 16	Samuel the Lamanite cannot be slain upon the wall.
3 Nephi 4	Gadianton Robbers defeated.
3 Nephi 7	Government overthrown. Nephi raises Timothy from the dead.
3 Nephi 8	Destructions at Christ's death. Cities destroyed. Three days of darkness.
3 Nephi 9	Voice of Christ heard. "Behold I am Jesus Christ."
3 Nephi 11	Christ appears in Bountiful.
3 Nephi 12	Christ calls the Twelve.
3 Nephi 15	Ye are the . . . other sheep.
3 Nephi 16	When the Gentiles reject the fulness of my gospel, I will bring my gospel from among them. Tread them down as salt that has lost its savor.

3 Nephi 17	Jesus heals the sick. Angels minister to the little ones.
3 Nephi 18	Jesus institutes the sacrament.
3 Nephi 21	Latter-day prophecies. New Jerusalem, return of ten tribes.
3 Nephi 26	Jesus expounds all things. Babes utter marvelous things.
3 Nephi 27	This is my gospel, that I might be lifted up to draw all men unto me.
3 Nephi 28	Three Nephites are translated. Nine are promised speedy exaltation.
4 Nephi	All are converted. 200 years of peace.
Mormon 1	Three Nephites are taken away. People have become wicked.
Mormon 3	War and carnage.
Mormon 6	Nephites defeated at Cumorah.
Mormon 8	Moroni begins his record.
Ether 2	Jaredites build barges.
Ether 3	Sixteen stones lighted by the finger of the Lord. Christ shows himself to the Brother of Jared.
Ether 4	When Gentiles exercise faith as the brother of Jared, then they will see the things the brother of Jared saw, even all the revelations of God. Gentiles must rend the veil of unbelief. Barges arrive in the land of promise.
Ether 6	Moroni speaks of "the Heavenly Gift" and seeing God. Faith is things which are hoped for and not seen. Weaknesses make men humble. My grace is sufficient.
Ether 12	Ether speaks of the New Jerusalem.
Ether 13	Sacrament prayer on the bread.
Moroni 4	Sacrament prayer on the water.
Moroni 5	All good things come from God. All evil is inspired of the devil. How to lay hold upon every good thing. Ministering of Angels. Faith. Charity.
Moroni 7	Infant baptism is evil.
Moroni 8	"When ye shall receive these things." Gifts of the Spirit. Speaking from the dust of the earth. "Gospel in a Nutshell": Come unto Christ and be perfected in him.

Scripture Mastery Key: The Doctrine & Covenants

2	Elijah will reveal the priesthood before the coming of the Lord.
3	Lost book of Lehi. God cannot be frustrated.
7	Promise to John the Beloved.
8	Tell you in mind and heart. Spirit of revelation; Moses.
17	Three Witnesses.
19	Eternal punishment is God's punishment. Walk in the meekness of my Spirit.
20	Church established April 6, 1830. Justification. Sanctification. Grace just and true. Sacramental prayers.
29	Spiritual creation. All things unto God are spiritual.
33	The field is white, already to harvest. Missionary work.
45	Enoch. Gathering of Israel. Times of the Gentiles. Tribulations, earthquakes, and desolations. Second coming to Jerusalem. Parable of Ten Virgins fulfilled. Flee unto Zion for safety.
46	Gifts of the Spirit.
50	He that is ordained of God and sent forth is the servant of all. Light grows brighter and brighter until the perfect day. I have overcome the world, and you are of them that my Father hath given me. None shall be lost.
58	After much tribulation come the blessings. Not meet that I should command in all things.
59	Sabbath observance. In nothing doth man offend God save those who confess not his hand in all things.
67	The veil shall be rent and you shall see me and know that I am.
76	Vision of Degrees of Glory.
77	Q&A on the Book of Revelation.
84	Key of the mysteries of the kingdom, even the key of the knowledge of God. See the face of God. Oath and Covenant of the Priesthood. The Spirit giveth light to every man. Hearken to the voice of the Spirit and come unto God, even the Father. Condemnation upon the children of Zion. Signs of faith. Second Coming and Zion.

88	Light of Christ. Law of the celestial kingdom. Governed by law. God knows all things. Eye single to my glory—filled with light. The days will come that you shall see him. Events of the Second Coming. Trumpets. Resurrection. Seven seals revealed.
89	Word of Wisdom.
93	Ye shall see my face and know that I am. Testimony of John the Beloved. I am the Spirit of Truth. Intelligence or light of truth was not created. All truth is independent.
98	Constitutional law.
101	Tribulation. Gathering Zion. Millennium. Constitution.
107	Melchizedek Priesthood holds keys to all of the spiritual blessings of the church. Mysteries, heavens opened, Church of the Firstborn, communion and presence of God and Jesus Christ. Aaronic priesthood holds the keys to the ministering of angels.
109	Dedication of Kirtland Temple.
110	Visions of the dedication of the Kirtland Temple. Elias, Elijah, keys of the dispensation.
116	Adam-ondi-Ahman.
119	Tithing.
121	Liberty Jail. Many are called but few are chosen. Principles governing the priesthood include persuasion, long-suffering, and love. Let virtue garnish thy thoughts unceasingly.
124	Build the Nauvoo temple. Baptisms for the dead.
129	Recognizing spirits and angels.
130	There is a law irrevocably decreed upon which all blessings are predicated. Father has a body of flesh and bone.
132	Eternal marriage. Holy Spirit of Promise. Receive me in the world. This is eternal life. Blasphemy against the Holy Ghost. Plural marriage to multiply and replenish the earth.
133	Come out of Babylon. Return of lost tribes. Second Coming. Building of Zion.
134	Law of the land. Right to defend.
135	Martyrdom of Joseph and Hyrum. "I am going like a lamb to the slaughter."
138	Joseph F. Smith vision of the dead.

Index

About the Authors

J
ohn and Terri Pontius enjoyed a beautiful life together in Alaska until 2010, when the Lord sent them to Utah to continue their work there. They shared a mutual passion for three things: Jesus Christ, His gospel, and their family.

They felt their mission has always been to teach the truth of the redemption of our Savior to all with ears to hear. They both have a gift for music, and they enjoyed working together in spreading the message of Christ through music, theatre, and church callings.

John worked tirelessly in writing and in teaching the gospel, with two doctrinal books currently in print: *Following the Light of Christ into His Presence*, and *The Triumph of Zion*. While struggling with cancer, he penned his last book, *Visions of Glory*, began and maintained his popular blog, "UnBlog My Soul," and delighted in testifying of Christ and the restored gospel in every teaching setting imaginable.

In his last book biography, John wrote: "I could not have written this book or any other eternally weighty thing without the Lord's hand. His hand has led me to places I did not want to go, but when I actually got there, I recognized it as my 'far better land of promise.'"

And of Terri he wrote, "Terri is the love of my life, my best friend, and the kindest mortal I have ever met." Together their eternal family consists of eight children and twenty-two grandchildren, at last count.

John passed away in December 2012, a few weeks after the publication of *Visions of Glory*.